MODERNISM AND EUGENICS

In *Modernism and Eugenics*, Donald J. Childs shows how Virginia
Woolf, T. S. Eliot, and W. B. Yeats believed in eugenics, the
science of race improvement, and adapted this scientific
discourse to the language and purposes of the modern imagination. Childs traces the impact of the eugenics movement on
such modernist works as *Mrs. Dalloway, A Room of One's Own, The
Waste Land,* and Yeats's late poetry and early plays. The
language of eugenics moves, he claims, between public discourse
and personal perspectives. It informs Woolf's theorization of
woman's imagination; in Eliot's poetry, it pictures as a nightmare the myriad contemporary eugenical threats to humankind's biological and cultural future. And for Yeats, it becomes
integral to his engagement with the occult and his commitment
to Irish nationalism. This is an original study of a controversial
theme which reveals the centrality of eugenics in the life and
work of several major modernist writers.

DONALD J. CHILDS is Associate Professor in the English
Department at the University of Ottawa. He is the author of
T. S. Eliot: Mystic, Son and Lover (1997) and of numerous articles
on T. S. Eliot, Virginia Woolf, and Modernism.

MODERNISM AND EUGENICS

Woolf, Eliot, Yeats, and the
Culture of Degeneration

DONALD J. CHILDS

CAMBRIDGE
UNIVERSITY PRESS

PUBLISHED BY THE PRESS SYNDICATE OF THE UNIVERSITY OF CAMBRIDGE
The Pitt Building, Trumpington Street, Cambridge, United Kingdom

CAMBRIDGE UNIVERSITY PRESS
The Edinburgh Building, Cambridge CB2 2RU, UK
40 West 20th Street, New York NY 10011–4211, USA
10 Stamford Road, Oakleigh, VIC 3166, Australia
Ruiz de Alarcón 13, 28014 Madrid, Spain
Dock House, The Waterfront, Cape Town 8001, South Africa

http://www.cambridge.org

First published 2001

Printed in the United Kingdom at the University Press, Cambridge

Typeface Baskerville 11/12.5 pt   *System* 3b2   [CE]

A catalogue record for this book is available from the British Library

ISBN 0 521 80601 1 hardback

For Janet, Kathleen, and Emma

Contents

Introduction

Before eugenics was born as a science in the work of Francis Galton late in the nineteenth century, the concerns that it would address were gathering. On the one hand, the age of European exploration confronted Europe with races and cultures that had to be explained in terms of the assurance in the Book of Genesis that we all descend from Adam and Eve. As late as the nineteenth century, many ethnologists and anthropologists were content to assume that all human beings indeed descended from Adam and Eve, but that some branches of the human species had been cursed for their sins and so had degenerated from their original noble state. On the other hand, in Galton's Britain, increasing urbanization confronted the middle class with an apparently permanent underclass of poor people – beggars, thieves, prostitutes – often in poor health, apparently indolent and lazy. This underclass, moreover, was increasing in size relative to the middle class because of the differential birthrate, and increasing also was the frequency of such social problems as murder, pauperism, disease, mental illness, alcoholism, and prostitution. Was the British nation degenerating – its very survival threatened by the potentially fatal fertility of its degenerates?

As early as 1871, analysis of records of the height, weight, and general health of army recruits throughout the nineteenth century in Britain suggested "a progressive physical degeneracy of race."[1] The early defeats of the British army in the Boer War (1899–1902) confirmed for many that degeneration had become a national problem. In *Degeneration, Culture and the Novel: 1880–1940*, William Greenslade offers an excellent history of the emergence of belief in degeneration during the last half of the nineteenth century, a belief that could explain "the growing sense in the last decades of the century of a lack of synchrony between the rhetoric of progress . . . and the facts on the ground, the evidence in front of people's eyes, of

poverty and degradation at the heart of ever richer empires."
Analyzing the role of medicine, psychology, urbanization, feminism,
and politics (among other factors) in the emergence of this discourse,
Greenslade notes that at the turn of the century "the crucial topic of
the differential birth-rate . . . emerged into social, medical, and
political discourse." Observing that less desirable elements in the
population were out-breeding all others, "Edwardian race-
improvers" undertook to "save the nation from degeneration."[2]

Alarmists like the eugenist R. R. Rentoul raised the spectre of
"race suicide": "Day by day, hour by hour, and year after year we
add diseased humanity – the children begotten by the diseased,
idiots, imbeciles, epileptics, the insane . . . Does any one contend
that such a scheme of pollution works for race culture? Rather, I
contend, that it works for race suicide."[3] Karl Pearson, Galton's
"principal successor in eugenics," lectured in similar terms:

It would be possible to paint a lurid picture – and label it Race Suicide.
That is feasible to any one who has seen, even from afar, the nine circles of
that dread region which stretches from slum to reformatory, from . . .
hospital and sanatorium to asylum and special school; that infernal lake
which sends its unregarded rivulets to befoul more fertile social tracts.[4]

Ensuring that fears about national degeneration and race suicide
would receive serious attention in the newspapers and in parliament
was the international political context. As Greta Jones points out,
"[t]he growing imperial rivalry between the European nations
increased the fear that British resources of fit and healthy manpower
were on the decline. Moreover, industry also paid a heavy price for
the diseased and the debilitated among the working class."[5] How
long would Britain's imperial and industrial sway continue in the face
of degeneration?

Charles Darwin's theory of natural selection and his cousin Francis
Galton's studies of heredity made it possible to understand these
problems in biological terms. Many argued that natural selection
had ceased to operate in the British population because public and
private charity now enabled the weakest to survive. Herbert Spencer
therefore called for a social Darwinism that would allow natural
selection once more to take its course:

[T]he well-being of existing humanity and the unfolding of it into . . .
ultimate perfection, are both secured by that same beneficial though severe
discipline, to which the animate creation at large is subject. It seems hard
that an unskilfulness . . . should entail hunger upon the artisan. It seems

hard that a laborer incapacitated by sickness . . . should have to bear the resulting privations. It seems hard that widows and orphans should be left to struggle for life or death. Nevertheless, when regarded not separately but in connexion with the interests of universal humanity, these harsh fatalities are seen to be full of beneficence. . .[6]

Similarly, Galton called for a "science of improving stock" that would study "all influences that tend in however remote a degree to give to the more suitable races or strains of blood a better chance of prevailing speedily over the less suitable than they otherwise would have had."[7]

Called eugenics, this new science of human breeding would supplement natural selection in two ways – negatively and positively. As the philosopher and eugenist F. C. S. Schiller explains, "Negative eugenics aims at checking the deterioration to which the human stock is exposed, owing to the rapid proliferation of what may be called human weeds." He warns that "negative eugenics is not enough," however, for it "can only arrest deterioration": "If we want improvement, progress, the creation of superior types of humanity . . ., we must look to positive eugenics, which sets itself to inquire by what means the human race may be rendered intrinsically better, higher, stronger, healthier, more capable."[8] Judged unfit to propagate, human weeds are to be eliminated by segregation, sterilization, or euthanasia; judged fit to propagate, the flowers of humankind are encouraged to have large families.

According to Galton, eugenics would inevitably come to supplement conventional religion:

[Eugenics] must be introduced into the national conscience, like a new religion. It has, indeed, strong claims to become an orthodox religious tenet of the future, for Eugenics co-operate with the works of Nature by securing that humanity shall be represented by the fittest races. What nature does blindly, slowly, and ruthlessly, man may do providently, quickly, and kindly.[9]

William and Catherine Whetham, a potent husband-and-wife team of eugenists, pushed this line by adapting the language of the New Testament to eugenics:

Not only are we our brother's keeper, but the guardian of the physical, mental, and moral character of his remotest descendents. . . The first care must always be to ask with regard to each proposal . . . "Will it help to increase our knowledge of mankind, so that we shall be able to separate the sheep from the goats, and to discover what elements among the people are best and most worthy of encouragement?"[10]

Rentoul did the same with a more Old Testament turn of phrase: "I consider that the most fiendish form of Christian devilry and torture is in our permitting diseased parents to beget diseased offspring. . . We seem, indeed, to forget that the Almighty has practically said to man and womankind – 'I shall no longer create human beings. I appoint you to act as my deputy. . .'"[11]

A generation later, the rhetoric was the same. Schiller asked: "is it not very near blasphemy to assume that the creative *nisus* was exhausted in evolving us, and cannot be trusted to sustain further efforts if we will make them?"[12] Albert E. Wiggam argued that "the biological Golden Rule, the completed Golden Rule of science, [is] . . . *Do unto both the born and the unborn as you would have both the born and the unborn do unto you.*"[13] Even Julian Huxley, a perceptive critic of the "right-wing" and "nationalist and imperialist politics" implicit in much of main-line eugenics, still saw eugenics as the religion of the future: "Once the full implications of evolutionary biology are grasped, eugenics will inevitably become part of the religion of the future, or of whatever complex of sentiments may in the future take the place of organized religion."[14] Thus eugenics was positioned by writers from the 1880s to the 1930s to assume responsibility for a creation recently orphaned by the death of God.

Of course not all scientists, politicians, and social reformers accepted the eugenist's model for addressing social problems. Indeed, the majority did not. In particular, Catholics resisted the suggestion that some lives were more or less sacred than others. Conservatives resisted the central planning that would be necessary to implement most eugenical schemes. Representatives of the working class resisted the tendency to elide the differences between poverty and feeblemindedness. Feminists resisted the suggestion that educated middle-class women who chose careers over childbearing were neglecting their duties to the race. And of course squeamish "Victorians" of all stripes did not want to talk about reproduction at all.

Opponents of eugenics could take heart from the fact that the nature versus nurture argument was no more settled in the early twentieth century than it is now. Many believed that the social environment was more responsible than biological determinism for such problems as pauperism, disease, alcoholism, and prostitution. Eugenists themselves often acknowledged the importance of environment in shaping human nature and behavior by incorporating within their explanation of heredity Lamarck's theory that acquired characteristics could be inherited. In fact, because of its usefulness in this regard, Lamarckism continued to influence eugenics long after most biologists had dismissed Lamarck in the neo-Darwinism that prevailed after August Weismann's publication of his germ plasm theory (1892) and the rediscovery of Gregor Mendel's experiments in heredity (1900) combined to suggest that germ plasm was unaffected by the acquired characteristics of its host.[15] Laypeople like T. S. Eliot could be forgiven for thinking that Jean Baptiste Lamarck was still an important figure in the science of heredity long after serious scientists had abandoned him, for in 1916–17 the *Eugenics Review* gave space in four successive issues to E. W. MacBride's Lamarckian "Study of Heredity," which Eliot called "the most valuable contribution" to its field that year. Eliot's summary of the essay reveals this Lamarckian eugenist's interest in both biological and environmental reforms:

Professor MacBride draws two conclusions of social importance: (1) That in former times the struggle for existence was enough to keep down the defective element in the population; but under present conditions these people are protected and multiply. He advocates therefore segregation and sterilization for the benefit of society. (2) The transmissibility of acquired characters makes the problem of education of the highest importance: we must adopt such a system of education that "the next generation may start at a very slightly higher level of capacity than their fathers."[16]

At least in part as a function of the great desire to find a compromise between the extremes of the environmental and strict hereditarian positions, Lamarckian eugenists – scientists and laypeople alike – flourished well into the 1920s.

Belated Lamarckians aside, however, eugenists increasingly discounted the practical value of social reform of the environment, especially scientists like Pearson, who headed the Galton Eugenics Laboratory:

If the bad man can by the influence of education and surroundings be made good, but the bad stock can never be converted into good stock – then we see how grave a responsibility is cast at the present day upon every citizen, who directly or indirectly has to consider problems relating to the state endowment of education, the revision of the administration of the Poor Law, and, above all, the conduct of public and private charities.[17]

Ethel Elderton, a researcher in Pearson's laboratory, argued that "[p]ractically all social legislation has been based on the assumption that better environment meant race progress, whereas the link between the two is probably that a genuine race progress will result in a better environment."[18] As Lyndsay Farrell notes, "[c]onvinced that 'social problems' were due to inherited factors . . . Pearson directed research based on these convictions. He expected to confirm that 'environmentalism' was not the way to eliminate the social problems under investigation."[19]

In addition to environmental explanations of social problems, however, opponents of eugenics could also counter it with critiques of its racism, classism, and sexism. As Farrell points out, "Pearson and Galton were representative of the eugenics movement in believing in the innate superiority of the white races over all other human populations. Such racist views were often combined with a vigorous nationalism in the writings of many eugenists in the years immediately before the First World War."[20] Julian Huxley recognized this problem and warned against the "danger of mistaking for our eugenic ideal a mere glorification of our prejudices": "It is not eugenics but nationalist and imperialist politics if we speak in such terms as subject races or miscegenation."[21]

Eliot, blind to Leonard Darwin's prejudices on class, wrote approvingly of Darwin's essay (his "articles always deserve attention") on "methods for encouraging reproduction on the part of the best classes in the community, and for discouraging reproduction on the part of the incompetent, thriftless, and pauper element."[22] Representatives of the working class, however, were particularly suspicious of a point of view that regarded the class war as a biological war. Not surprisingly, opposition to the Mental Deficiency Act of 1913, which allowed the detention in mental deficiency institutions of "moral imbeciles" and those who "should be deprived of the opportunity of producing children," and opposition to the defeated Sterilization Bill of 1931 was centered in the Labour movement.[23] The eugenist C. P. Blacker acknowledged the classism and the need to "undo the unfavorable impression" created by those who had emphasized "the question of class": "If you want the help of the dysgenic you are not very likely to enlist their sympathy if you speak about them as dregs and scum."[24] Huxley's observation is on the mark again: "It is not eugenics but right-wing politics if we merely talk of favoring the breeding of the upper classes of our present social system at the expense of the lower."[25]

Similarly, feminists complained of sexism. When the Whethams blamed working women for the low middle-class birthrate ("As soon as the married woman becomes a wage-earner, the birth-rate drops disastrously"[26]), Edith Bethune-Baker complained that they were "prejudiced against the woman's movement."[27] In the face of the Whethams' suggestion that it is "essential to the race that the ablest, healthiest, and finest women should be encouraged, tempted, compelled if necessary . . . to devote themselves to family life," Bethune-Baker responds: "A declining birth-rate would be for some of us no matter for regret if the race can only be perpetuated on such terms . . . Better 'race-destroying occupations' . . . than the soul-destroying atmosphere of the eugenic materialism which is advocated here."[28]

The Roman Catholic Church was another prominent opponent of eugenics, opposing the eugenist's discrimination between human weeds and human flowers with the argument that all life is equally sacred. In *The Church and Eugenics* (1912), Father Thomas J. Gerrard saw in the assumption of certain eugenists that humankind's "betterment is chiefly if not entirely a matter of germ plasm, milk, fresh air, sentimental art, and illuminated certificates" of eugenical worth the danger of "a complete return to the life of the beast."[29] In "The Catholic Church and Race Culture" (1911), he reminded readers of *The Dublin Review* that "[t]he Church declares the root cause of degeneracy to be sin . . . and the root cause of betterment to be virtue."[30] Ultimately, eugenics was among the modern tendencies (like divorce and birth control) condemned by Pope Pius XI in the 1930 encyclical *Casti Connubii*.[31]

Yet Galton's eugenics made for a church as broad as that of its opponents. For all Huxley's awareness of the dangerous prejudices exemplified in mainline eugenics, he was nonetheless a eugenist. Similarly, dissenting voices notwithstanding, many socialists were eugenists.[32] The Fabian socialist George Bernard Shaw was a eugenist whose sense of eugenics' religious mission matched Galton's:

I believe that if we can drive into the heads of men the full consciousness of moral responsibility that comes to men with the knowledge that there never will be a God unless we make one – that we are the instruments through which that ideal is trying to make itself reality – we can work towards that ideal until we get to be supermen, and then super-supermen, and then a world of organisms who have achieved and realized God.[33]

Man and Superman's John Tanner explains the socialist element in Shaw's eugenics: "Equality is essential to good breeding; and equality . . . is incompatible with property."[34] Similarly, the Webbs were both Fabian socialists and eugenists – Beatrice thanking Shaw for discussing in *Man and Superman* "the breeding of the right sort of man" (a discussion that this "Angel in the House" was too delicate to undertake herself), Sidney arguing that the unregulated birth in Great Britain of "Irish Roman Catholics and the Polish, Russian, and German Jews, on the one hand, and the thriftless and irresponsible . . ., on the other, . . . can hardly result in anything but national deterioration."[35] In *The English Review,* the editor Austin Harrison argued that the working class could force employers to meet their demands if they were to launch a "strike of human life" by refusing to reproduce the next generation of workers:

A strike on those lines would paralyze the whole foundations of capitalism, while economically vastly improving the lot of the working-man. He might still marry, but like those in better conditions, he would avoid a family. . . With a population falling to pieces, the State would have to yield to any demands imposed upon it; would, as a consequence, have to take upon itself the problem of the proletarian family; see that it was adequately housed, fed, educated, and buried, for the alternative would be race extinction.[36]

As Feisal Mohamed points out, the "lament about the degeneracy of the lower classes usually found in eugenic discourse is here turned on its head. The working class becomes the truly valuable genetic stock of the nation, for it is the foundation of capitalism."[37]

Similarly, some feminisms were compatible with eugenics. Bethune-Baker described herself as "a believer in 'eugenic' thinking," despite her reservations about the Whethams' attitude toward women – and she was joined in her eugenical beliefs by many other women.[38] Daniel Kevles notes that in the early years of the Eugenics Education Society (established 1907) "[f]ully half the membership . . . consisted of women, and so did about a quarter of its officers."[39] Jones observes that as late as 1937 "The Eugenics Society had a high female membership of just over 40 per cent."[40] In explanation of these facts, Kevles suggests that on the one hand "[e]ugenics . . . focused on issues that, by virtue of biology and prevailing middle-class standards, were naturally women's own" and that, on the other, certain feminists found in the eugenics movement a legitimate public platform for engagement in social activism and involvement with the world of science – a platform not otherwise easy for women to come by.[41] Jones, however, argues that "women in the social hygiene movement, drawn as they were from largely conventional middle class and upper class backgrounds, were socially conservative in their views" and that "even the female social hygienists who were feminists were often ferocious economic moralists of the old *laissez-faire* school."[42] Yet the "feminist" socialist eugenist Herman Muller shows that even socialist feminists could find a point of contact with eugenics: urging that the workplace be made woman-friendly, that community child-care and mother-support programmes be established, that the medical profession's attitudes toward childbirth become woman-centered, and that birth control be promoted, he argues that "[o]nly by lightening the physiological, the psychological, the economic, and the social burdens on the mother now caused by child-bearing and child-rearing can we attain to a state in which real eugenics is feasible."[43]

There were many ways, then, in which eugenics could be incorporated both into one's understanding of the past and present *and*, more interestingly and more controversially, into one's vision of the future – whether that vision was progressive or reactionary. Although it by no means earned everyone's trust and support, the science of eugenics and the social-policy debates to which it gave rise interested everyone in the early years of the twentieth century. Neither the variety of writers interested in eugenics nor the variety of ends that their interest in eugenics served, therefore, should surprise us.

Notwithstanding the Nazi atrocities in the name of eugenics that were still to follow, the eugenics of some writers was notorious even in their own day. The Fabian Shaw's eugenics was at times extreme: "Extermination must be put on a scientific basis if it is ever to be carried out humanely and apologetically as well as thoroughly . . . [I]f we desire a certain type of civilization and culture, we must exterminate the sort of people who do not fit in."[44] In his equally notorious book *Anticipations*, the equally Fabian H. G. Wells contemplates the threat to the New Republic of the future represented by the proliferation of "vicious, helpless and pauper masses":

It has become apparent that whole masses of human population are, as a whole, inferior in their claim upon the future, to other masses, that . . . their characteristic weaknesses are contagious and detrimental in the civilizing fabric, and that their range of incapacity tempts and demoralizes the strong. To give them equality is to sink to their level, to protect and cherish them is to be swamped in their fecundity.

Whereas in the old world the fatal fertility of the degenerate masses was unopposed, in this new world, "[t]he new ethics will hold life to be a privilege and a responsibility . . . and the alternative in right

conduct between living fully, beautifully and efficiently will be to die"
– a "merciful obliteration of weak and silly and pointless things."[45]
Pregnant by Wells, Rebecca West gestured toward the eugenical
beliefs of her Fabian friends as justification of her ostensibly hypocri-
tical secrecy about her pregnancy (given her articles at this time
criticizing society's attitude toward unwed mothers): "Pale Fabians
would say that I was The Free Woman and that I had wanted to be
the Mother of the Superman."[46] The notoriety of its superstar
eugenists was sufficient to make the discourse of eugenics an
important part of Fabian public policy and private gossip alike.

No Fabian, but as extreme in his negative eugenics as Shaw and
Wells, D. H. Lawrence outlines a plan of extermination for society's
outcasts as early as 1908:

If I had my way, I would build a lethal chamber as big as the Crystal Palace,
with a military band playing softly, and a Cinematograph working brightly;
then I'd go out in the back streets and main streets and bring them in, all
the sick, the halt, and the maimed; I would lead them gently, and they
would smile me a weary thanks.[47]

He displays at least the virtue of consistency in a similar comment in
1923: "we must look after the quality of life, not the quantity.
Hopeless life should be put to sleep, the idiots and the hopeless sick
and the true criminal. And the birth-rate should be controlled."[48]
The solutions proposed by Lawrence, Wells, and Shaw testify to the
magnitude of the problem of fatal fertility that seemed to them to
loom over the future of humankind.

Of course the negative eugenics of other writers was not necessarily so extreme, and there was also a widespread interest in positive
eugenics. In *The Playboy of the Western World*, J. M. Synge's publican
Michael Flaherty expresses the eugenist's fear of human weeds when
explaining his preference for Christy Mahon over Shawn Keogh as
his daughter Margaret's husband: "it's the will of God that all should
rear up lengthy families for the nurture of the earth. . . and I liefer
face the grave untimely and I seeing a score of grandsons growing up
little gallant swearers by the name of God, than go peopling my
bedside with puny weeds the like of what you'd breed, I'm thinking,
out of Shaneen Keogh."[49] How much of Michael Flaherty's positive
eugenics is Synge's is impossible to determine because of Synge's
pervasive irony, but it is clear that Synge knows something of the
eugenical discourse concerning human weeds.

Aldous Huxley speaks in his own voice to much the same effect as

Synge's publican. As much a eugenist as his brother, although lacking the latter's alertness to the strains of classism and racism in his eugenics, Huxley takes up the same concern about the proliferation of human weeds. Just months after finishing *Brave New World* (1931), he observes: "So far as our knowledge goes, negative eugenics – or the sterilization of the unfit – might already be practised with tolerable safety. On the positive side we are still very ignorant – though we know enough . . . to foresee the rapid deterioration, unless we take remedial measures, of the whole West European stock."[50] Two years later, after the introduction of the Nazi Eugenical Sterilization Law, his thinking remains the same: "What is the remedy for the present deplorable state of affairs? It consists, obviously, in encouraging the normal and super-normal members of the population to have larger families and in preventing the sub-normal from having any families at all."[51]

Of course there were many writers who remained suspicious of eugenics or condemned it outright. It was the newspaper founded by Hilaire Belloc, *Eyewitness*, that, as Jones points out, "ran the toughest campaign against the 1913 Mental Deficiency Bill."[52] As early as 1901, G. K. Chesterton had accused Pearson of preaching "the great principle of the survival of the nastiest."[53] Jones sees Chesterton and Belloc united in "a variety of Catholic radicalism" that "believed an intimate connection existed between capitalism and eugenics."[54] Yet Chesterton's anti-eugenical essays also articulate a more secular humanism. Negative eugenics is "the social justification of murder" – but murder nonetheless, however much its proponents might prefer to call it "Social Subtraction" or "Life Control."[55] According to Chesterton, for Dean Inge to believe that "some absurd American statistics or experiments show that heredity is an incurable disease and that education is no cure for it," and for Arnold Bennett to believe that although "many of his friends drink too much . . . it cannot be helped, because they cannot help it," is a "humiliating heresy" – "the really intolerable insult to human dignity" of saying that "human life is not determined by human will."[56]

James Joyce attributes the same Catholic and humanist suspicion of eugenics to Stephen Dedalus in *A Portrait of the Artist as a Young Man* when Stephen dismisses the hypothesis "that every physical quality admired by men in women is in direct connection with the manifold functions of women for the propagation of the species." Stephen dislikes this explanation of woman's beauty: "It leads to eugenics rather than to esthetic." He caricatures eugenists (like Galton, Rentoul, and the Whethams) for whom eugenics has become the new religion: in his "new gaudy lectureroom," the eugenist stands "with one hand on *The Origin of the Species* and the other hand on the new testament" and "tells you that you admired the great flanks of Venus because you thought that she would bear you burly offspring and admired her great breasts because you felt that she would give good milk to her children and yours."[57] Although at virtually the same time in the United States, the undergraduate F. Scott Fitzgerald was framing the same issue much more ambiguously in his poem "Love or Eugenics" – "Men, which would you like to come and pour your tea, / Kisses that set your heart aflame, / Or Love from a prophylactic dame" – Stephen clearly declares that he, like Chesterton, will not accept a definition of the human in terms of the animal.[58]

The novel's timeframe indicates that this conversation is set in 1902 – implying that *both* the academic Stephen *and* the vigilantly non-academic Lynch to whom he is speaking are familiar with the term "eugenics." This word was first used by Galton and other scientists in the mid-1880s and was being used occasionally in the English periodical press of the 1890s, so it is just possible that these two university students could have used the word in this casual way without the much weaker student Lynch, not otherwise reluctant to push Stephen for definitions, having to ask for an explanation of it.[59] Given, however, that Stephen does not mention eugenics in very similar conversations with Lynch in *Stephen Hero* (1904–06), and given that the fifth chapter of *A Portrait of the Artist as a Young Man* in which eugenics is for the first time mentioned was not completed until 1914 (after the founding of the Eugenics Education Society in 1907, after the publication in *The Dublin Review* of Father Gerrard's 1911 essay "The Catholic Church and Race Culture," and after the controversy about the 1913 Mental Deficiency Bill, including the controversy about whether it should be extended to Ireland), it is likely that the conversation represents a mild anachronism. That is, it presumably reflects not so much Stephen's concern about eugenics in turn-of-the-century Dublin as Joyce's own concern about eugenics at the time he was writing the novel's concluding chapter.

Clearly, although not all writers were eugenists or sympathetic to eugenics, eugenics touched upon the interests – if not the very lives – of many more of them than were eugenists. The list of major and minor writers that a history of eugenics and modern literature must address is therefore extensive: Virginia Woolf, T. S. Eliot, W. B. Yeats, George Bernard Shaw, D. H. Lawrence, H. G. Wells, Rebecca West, Arnold Bennett, J. M. Synge, Aldous Huxley, F. Scott Fitzgerald – I list only those mentioned above. One could also add the names of many others: C. P. Snow, Olive Schreiner, Marie Stopes (who published *Married Love* in 1918 as Mary Carmichael), Naomi Mitchison, H. L. Mencken, and Jack London – to name but a few.[60] Furthermore, in any such history, James Joyce, G. K. Chesterton, Hilaire Belloc, and a host of other literary dissenters from eugenics would also have an important place.[61]

Such a history will of necessity be more than a story of the positions that individual writers took *vis-à-vis* eugenics. It will also be a story of the position that eugenics itself took in the modern world by speaking through the lives and works of these writers. From this point of view, perhaps the most suggestive account of the relationship between writers like these and the science of heredity that captured their attention is Michel Foucault's in *The History of Sexuality.*

Foucault claims that since the seventeenth century the state has arrogated to itself a "bio-power" by which it assumes the right to eliminate "biological danger to others." He suggests that "between the state and the individual, sex became an issue, and a public issue no less." Sex was put into discourse "to transform the sexual conduct of couples into a concerted economic and political behavior." This discourse became the science of sex, which

set itself up as the supreme authority in matters of hygienic necessity, taking up the old fears of venereal affliction and combining them with the new themes of asepsis, and the great evolutionist myths with the recent institutions of public health; it claimed to ensure the physical vigor and moral cleanliness of the social body; it promised to eliminate defective individuals, degenerate and bastardized populations. In the name of a biological and historical urgency, it justified the racisms of the state . . .

The eugenics latent in this discourse was not fully actualized until the late nineteenth and early twentieth centuries, when the science of eugenics was born – "the programs of eugenics" constituting one of the "great innovations in the technology of sex of the second half of the nineteenth century."[62]

I have chosen to focus on Woolf, Eliot, and Yeats as the subject of this study not only because they are traditionally regarded as among

the most important of the many modern writers interested in
eugenics, but also because the history of their engagement with
eugenics needs to be read against the background of Foucault's
general claim. All three pretend to adapt the scientific discourse of
the body as used by the eugenist to the language and purposes of the
imagination. In Woolf's case, the language of eugenics moves from
conversations in the consulting rooms and at the dinner tables of her
doctors into both her fiction and, ultimately, her feminist theorization
of woman's imagination in *A Room of One's Own*. In Eliot's case, the
language of eugenics moves from the realm of public debate into his
marriage bed, issuing therefrom in poetry and prose that imagines as
nightmare the myriad contemporary eugenical threats to the continued biological and cultural development of humankind. In Yeats's
case, the language of eugenics becomes involved in the projects of the
occult adept, the romantic poet, and the nationalist politician –
projects that Yeats seeks to advance by informing the Irish mind with
poetic images that will enable the nation to procreate its way to a
better race. Woolf, Eliot, and Yeats all appropriate the language of
eugenical biology as a metaphor in aid of ostensibly non-biological
cultural projects. In each case, however, the writer seems to serve as
an agent – whether witting or unwitting – of what Foucault calls
"bio-power." Each extends the imperial sway of the scientific
discourse of the body into a realm long thought most different from it
(if not most hostile to it): the realm of the imagination.

I do not at all attempt a comprehensive survey of the complete
work of any one of these writers. Instead, I draw attention on the one
hand to eugenical aspects of the lives they led, and I draw attention
on the other hand to eugenical dimensions of some of their most
famous poems, plays, and novels. My purpose is to show how much
more work remains to be done in the way of close readings of
modernist lives and modernist literature in the wake of the attention
to eugenics that has been stimulated by recent scholarship.

In the course of this study, I attempt to document wherever
possible the actual eugenical texts – books, diaries, letters, conversations, lectures, public debates, and so on – that introduced Woolf,
Eliot, and Yeats to eugenics and influenced their understanding of
this science and this social movement. Even when the so-called
smoking-gun that proves the specific influence of specific texts is
unavailable, however, I draw attention to significant parallels
between eugenical texts in general and particular texts by these

writers – texts that might otherwise seem remote from eugenical influence. Such parallels, however, provide compelling circumstantial evidence of these writers' implicitly eugenical beliefs. As Bernhard Radloff suggests, "correspondences of discursive structures are not always evidenced by demonstrable influences and sources, but are no less real than these . . ."[63] In remarking such correspondences, we are on the trail of what Gillian Beer calls the "hermeneutic circle" of the text and its first readers – "the complexity of whose relations is written into the work" as voices (both explicit and implicit) "arguing, repeating, refusing, diversifying the range of the book's linguistic community."[64] Even when we need to tease it out of sometimes recalcitrant poems, plays, novels, and essays, the voice of eugenical discourse is nonetheless present and nonetheless significant for its reticence about being seen and heard.

Reticence in the matter of eugenics is overdetermined. After the Nazi atrocities in the name of eugenics in the 1930s and 1940s, most countries apart from Germany conveniently forgot their complicity in the eugenics movement of the early years of the twentieth century. Before the Nazi Eugenic Sterilization Law came into effect on 1 January 1934, however, sterilization laws had already been enacted in thirty American states, as well as a number of other countries, including Denmark, Finland, Sweden, Norway, Iceland, Switzerland, and Canada.[65] The thoroughness of these countries' repression of awareness of their eugenical history helps to explain the shock occasioned by newspaper accounts in the late 1990s of the effects of such laws: 2,845 Canadians were sterilized by the Alberta Eugenics Board between 1929 and 1972! 11,000 eugenically unfit Finns were sterilized between 1935 and 1970! 63,000 eugenically unfit Swedes were sterilized between 1935 and 1976! Sterilizations in the name of eugenics continued in Switzerland and France to the end of the twentieth century! The repressed history has returned – accompanied both by lawsuits on behalf of those sterilized and by government investigations on behalf of the conscience-stricken sterilizing countries.[66]

The progressive sensibility has been particularly tormented by the return of eugenics to public consciousness. The sterilization laws in Sweden were enacted and administered by leftwing, welfare-minded Social Democratic governments. Similarly, although Britain never enacted sterilization laws, it "has some soul-searching of its own to do," suggests Jonathan Freedland, for "eugenics is the dirty little secret of the British left":

The names of the first champions read like a rollcall of British socialism's best and brightest: Sidney and Beatrice Webb, George Bernard Shaw, Harold Laski, John Maynard Keynes, Marie Stopes, the *New Statesman*, even, lamentably, the *Manchester Guardian*. Nearly every one of the left's most cherished, iconic figures espoused views which today's progressives would find repulsive.

Observing that "in the shadow of Auschwitz, Treblinka and Sobibor, the British left gave up its flirtation with eugenics," Freedland complains that "[t]hey escaped the reckoning": "their past was buried too quickly – and forgotten. . . despite their association with the foulest idea of the twentieth century."[67]

Similar patterns of shock and denial are evident in the literary community's attempt to reckon eugenics in the history of modern literature. In her biography of Virginia Woolf, Hermione Lee confronts Woolf's suggestion that the institutionalized "imbeciles" that she has seen "should certainly be killed."[68] Although Lee elsewhere writes "I feel the need to swallow her whole, not spit out the bits of her which I may find distasteful," she apologizes in the biography for both the form and the substance of Woolf's remark: "It may seem to most of us reprehensible and cruel to speak about 'idiots' and 'imbeciles,' and it is horrid to find Virginia Woolf doing so," but "we have to remember that these were standard terms" and that Woolf's "violent endorsement of an extreme theory of eugenics, written between two very severe breakdowns, must be understood as expressing her dread and horror of what she thought of as her own loss of control."[69] Invoking the yet to occur second breakdown as somehow a mitigation of this endorsement of eugenics shows how hard it is for Lee not to spit out this distasteful bit of Woolf.

Scholars have had to confront similar statements by Yeats and Eliot, and they have often accounted for them in similarly mitigating ways. According to Yeats,

Since about 1900 the better stocks have not been replacing their numbers, while the stupider and less healthy have been more than replacing theirs. . . If some financial reorganization . . . enable everybody without effort to procure all necessities of life and so remove the last check upon the multiplication of the uneducatable masses, it will become the duty of the educated classes to seize and control one or more of those necessities. The drilled and docile masses may submit, but a prolonged civil war seems more likely, with the victory of the skilful, riding their machines as did the feudal knights their armoured horses.[70]

We must remember, says Paul Scott Stanfield, that "in the years before World War II, when Yeats became interested in eugenics, it was respected, widely influential and had even started to seem orthodox."[71] Elizabeth Cullingford suggests that Yeats's "style may obscure the fact that the problem he raises is genuine": the statement above – "a horrendous and probably metaphorical vision of the forcible control of the multiplying masses by the skilled few" – obscures his interest in "family planning," and "[t]o do Yeats justice, life in Catholic Ireland must have highlighted the need for a birth control policy."[72] Cullingford implies that Yeats was driven to his scathing modest proposal by what W. H. Auden called "mad Ireland"; like Swift, he could claim: "I calculate my Remedy *for this one individual Kingdom of* IRELAND *and for no other that ever was, is, or I think ever can be upon Earth.*"[73]

Eliot reveals similar prejudices about the multiplying masses. The eugenist speaks "very justly," he says, when insisting that there is no help for the poor "if parental responsibility be removed and reckless reproduction encouraged."[74] Eliot's language is less sensational than Yeats's, but their fears about the potentially fatal fertility represented by the reproductive power of the masses is the same: "There is no doubt that in our headlong rush to educate everybody, we are lowering our standards . . . destroying our ancient edifices to make ready the ground upon which the barbarian nomads of the future will encamp in their mechanized caravans."[75] Criticizing this aspect of Eliot's pride and prejudices, John Carey does not pull his punch: he suggests that the description of the Jew in "Gerontion" as "Spawned in some estaminet of Antwerp" reveals "a belief in the importance of good breeding which would have been readily understood in eugenicist circles."[76] Juan Leon's survey of the eugenics implicit in "Gerontion" and other poems like *The Waste Land*, in which "the city festers as the breeding ground of disturbing populations and eugenic terrors," concludes with a more familiar gesture: "Eliot's eugenic fears must be considered . . . in perspective. They were far less an anomaly than a characteristic of his age."[77] Robert Crawford goes one step further and suggests that in the poem's horror of abortion and emotionless lovemaking, "A grotesque critique of eugenic ideas permeates *The Waste Land*."[78]

Find a writer – almost any modern British, Irish, or American writer – who is accused of endorsing eugenics and one will also find an apologetic defender of that writer's moral values. To Michael Coren's charge that H. G. Wells offers in *Anticipations* (1901) "the most structured and complete manual of eugenics ever to be written by a reputed author," Michael Foot answers that Wells's progressive heart was in the right place, for he "was the pioneer in advocating the combination between social reformist eugenics and sexual liberation for men and women."[79] In 1995, David Bradshaw presented extensive evidence of Aldous Huxley's support for eugenics at the time of writing *Brave New World*, concluding that the novel "embodies in an absurd and distorted form ideas and opinions that Huxley framed in earnest beyond his novel's satirical parameters."[80] As though called forth once more by this charge, Donald Watt's twenty-year-old essay was republished the very next year to argue again that Huxley's manuscript revisions "intensify" the irony that he "uses implicitly to deplore the values celebrated in his brave new world." Watt wonders "how so many of his [Huxley's] book's early reviewers could have thought he was advocating its view of the future."[81] And so it goes.

In the debate about the values of modernism itself, these two tendencies are represented by Carey and Greenslade. Carey regards the interest in eugenics on the part of many modernist poets and novelists as a particular expression of a more general fear of and contempt for the masses: "the principle around which modernist literature and culture fashioned themselves was the exclusion of the masses, the defeat of their power, the removal of their literacy, the denial of their humanity."[82] The indictment he prefers against modernism is impressive. Yet so is the defense that Greenslade mounts. The latter argues that "the widespread attribution of deviancy and degeneracy to modern culture" effectively placed modern writers themselves under the surveillance of eugenical discourse and so prompted in their work a complex defense of the rights of the individual as narrators and characters in their works explicitly or implicitly took on the role of "critical, combative humanist."[83]

I am interested neither to condemn nor to apologize for either the writers in question or the phenomenon of modernism itself. The apologetic reflex too often prevents a full accounting of a writer's engagement with eugenics by prejudging eugenical beliefs always and everywhere an aberration – pathologizing what we find "reprehensible," "cruel," and "horrendous," making it a function of emotional distress, marking it a lapse in judgment, a letting down of one's moral guard in the privacy of a diary or confidential letter (the result of a bad day, a bad year, or a bad decade). The urge to condemn can function as an instance of the imperialism of contemporary absolutes – an insistence that writers share the moral values of today's progressives if they are not to be kicked out of the canon of great writers. A dialogue with the past that begins with either a condemnation of or an apology for eugenical beliefs risks being no less colonial than dialogue with any other Other in which the so-called dialogue begins with the prejudice that a foreign consciousness is false and illegitimate.

As Jerome McGann suggests, "in attempting to specify historical distinctions, we set a gulf between our past and our present. It is this gulf which enables us to judge and criticize the past, but it is equally this gulf which enables the past . . . to judge and criticize us."[84] How might the eugenists of the past judge and criticize us? They might point out the unwisdom of stone-throwing inhabitants of glass houses. At the very least, their example should make us beware the hubris in any confidence we might have that *today's* science of heredity is significantly sounder than yesterday's, or that we can foresee any better than the eugenists could the implications for the future of the science that we embrace today – whether we call that science eugenics or genetics. And their example might also make us beware the hubris of assuming that because we can no longer believe what early eugenists believed we are therefore better moralists and scientists than our benighted forbears – the hubris of assuming that we do not believe things today that our descendents will criticize a century hence (as we now criticize eugenics) as an example of egregious moral and scientific failure on our part.

A century after Francis Galton inaugurated the science of eugenics, some things have not changed: it is still the case, for instance, that everything from alcoholism to homosexuality is liable to receive an explanation in terms of biological heredity – an explanation that has been turned to their own advantage by both progressives and reactionaries, just as it was a century ago. At the beginning of the twenty-first century, however, genetic technology makes available to prospective parents a genetic counseling almost unimaginable at the beginning of the twentieth century – a genetic counseling that invites people to make implicitly or explicitly eugenical decisions about the immediate genetic future of their offspring and the long-term genetic future of the species.

If history is repeating itself, we must beware the tendency to treat the first engagement with eugenics as farce. As Marouf Arif Hasian, Jr., suggests: "If our society is going to engage in profitable public debate on the issue of eugenics, we need rhetorical histories that look at the ways in which eugenical arguments have been deployed and reconfigured."[85] That eugenics served projects as diverse as Yeats's Irish nationalism, Shaw's Fabian socialism, Woolf's feminism, Lawrence's vitalism, and Eliot's conservatism makes it a force to be reckoned with. It is incumbent upon literary critics to investigate the ways in which a discourse ostensibly so racist, classist, and sexist as eugenics apparently circulated in turn-of-the-century Europe and America to simultaneously oppressive and emancipatory effect – both in the realm of modern social policy and in the realm of the modern literary imagination.

Of course the historical investigation prerequisite to any attempt to appreciate a literary consciousness informed by the eugenics of the early years of the twentieth century requires considerable effort. We must first attempt to repossess the discourse of eugenics – ostensibly a scientific discourse in its own right, but also a discourse implicated in imperialist politics, the economics of overpopulation and depopulation, the prostitution or social hygiene problem, the birth control campaign, the movement for the emancipation of women, and so on. I attempt to repossess important aspects of the eugenics discourse in this Introduction and I introduce further information, as necessary, in the chapters that follow. We must also examine the writer's life as lived within the discourse of eugenics, and we must read closely and carefully the writer's texts – texts written not only within that discourse, but with and against its grain.

I bear in mind that contemporary theories of discourse such as Foucault's provide for the possibility of resistance to the kind of hegemonic discourse that the eugenical science of sex represents: "Discourse transmits and produces power; it reinforces it, but also undermines and exposes it, renders it fragile and makes it possible to thwart it." Discourse can become "a hindrance, a stumbling-block, a point of resistance and a starting point for an opposing strategy" – for instance, through silence. Silence "is less the absolute limit of discourse . . . than an element that functions alongside the things said, with them and in relation to them within over-all strategies."

Silence can be "a shelter for power," but it can also "loosen its hold and provide for relatively obscure areas of tolerance."[86] Reticence, in short, can be good and/or bad.

In attempting to restore a voice to the neglected eugenical selves of Woolf, Eliot, and Yeats, and in attempting to tell a tale about their eugenical lives, therefore, I would not want to suggest that the eugenical voice in question is unsilently single or that the eugenical life in question is unthwartedly whole. Investigation of the multiplicity of the eugenical voice and of the silences that bedevil the telling of the eugenical life, however, must await the information and the interpretation of others. My proposal with regard to the history of modern literature and eugenics is more modest: let us document the eugenics in the life and literature of our favorite writers, and let us face it squarely. As Thomas Hardy urged at the turn of the last century, "if way to the Better there be, it exacts a full look at the Worst."[87]

CHAPTER I

Virginia Woolf's hereditary taint

Virginia Woolf's eugenical self has gone largely unremarked – perhaps not surprisingly. On the one hand, as Woolf's latest biographer Lee observes: "Virginia Woolf doesn't have a life, she has lives."[1] Similarly, as Woolf herself notes of Orlando, "she had a great variety of selves to call upon, far more than we have been able to find room for, since a biography is considered complete if it merely accounts for six or seven selves, whereas a person may have as many thousand."[2] So the fact that one of Woolf's selves has gone unheard and one of her lives untold is not surprising in itself. On the other hand, this silence may be a function of the fact that such a self and such a life do not accord with today's received myths. As Lee notes, "from the 1960s onwards, rival myths took shape out of the libertarian, radical and feminist movements of the time, constructing Virginia Woolf as a bold, revolutionary pioneer, a Marxist and lesbian heroine, a subversive cultural analyst and a historian of women's hidden lives."[3] Some of those who subscribe to such myths may regard the thesis that Woolf was a eugenist as an attack upon her, and since, as Eliot observes, "[t]here is a large class of persons, including some who appear in print as critics, who regard any censure upon a 'great' [writer] as a breach of the peace, as an act of wanton iconoclasm, or even hoodlumism," I must hasten to add that this essay is not part of what Lee calls the "hostile Leavisite attack on Woolf . . . as a pernicious and typical representative of Bloomsbury elitism, prejudice and complacency."[4] I simply agree with Lee: "all the information and all the interpretations should be written, or re-written, as accurately as possible."[5] Therefore, the eugenical self needs a voice; the eugenical life, a telling.

As we know, eugenics comes in two forms – negative and positive – and Woolf supported both. Her negative eugenics appears in a 1915 diary entry, where she records her thoughts about a group of people she encountered on a walk – people apparently institutionalized on account of defective mental development:

we met & had to pass a long line of imbeciles. The first was a very tall young man, just queer enough to look at twice, but no more; the second shuffled, & looked aside; and then one realised that every one in that long line was a miserable ineffective shuffling idiotic creature, with no forehead, or no chin, & an imbecile grin, or a wild suspicious stare. It was perfectly horrible.

Her conclusion – "They should certainly be killed" – represents a most negative eugenics.[6] Years later in *Three Guineas* (1938), Woolf's eugenics is more positive. Surveying the many "duties . . . which are specially appropriate to the daughters of educated men," Woolf contemplates the role of such daughters become "the mothers of educated men" and urges that "a wage . . . be paid by the State to those whose profession is marriage and motherhood." Her justification of such a policy is positively eugenic:

Consider . . . what effect this would have upon the birth-rate, in the very class where births are desirable – the educated class. Just as the increase in the pay of soldiers has resulted . . . in additional recruits to the force of arm-bearers, so the same inducement would serve to recruit the child-bearing force, which we can hardly deny to be as necessary and as honorable . . .

In her otherwise anti-war tract, Woolf recruits soldiers for the biological war that must be won by positive eugenics if England is to produce the "desirable" kind of future citizen who will help to create "peace and freedom for the whole world."[7]

Woolf's eugenics has not gone completely unremarked. Apologizing for Yeats's well-known enthusiasm for eugenics, Cullingford quotes this passage from *Three Guineas* as part of her argument that "[t]he decline in the European birthrate between 1880 and the Second World War caused observers of all shades of the political spectrum to embrace eugenic ideals."[8] Jonathan Rose apologizes for Edwardian enthusiasm for eugenics by means of a similar gesture towards Woolf: "Very few eugenists openly advocated the extermination of the subnormal, but the suggestion was sometimes made in private, even by Virginia Woolf."[9] So high today is the estimation of Woolf's politics, and so low the estimation of the politics of Yeats and modernism generally, that the ignominy of one's eugenics is apparently mitigated by Woolf's having kept company with the same ideas.

Woolf scholars themselves, however, have been less inclined to allow that she could even have entertained eugenical ideas. Stephen

Trombley reveals that many of Woolf's doctors were thoroughgoing eugenists, but he hastens to assure us that so far as eugenics is concerned, "[w]e can be certain that doctor and patient were hopelessly at odds."[10] Roger Poole singles out Dr. T. B. Hyslop for contempt, speculating that his paralyzing neurosis in old age was "[a] curious latter-day revenge taken by the spirit" for his eugenical beliefs. He mocks Hyslop for his "naive, almost crazy theory, that the vital energies of the Empire were being sapped, and that strong measures were to be taken against further decline." Unaware of how typical and how widespread Hyslop's eugenical beliefs were, and apparently unaware of Woolf's very similar eugenical ideas in *Three Guineas*, he concludes that "Hyslop's eugenics, mixed with his concern for the Empire and a kind of Gilbert and Sullivan grasp of Darwinism, is beyond serious comment."[11]

Woolf herself clearly disagrees about what deserves serious comment. Her diary and *Three Guineas* constitute serious enough comment about just this sort of eugenics. And of course Foucault disagrees: the discourse of "bio-power," by which the state assumes the right to eliminate "biological danger to others," certainly receives serious comment from him. Our contempt today for early twentieth-century eugenics must not blind us to the quite different attitudes of quite different people in quite different times.

In the following chapters, I outline briefly the nature of the eugenics that Woolf knew, the social and political context in which she encountered it, and the ways that eugenical ideas impinged upon her sex-life and marriage. I argue that the issues raised by eugenics were so important to Woolf as to force their way not just into her diary and *Three Guineas*, but also into one of her most important novels, *Mrs. Dalloway* (1925), and one of her most important essays, *A Room of One's Own* (1928). In the course of this argument, I focus upon many other texts – other essays, other novels, diaries, letters, and so on – yet my purpose is not to provide a comprehensive account of the influence of eugenics upon everything that Woolf wrote, but rather to detail two examples of the kind of readings of her work enabled by awareness of the eugenical discourse that surrounded her and at times took voice through her.

In *Mrs. Dalloway*, the problems raised by eugenists are contemplated both by a wide variety of characters and by the third-person narrator – a narrator whose attitudes often reflect those of the author herself. Close attention to the role of eugenics in *Mrs. Dalloway* reveals the extent to which Woolf accepted eugenics, regarding it as a literally unremarkable response to certain problems in the modern world. In *A Room of One's Own*, Woolf's conception of a woman's literary tradition as a pattern of influence grounded in the enabling priority of women precursors is itself facilitated by eugenical thinking – a thinking that extends "bio-power" into the realm of woman's imagination.

Woolf was introduced to the science and the ideology of the eugenics movement in a variety of ways. Eugenics was the focus of published controversy, for instance, in three main areas: where its claims impinged upon the domain of other sciences, where its claims to provide the remedy of social ills contradicted the beliefs of social reformers, and where its claims implied consequences for everyday life.[12] Woolf need not have read the specialized scientific journals to have learned of eugenics at this time. From 1900 to the First World War, there were many articles on eugenics in newspapers, magazines, and popular journals such as *The Times*, *The Nineteenth Century*, *The Monthly Review*, *The Westminster Review*, *The Hibbert Journal*, and so on.[13] In 1910, for instance, an editorial in *The Times* sparked controversy by celebrating the research at the Galton Eugenics Laboratory by which Elderton concluded that the children of alcoholic parents did not inherit their parents' defects. Temperance supporters like Alfred Marshall and believers in the inheritance of acquired characteristics like John Maynard Keynes publicly attacked this conclusion during a letter-to-the-editor controversy that lasted two years.[14]

So ubiquitous was eugenics, in fact, that Woolf found one of her early book reviews in *The Cornhill Magazine* published alongside an essay clearly reflecting eugenical thinking: Henrietta Barnett's "Some Principles of the Poor Law" (1908). Contemplating revisions in the administration of the Poor Law, and noting both the increasing numbers of the poor in Britain and the inconsistent regional policies in the implementation of the Poor Law, Barnett urged that the poor everywhere be treated with a view to their "restoration to Industrial Efficiency":

first . . . the nation must be willing to believe in the possibility of such men's restoration; secondly, to pay for it; and thirdly (and this is the most alien to the present lawless attitude of public thought), to agree that he should be controlled while he is being restored to industrial efficiency, or permanently

detained if he fails to attain to a standard by which he can support himself
or is fit to call others into existence.

Prostitutes should also be detained until restored to industrial
efficiency: "How many girls have I seen go out of the lock wards
when they 'felt better' to spread sin and suffering, when powers of
detention would have kept them long enough to have broken their
lawless connections and discipline taught them self-control."[15] One
notices the general eugenical concern about the unrestricted ability
of the unfit to propagate, and the apparently neo-Lamarckian
proposal to allow propagation only by those who have acquired and
therefore can pass on good character.

Did Woolf read Barnett's essay? As part of Beatrice Webb's circle,
Barnett was known to Woolf, and so Woolf may have read the essay
of someone she was likely to meet socially. And of course authors
often note the work appearing alongside their own in magazines and
journals. Moreover, Woolf was alert to the sorts of problems raised by
Barnett. In her own essay, she criticizes Lady Dorothy Nevill as naive
because of her nostalgia for the elegantly witty society of her youth:
"life is not merely a matter of dinner parties; there are the 'lower
classes,' country houses, politics and arts. In order that you may have
a society such as she laments, all these surroundings must be properly
arranged in due relation to it."[16] Barnett's essay offers advice about
precisely such arrangements. Furthermore, Woolf implies familiarity
with "the principle of . . . Industrial Efficiency" promoted by social
hygienists like Barnett, for her later diary entry criticizing imbeciles
as "ineffective" suggests neither the language of medicine nor the
language of common prejudice, but rather the very language of
Industrial Efficiency. So whether or not Woolf read this particular
essay by Barnett, she was certainly familiar with the text that the
Barnetts of the turn of the century were circulating – what Foucault
calls the eugenical discourse of the body, a scientific discourse
designed "to transform the sexual conduct of couples into a concerted economic and political behavior."

It is also clear from the diary entry cited above that Woolf was
familiar with an even more negative eugenics. W. Duncan McKim,
for instance, proposed that

[t]he surest, the simplest, the kindest, and most humane means for
preventing reproduction among those whom we deem unworthy of this
high privilege, is a gentle, painless death; and this should be administered
not as a punishment, but as an expression of enlightened pity for the victims

– too defective by nature to find true happiness in life – and as a duty toward the community and toward our own offspring.[17]

In fact, the emphatic word "certainly" in Woolf's assertion about imbeciles – "They should certainly be killed" – can be read as an indication that Woolf is here confirming either a conclusion that she knows others have reached or a conclusion that she herself had reached even before this experience. That is, she seems to understand her particular observations to corroborate a general eugenical argument (like that of McKim, Shaw, Wells, and Lawrence) – an argument so familiar to her that her train of thought seems to run, "Yes, the eugenical conclusion is right: imbeciles should be killed."

Another way that the eugenics in the air reached Woolf was by means of friends and acquaintances like the Webbs who were active in the eugenics debate. Even more intimate friends with whom she socialized more regularly – Goldsworthy ("Goldie") Lowes Dickinson, John Maynard Keynes, and Ottoline Morrell – were members of the Eugenics Education Society itself.[18] Charles Darwin's son Leonard, whom Woolf knew as the "widower of 50" who married her childhood friend "dear old Mildred Massingberd," became the very visible, long-serving president of the Eugenics Education Society in 1911. Dear old Mildred herself served on the Reception Committee of the First International Eugenics Congress in 1912.[19] Josiah Wedgwood, another of Woolf's acquaintances, was the Liberal MP who led the spirited and widely reported opposition to the Mental Deficiency Bill in 1913.[20] He protested that "[t]he only interest of Hon. Members who support this Bill is the production of wealth by the community"; as Jones notes, he believed that the Bill "exemplified the attitude of mind which saw the working class solely in the light of their economic efficiency or inefficiency."[21] Woolf – condemning imbeciles as "ineffective" – would have recognized that Wedgwood's campaign against views like Barnett's also implied criticism of views like those she expressed in her diary. Another way of reading her conclusion that "ineffective" imbeciles should "certainly be killed," therefore, is as an emphatic rejection of the criticism of her own views that she perceived in Wedgwood's arguments: "I am right, and Wedgwood is wrong: they should certainly be killed."

Shaw also played a noteworthy role in introducing Woolf to eugenics – particularly Lamarckian eugenics. In 1916, Woolf attended Shaw's lecture "Religion" – the last in the Fabian lecture series "The World in Chains," which was chaired by the "widely known eugenist" C. W. Saleeby.[22] "Religion" was never published, but it is clear that Shaw lectured on his philosophy of the Life Force, described in the Introduction above (p. 7) in the quotation from his contemporaneous essay "The Religion of the Future." Shaw's thesis – that "there never will be a God unless we make one" and "that we are the instruments through which that ideal is trying to make itself reality" – echoes years later in Woolf's own "philosophy" about the elision of God and humanity: "the whole world is a work of art . . . But there is no Shakespeare, there is no Beethoven; certainly and emphatically there is no God; we are the words; we are the music; we are the thing itself."[23] Furthermore, Shaw advocated a Lamarckian version of eugenics: "My biology is all right: I explained it before the amazed Saleeby at my first lecture. You will find it all in the third act of *Man and Superman*, in . . . the passage from my essay on Darwin in which I sweep away the silly controversy about the inheritance of acquired habits – as if, Good God! there were any habits but acquired habits to an evolutionist . . ." Shaw's defense of Lamarckian eugenics was particularly vigorous because of the presence of Saleeby, who seems to have represented for Shaw the turn-of-the century "Neo-Darwinian lunacy, when it was scientific to think of Darwin as a giant and of Butler as a nobody."[24] Inspired by Samuel Butler's defense of the inheritance of acquired characteristics in *Luck, or Cunning?*, Shaw depicted a future to be realized, in part, through a cunning eugenics.

Woolf's doctors were another likely source of her knowledge of eugenics. Poole describes Hyslop as a "guardian of the purity of the blood of the race."[25] Hyslop felt compelled to comment upon the Mental Deficiency Bill in the *Journal of Mental Science*: "One point for our consideration is whether this matter of preventing procreation by the mentally defective is of equal urgency to the other matters referred to in the Bill. I, for my part, believe that it is one of the most important and farthest reaching of the benefits proposed." He anticipated opposition to such a prophylactic eugenics – "in spite of the overwhelming evidence of much evil inheritance that tends to destroy the vital energies of the nation, there are many who will raise their voices in indignant protestation" – but dismissed it as "owing to fetish worship of the liberty of the subject."[26] In *Roger Fry* (1940), Woolf recalled that Hyslop not only opposed the modernism represented by Roger Fry's Post-Impressionist exhibition "Manet and the Post-Impressionists" (London, November 1910 to January 1911), but did so by associating the art with degeneration – giving "his opinion before an audience of artists and craftsmen that the paintings were the work of madmen."[27]

Another of Woolf's doctors, Maurice Craig, held similar views. In his popular medical textbook of 1905 he drew attention to the dangers of race suicide: "alcohol is the curse of the British race, and is slowly but surely undermining the moral energy of the nation. . . [It] deranges the nervous system and leads to early decay of the intellectual faculties of the individual, it produces degeneracy in the offspring, and finally extinction of the race."[28] In a later essay (1922), he argues that "[t]he country is learning that the greatest asset to a nation is good health and that a small number of A1 men count for infinitely more than a crowd of the C3 class."[29]

Although Trombley is wrong to suggest that "Craig's attitude is in fundamental opposition to that of Virginia Woolf," it is unlikely that Woolf directly gathered her knowledge of eugenics from either Craig or Hyslop.[30] Certainly she consulted Craig regularly after 1912, and her husband Leonard consulted Hyslop about her health in the same year, but Woolf did not consult Hyslop herself and she did not socialize with either of these doctors. It is quite likely, however, that Leonard himself represented their eugenical views to Woolf as part of his argument that the couple should not have children.

Peter Alexander points out that despite Virginia Woolf's love of children and despite her gloom at the prospect of childlessness, Leonard became determined that they should not have children and so was disconcerted when

Sir George Savage . . . said that he considered children were exactly what Virginia needed . . . This was not what Leonard wanted to hear, as he showed by seeking, not just a second, but a third, fourth and fifth opinion. He took the advice of Jean Thomas, the woman who ran the Twickenham asylum in which Virginia had several times been treated, and his diary records that he also took the advice of three doctors, Maurice Craig, Maurice Wright and T. B. Hyslop . . . Of these doctors, only Craig considered that having children might be too risky for Virginia . . .[31]

Leonard himself did not like children. Moreover, he was genuinely concerned that having children would risk his wife's fragile mental health. Yet he may also have been influenced by eugenical concerns about passing on Virginia's supposedly tainted blood.[32] He was himself conscious of questions about purity of blood and about the relative value of races: he experienced anti-Semitism (including his

wife's); his family was against mixed marriages (his grandfather
disinherited children who married outside the faith); he believed his
race superior to others ("You may say what you like, but the Semitic
is worth . . . 30 Aryans").[33]

In fact, if we read the views attributed to the psychologist Sir
William Bradshaw in *Mrs. Dalloway* as representing Virginia's understanding of her own doctors' views (as these views were represented
to her by Leonard), then the novel implies that when Leonard
(mis)represented to Virginia her doctors' advice that she should have
no children, he explained such advice as having been based at least
in part upon eugenical considerations: "Sir William not only pros-
pered himself but made England prosper, secluded her lunatics,
forbade childbirth, penalized despair, made it impossible for the unfit
to propagate their views until they, too, shared his sense of proportion."[34] Woolf's narrator imputes to Bradshaw eugenical interests in
industrial efficiency, segregation of the feeble-minded, and laws
against the propagation of illness and acquired bad character.
Bradshaw's eugenics can thus be read as a figure for the eugenical
advice borne to Woolf by Leonard – advice that was an amalgam of
the eugenics of Hyslop, Craig, and perhaps Leonard himself.[35]

Although Sir George Savage has long been recognized as another
of the models for certain aspects of Bradshaw, no one has suspected
that he was a major source of Woolf's information about eugenics –
perhaps because his eugenical beliefs are masked by his apparently
anti-eugenical advice that children were just what Woolf needed
(advice offered in full awareness as family doctor of the Stephens'
apparently inherited predisposition to mental illness). Certainly
Trombley notes that Savage was a eugenist, but he notes only that so
far as Woolf was concerned Savage did not practice what he
preached. He draws attention to the latter's 1911 essay in which
Savage identifies mental illnesses that doctors should treat as a basis
for forbidding marriage: "In no case should it be allowed where
there is a history of periodic recurrences, and it is certain that there is
a very grave risk in those cases of adolescents who at puberty and
with adolescence have periods of depression and buoyancy. I have
seen a good many such cases in which there has been marriage in
haste with a leisure of repentance." Furthermore, "[m]arriage
should never be recommended as a means of cure."[36] Having in 1910
advised Virginia Woolf to get married – knowing that she had had
recurring periods of depression and buoyancy since adolescence –

Savage seems to contradict himself.[37] Yet in a speech as the Royal Society of Medicine delegate to the First International Eugenics Congress – a speech not reviewed by Trombley in his otherwise comprehensive survey of Savage's attitudes – Savage qualifies his advice that mental illness is a basis for forbidding marriage. On the one hand, "[i]nsanity in many cases had to be looked upon as very much like genius; but genius never bred true, and scarcely ever produced a genius in the second generation. It was comforting to know that many cases of so-called sporadic insanity were like genius and did not propagate." On the other hand,

[h]e recalled a number of families that seemed almost saturated with insanity. In one, three or four members had given evidence of mental disorder. The offspring of one of these . . . married into wholly unrelated families, with the result that they had perfectly healthy children. There was a natural tendency to breed out, as well as a terrible responsibility for breeding in. One could not exclude all neurosis, by marriage, by eugenics, or anything else. If one could, it would reduce the world to such a dead level of respectability that it would be hardly worth living in.[38]

This is neither the advice nor the voice of Sir William Bradshaw, prophet of the goddesses Proportion and Conversion. Savage seems to have regarded Woolf's mental illness as an instance of sporadic insanity, perhaps a byproduct of genius itself. His advice that she marry and have children suggests that he agreed with F. W. Mott (to whose paper his speech at the Eugenics Congress was a response) that marriage and childbirth were to be recommended in the case of certain women liable to insanity: "an important and perhaps the only cause [of insanity] in many instances [is] the enforced suppression by modern social conditions of the reproductive functions and the maternal instincts in women of an emotional temperament and mental instability."[39] Savage may have regarded Woolf as a woman of this type and the Stephen family more generally as a type of the family that can breed out hereditary mental illness.

Refusing to support Leonard's opinion that Woolf be advised not to have children – whether on the basis of her fragile health or on the basis of eugenical concerns – Savage is likely to have introduced Woolf to eugenics at the dinners to which he often invited her. He was the only one of her doctors with whom she socialized. Pronouncing her well after his first treatment of her, Savage invited her to dinner in February of 1905: "He asked me to go and dine with him!" She later remarked of the evening that it "was more heavy and dreary than you can conceive." Invited for dinner again in July, she teased her friend Violet Dickinson that she would ask Savage why her letters to Dickinson were at times so silly: "I think I shall ask him what bee gets into my bonnet when I write to you. Sympathetic insanity, I expect it is."[40] Woolf's joke acknowledges Savage's reputation: in the language Mott used to describe him at the Eugenics Congress, Savage was the one "to whom they all looked up as the greatest living authority on insanity."[41] Furthermore, the joke shows that Woolf believes that she can depend on Dickinson's knowing this reputation, too. There are hints here of a one-dimensional reputation and perhaps a one-dimensional dinner conversation: Savage is the expert on insanity and the conversation acknowledges this fact; it is all rather dreary.

However many more times she may have dined with him in the interval, Woolf next records dining with Savage in 1911. Savage was trying to put together a guest list that included Dr. Seymour Sharkey and Jean Thomas, the proprietor of the nursing home where Savage occasionally sent Woolf, so Woolf may even have found her own case the subject of conversation at such meals.[42] Her experience of dreariness and heaviness, on the one hand, and the likelihood of table talk about Savage's professional opinions about insanity (a likelihood that Woolf's letter to Dickinson acknowledges), on the other, suggest that Woolf recalls such dinners in *Mrs. Dalloway* when she describes the Bradshaws' "large dinner-parties": "without knowing precisely what made the evening disagreeable, and caused this pressure on the top of the head (which might well be imputed to the professional conversation . . .) disagreeable it was: so that guests, when the clock struck ten, breathed in the air of Harley Street even with rapture . . ." (pp. 143, 152–53). The contrast that Woolf draws between the Lady Bradshaw "feeding ten or fifteen guests of the professional classes" and the Lady Bradshaw who "[o]nce, long ago, . . . had caught salmon freely" presumably originates in table-talk about one of Savage's favorite recreations: "fishing" (p. 152).[43] The description of Sir William Bradshaw as toiling "to raise funds, propagate reforms, initiate institutions!" (p. 152) may well derive from table talk about Savage's work on behalf of the National Association for the Feeble-Minded. Savage gave the opening address to the Association's annual meeting in 1909 (advising that "in view of the alarming increase of the feeble-minded class . . . the only remedy seemed to lie in measures for the early detection of the unfit and the prevention of their propagation"). The Association's policy was to propagate reforms that would segregate the feebleminded permanently in industrial colonies – a version of Lady Bruton's plan in *Mrs. Dalloway* to colonize Canada with Britain's orphans. Toward this end, the Association established "The Colony Fund," the 1909 meeting concluding with a report on the funds raised to date.[44] It is clear that the "professional conversation" at Savage's dinner table made a strong impression upon Woolf, and it is likely that explicitly or implicitly eugenics informed much of this conversation.

One can see the pervasiveness of eugenical discourse at dinner tables like Savage's in another fictional instance of such dinner table conversation in *To the Lighthouse*. During an argument about politics between Charles Tansley and William Bankes, Mrs. Ramsay suddenly reveals her enthusiasm about certain social and political problems by seizing on the slenderest of opportunities – Bankes's reference to bad English coffee – to turn the conversation to the subject of milk:

"Oh, coffee!" said Mrs. Ramsay. But it was much rather a question (she was thoroughly roused, Lily could see, and talked very emphatically) of real butter and clean milk. Speaking with warmth and eloquence, she described the iniquity of the English dairy system, and in what state milk was delivered at the door, and was about to prove her charges, for she had gone into the matter, when all around the table . . . she was laughed at . . .[45]

Her husband and children presumably laugh at the familiar signs of enthusiasm – an enthusiasm here producing something of a conversational *non sequitur* – and not at the equally familiar social conscience that she reveals. Mrs. Ramsay's zeal for social work is such that, although busy enough in London with her own acts of charity, she dreams that someday "she would cease to be a private woman whose charity was half a sop to her own indignation, half a relief to her own curiosity, and become what with her untrained mind she greatly admired, an investigator, elucidating the social problem" (p. 18).

Mrs. Ramsay has "gone into the matter" of milk production and delivery, and in doing so she has also entered the eugenics debate. As Megumi Kato points out:

In late Victorian Britain, the redistribution of the population to cities created a demand for milk far removed from its source. In the intervening period from farmers to consumers, milk was subjected to contamination and infection. Bacteriological findings in the 1880s that the milk supply was a source of infectious diseases gave an impetus to much discussion that measures for the prevention of milk-borne diseases were needed.[46]

Self-styled advocate on behalf of London's poor, Mrs. Ramsay thinks, "[i]t was a disgrace. Milk delivered at your door in London positively brown with dirt. It should be made illegal" (*To the Lighthouse*, p. 89). Kato points out that by 1904, this issue had been appropriated by eugenists: in his "Discussion of the Control of the Milk Supply," George Newman argues that "[t]he control of the milk supply is not only a concern of preventive medicine, but one of national importance."[47] An essay earlier the same year – "Milk and National Degeneration" – asserts that lack of milk is "an essential and primary cause of degeneration": "healthy babies are impossible without clean and wholesome cow's milk. . . It is here that the question of physical deterioration of the nation comes in, for a few generations of weakly babies necessarily spell a nation with an undue proportion of defective citizens."[48] Uncertain whether Mrs. Ramsay "was aware of the political agenda of this discourse," Kato suggests that "contextualizing the milk problem reveals the racial character of this allusion" and allows us to see "how politicized her character actually is."[49]

The nature of Mrs. Ramsay's politicization in this matter is implied much earlier in the novel – and precisely in the context of questions of race, blood, and heredity. "Inventing differences," she thinks, is nonsense "when people, heaven knows, were different enough without that." The "real differences" that she has in mind are the differences between "rich and poor, high and low." According to Mrs. Ramsay, these are two distinct differences. The difference between rich and poor causes her to ruminate "more profoundly" than the other one, Woolf implies, because Mrs. Ramsay sees here the possibility of effective intervention on her part: she can take a "bag" of provisions to poor widows; she can record poor people's "wages and spending, employment and unemployment" in "a note-book." It is not clear to Mrs. Ramsay that the difference between "high and low" is a problem that deserves to be ruminated as profoundly as "the other problem" – "the great in birth receiving from her, some half grudgingly, half respect, for had she not in her veins the blood of that very noble . . . Italian house, whose daughters . . . [were] scattered about English drawing-rooms in the nineteenth century." The virtue of this blood, according to Mrs. Ramsay, is not only that it is noble, but also that it is Italian: "all her wit and her bearing and her temper came from them, and not from the sluggish English, or the cold Scotch" (*To the Lighthouse*, pp. 17–18). If Mrs. Ramsay is something of a socialist, her socialism is of the Fabian sort that Shaw, Wells, and the Webbs demonstrate – at least so far as her attitudes toward race, blood, and heredity are concerned. That her armchair socialism eventuates in dinner-table eugenics is at first perhaps hard to see, but in the end quite easy to explain.

Supplementing Savage's presumed conversation about eugenics was Jean Thomas's. Savage's loyal supporter, she certainly was not reluctant to share with Woolf her opinions about what ailed her, and in doing so she made clear her eugenical assumptions. Woolf had "long conversations" with Thomas, which she characterized as potentially disagreeable: "What a mercy we cant [sic] have at each other! or we should quarrel till midnight, and Clarissas [sic] deformities [Woolf's sister Vanessa Bell was expecting a baby; Clarissa was a possible name for a girl], inherited from generations of hard drinking Bells, would be laid at my door."[50] Woolf alludes to the eugenical assumption that children inherit deformities from alcoholic parents. She presumes that either the assumption itself or her own eugenical views are so well-known to her sister that the latter will recognize her allusion. She suggests that Thomas has made a eugenical assertion to the effect that deformity in the Stephen family can be traced to the mental illness that Woolf herself has inherited. Eventually their conversations did indeed become quarrels – Thomas promoting Christianity as a cure for Woolf, Woolf maintaining her atheism: "What will be the end of Jean I cant think. . . Suppose this ends in Atheism, and she gives up lunatic keeping: well, her blood will be on my head." Not surprisingly, as Savage's representative in "lunatic keeping," Thomas is criticized in *Mrs. Dalloway* for the same failing that is associated with the Savage figure: Thomas's desire to convert Woolf to Christianity is figured in Doris Kilman, a character devoted, like Bradshaw, to the goddess Conversion.[51]

Whatever its sources – and there were certainly many – the eugenical opinion that surrounded Woolf seems to have converged in her own mind on the question of abortion. Troubled all her life by the childlessness that was her lot, Woolf returns via a canceled passage in *The Years* to the year 1910 and the question then of the role of eugenics in decision-making about whether or not one should have a child:

"Look at those wretched little children" said Rose, looking down into the street.

"Stop them, then" said Maggie. "Stop them having children."

"But you cant" said Rose.

"Oh nonsense, my dear Rose," said Elvira. "What you do is this: you ring a bell in Harley Street. Sir John at home? Step this way ma'am. Now Sir John, you say, casting your eyes this way & that way, the fact of the matter is, whereupon you blush. Most inadvisable, most inadvisable, he says, the welfare of the human race – sacrifice, private interests – six words on half a sheet of paper."[52]

The passage is perfectly ambiguous – and more. In the context of the concern by Rose, Maggie, and Elvira about "wretched little children" produced by the apparently reckless reproduction of the working class, Elvira's narrative can be understood as a description of a hypothetical encounter between Sir John and a working-class woman. Sir John's advice may be that her pregnancy is indeed "inadvisable," that another wretched little child does not promote "the welfare of the human race." Or if Sir John is worried about depopulation, his advice may be that abortion is inadvisable and against the interests of the human race. His argument may be that she must "sacrifice" her "private interests" for the public good. Yet Rose objects that Elvira's narrative is unrealistic so far as the working-class woman goes: "But how is that woman down there going to Harley Street? with three guineas?" (three guineas being the cost of the abortion). She implies that Elvira has actually described a conversation between Sir John and a middle-class woman. If so, Sir John's advice might be understood as a complaint that abortion by the middle-class woman is "inadvisable." His concern would still be about depopulation, but it would be the more class-based eugenical concern about the differential birthrate. The middle-class woman must sacrifice her private interests for the welfare of the human race. If so, Sir John's argument against abortion is similar to Woolf's argument against middle-class childlessness in the essay named for the price of an abortion: *Three Guineas*.

Yet there is also the biographical reading invited by Woolf's own experience of these matters. The middle-class woman visiting the Harley Street doctor can be read as a figure for Woolf herself, the doctor's advice being that for a woman such as Woolf – bearing a hereditary taint – to have a child is "inadvisable" (precisely the advice that Leonard seems to have conveyed to Virginia from her doctors). To risk passing on polluted germ plasm is to neglect the welfare of the human race. Regardless of her personal desire for a child, she must make this sacrifice of her private interests. If the one most forcefully making this eugenical argument to Woolf during the early years of her marriage was in fact her husband Leonard, then a canceled phrase in the passage above lends further support to this biographical reading, for the woman first raises the subject of abortion by hinting that the idea is her husband's: "the fact of the matter is, my husband . . ."[53] Lee speculates that Woolf herself may actually have had an abortion in 1913.[54]

In each of these readings, Sir John's advice is eugenical: reproductive issues concern us all, for they bear on "the welfare of the human race." This canceled passage from *The Years* bitterly highlights the power of eugenics in 1910 – a power wielded here by doctors over patients, husbands over wives, middle-class women over working-class women. Contemplating the relation between domestic and public tyranny as much here as in *Three Guineas*, Woolf stands amazed before the "bio-power" that in 1910 coordinated money and words in an effort to preserve the national germ plasm: when Woolf got married, "Three guineas" and "six words on half a sheet of paper" – the six-word eugenical criterion "the welfare of the human race" – could determine whether or not one had a child.

CHAPTER 2

Boers, whores, and Mongols in Mrs. Dalloway

And so Virginia Woolf came to consciousness in a world in which eugenics was seen to deserve very serious comment – from both the right and the left of the political spectrum, and from every variously interested point of view in between. Furthermore, the discourse of eugenics was borne in upon her both publicly and privately – on the one hand, as a matter of national urgency, and on the other hand, as a matter of great personal consequence with regard to decisions about marriage and having children. Not surprisingly, then, insofar as *Mrs. Dalloway* bears the traces of Woolf's engagement with her time and place, so it bears the traces of her engagement with eugenics. As we have seen, Bradshaw is a eugenist and the Christian Kilman is based in part upon the Christian eugenist Jean Thomas. Woolf's narrator (seeming to speak as Woolf herself on many occasions) certainly criticizes these figures devoted to goddesses like Proportion and Conversion, but it is by no means clear that she criticizes eugenics itself.

The eugenical subtext in *Mrs. Dalloway* appears in a number of ways. Lady Bruton, for instance, is a eugenist. Hugh Whitbread and Richard Dalloway are invited to lunch to help her with her "project for emigrating young people of both sexes born of respectable parents and setting them up with a fair prospect of doing well in Canada" (p. 164). Happily day-dreaming of "commanding battalions marching to Canada," Lady Bruton at other times lacks confidence in her proposal: "She exaggerated. She had perhaps lost her sense of proportion. Emigration was not to others the obvious remedy" (pp. 169–70, 164). To what problem is emigration the "remedy"? Lady Bruton's Britain is threatened by a differential birthrate; emigration of the least fit class is one solution.

Her emigration project is so clearly eugenical that Woolf might just as well have made her the delegate that the British Women's

Emigration Association sent to the First International Eugenics Congress in 1912.[1] The Congress attracted such a delegate because of the variety of concerns about migration that eugenists articulated: greater migration by one gender than another could change the sex ratio and thereby the birthrate; undesirable alien immigration could compromise the purity of the race; excessive emigration of the fit (for instance, as imperial administrators) could lead to national degeneration.[2] Thus Lady Bruton proposes emigration of "the superfluous youth of our ever-increasing population" (p. 166). These youths are fitter than *some* others insofar as it can be determined that their parents were "respectable"; Lady Bruton does not propose that Canada become the dumping ground for the hazardous waste of feeble-minded British prostitutes. Yet these children are not what Lady Bruton would regard as the most fit, for they are superfluous precisely because they are the orphans of the working class – the element responsible for the differential birthrate and thereby responsible for the "ever-increasing population."

Woolf goes to considerable lengths to explain the personal motivation for Lady Bruton's campaign. Psychologically, it is "the liberator of the pent egotism, which a strong martial woman, well nourished, well descended . . . feels rise within her, once youth is past, and must eject upon some object – it may be Emigration, it may be Emancipation" (pp. 164–65). In *Night and Day*, Woolf also associates these two projects, locating the society for the emigration of women in the same building as the society for the emancipation of women, but one floor closer to the ground.[3] Sociologically, one might suspect that Lady Bruton's project is emigration instead of emancipation because she comes of the well-nourished, well-descended class threatened by the differential birthrate.

Yet Woolf also provides another, more public history that accounts for Lady Bruton's enthusiasm: she was involved in the Boer War – an early and important stimulus to public concern about the degeneration of the British race. Lady Bruton recalls the war when thinking that writing letters to the editor "cost her more than to organize an expedition to South Africa (which she had done in the war)" (p. 165). Woolf is careful to signal that the war in question is the Boer War (as opposed to the recently ended First World War), for she does not capitalize the word "war," her usual habit elsewhere in the novel when referring to the European War as "the War."[4] Woolf also associates Lady Bruton with South Africa via her secretary, Miss Brush:

[Hugh] would never lunch . . . with Lady Bruton, whom he had known
these twenty years, without bringing her in his outstretched hand a bunch of
carnations and asking Miss Brush, Lady Bruton's secretary, after her
brother in South Africa, which, for some reason, Miss Brush . . . so much
resented that she said "Thank you, he's doing very well in South Africa,"
when, for half a dozen years, he had been doing badly in Portsmouth.
(pp. 156–57)

It is even possible to explain Hugh's mistake by means of the South
African connection. Millicent Brush and her brother seem to be from
South Africa. It seems to be only recently (six years ago) that the
brother left South Africa for Portsmouth, and so Hugh may well have
been correct for as many as fourteen years before this in asking after
the brother in South Africa. He has certainly known Lady Bruton for
twenty years – the twenty years during which he has been bringing
Lady Bruton carnations and asking after Miss Brush's brother – the
twenty years, it would seem, since Lady Bruton returned from her
South African expedition with Miss Brush in her employ.

The Boer War's centrality in the debate about national degeneration was well known. Pearson himself used early British losses in the
war as the pretext for stirring interest in eugenics: "The spirits of one
and all . . . were depressed in a manner probably never before
experienced by those of our countrymen now living. . . We had been
. . . badly defeated . . . by a social organism far less highly developed
and infinitely smaller than our own." The conclusion Pearson drew
was that Britain ought to attend to the role of natural selection both
in the battle amongst nations and in the battle within nations:

History shows me one way, and one way only, in which a high state of
civilization has been produced, namely, the struggle of race with race, and
the survival of the physically and mentally fitter race. . . Let us face [the]
question of increasing population boldly . . . for what I have said of the
struggle of race against race makes itself again felt within every community. . . [H]ow shall we be sure that . . . offspring are from the better and not
from the inferior stock?[5]

Pearson and Lady Bruton are both concerned with the "question of
increasing population," and both associate this problem with the war
in South Africa.

In *Mrs. Dalloway*, Pearson's elision of the Boer war and the
biological war echoes in the narrator's depiction of Lady Bruton's
enthusiasm for Emigration:

Emigration had become, in short, largely Lady Bruton.

But she had to write. And one letter to the Times, she used to say to Miss Brush, cost her more than to organize an expedition to South Africa (which she had done in the war). (p. 165)

Of all difficult things, why should the difficulty of writing a letter to the *Times* be compared to the difficulty of organizing an expedition to South Africa? Perhaps no logic connects these two seemingly very different tasks and Woolf simply illustrates here what the narrator later calls "some truancy. . . of the logical faculty" on Lady Bruton's part – the proof of which is that "she found it impossible to write a letter to the *Times*" (p. 275). Yet Woolf has provided enough information about Lady Bruton's experiences and attitudes for us to see that there is a plain enough logic of association enabling her stream of consciousness: the letter to the *Times* and the expedition to South Africa during the war are linked because the letter about emigration is a continuation of the eugenical project that she, like so many eugenists, associates with the turn-of-the-century shock in the Boer War. What non-truant logic she possesses is eugenical. In Lady Bruton's mind, the journey by ship to the site of degenerational shock is continuous with the journey by letter toward the solution to the problem of degenerate stock, and so the difficulty of organizing the expedition to South Africa is a reasonable point of reference in her explanation to herself of her surprise at the difficulty of writing the letter.

Woolf is no more an admirer of Lady Bruton than she is an admirer of Bradshaw or Kilman. Lady Bruton is an object of fun – overvaluing the world of men (she would "have worn the helmet and shot the arrow" like her male forbears), and undervaluing the world of women (women doubted "her interest in women who often got in their husband's way, prevented them from accepting posts abroad, and had to be taken to the seaside in the middle of the [parliamentary] session to recover from influenza" [pp. 274, 160]). Her enthusiasm for Emigration is explained as the result of "pent egoism"; her purpose is not so much to solve the overpopulation problem as to enable the wish-fulfilling day-dream in which her hand seems "curled upon some imaginary baton such as her grandfathers might have held" as she imagines herself "commanding battalions marching to Canada" (pp. 169–70). Yet the object of Woolf's disdain is not the eugenical project itself, but rather the ineffectualness of Lady Bruton's enthusiasm – an enthusiasm fueled by the same egoism that drives Bradshaw and Kilman. In fact, while the egoism that corrupts the emigration project is criticized, the eugenics once more remains largely invisible and relatively unscathed in the margins of Woolf's text.

The discussion of prostitutes and prostitution is another aspect of *Mrs. Dalloway* informed by eugenical concerns. Clarissa Dalloway, Sally Seton, and Richard Dalloway all contemplate the lot of prostitutes, and they do so in such a way as to cover the main bases of public discussion of this issue in the early twentieth century.

Many eugenists regarded prostitution as heritable. Charles B. Davenport saw prostitutes as "feebly inhibited," having inherited an abnormally enlarged erotic center.[6] Prostitutes were thought to suffer from feeblemindedness – the feeblemindedness that the Mental Deficiency Act was meant to address. With regard to prostitutes, this Act finally provided the state with a form of the "powers of detention" that Barnett had called for in 1908. As Jones notes, in the early twentieth century the assumption that nature dominated nurture was gaining the upper hand:

It was increasingly assumed that alcoholism, prostitution, vagrancy and to a large extent unemployment were a complex of problems with a single root – feeblemindedness. Since this was an innate and inherited condition, contemporary wisdom saw the institution as more important as a means of reproductive control than of rehabilitation.[7]

Not surprisingly, at the First International Eugenics Congress, as the minutes indicate, anti-eugenical arguments on this topic were not tolerated: "Dr. Holt emphasized the importance of the economic factor. The chief cause of prostitution and venereal disease was economic. The young women were prevented from earning an honest living . . . (Dr. Holt was proceeding to indicate legislative remedies, when the Chairman ruled him out of order.)"[8]

This question about the roles of nature and nurture in the creation of prostitutes is precisely the one that *Mrs. Dalloway* raises. Sally Seton implies an environmental explanation of prostitution when she chastises Hugh Whitbread for assaulting her with a kiss: "Sally suddenly lost her temper, flared up, and told Hugh that he represented all that was most detestable in British middle-class life. She told him that she considered him responsible for the state of 'those poor girls in Piccadilly'" (p. 110). These Piccadilly girls also draw Woolf's attention in *The Voyage Out*, becoming the subject of conversation between Rachel Vinrace and Helen Ambrose: "'Tell me,'

[Rachel] said suddenly, 'what are those women in Piccadilly?' 'In Piccadilly? They are prostitutes,' said Helen."[9] In the 1890s of the novel, the fictional feminist Sally Seton accuses the sexist Hugh of perpetuating with his kiss a habit of objectifying women that she regards as connected to the objectification of women in the phenomenon of prostitution. At the same time in the real world, the actual feminist Maria Sharpe (who was later to marry the eugenist Pearson) made the same observation about prostitution: it is "the region where women are possibly only bodies to men casting a dark shade across all their own relations to the other sex."[10] Sally Seton and Maria Sharpe agree on an environmental explanation of prostitution in particular and of the disempowering objectification of women in general.

Richard Dalloway also favors an environmental explanation of prostitution, and so he refuses to accept the eugenical belief that prostitution is innate: "prostitutes, good Lord, the fault wasn't in them, nor in young men either, but in our detestable social system and so forth" (p. 175). As a relatively left-leaning Conservative Member of Parliament, he is in a position to contemplate the possibility of legislative remedies for prostitution – remedies such as those that Dr. Holt was prepared to offer at the Eugenics Congress before he was ruled out of order. In fact, Richard Dalloway has already "championed the down-trodden . . . in the House of Commons" (p. 175). Unlike Dr. Holt, however, Richard Dalloway has no remedies to hand: "But what could be done for female vagrants like that poor creature, stretched on her elbow (as if she had flung herself on the earth, rid of all ties, to observe curiously, to speculate boldly, to consider the whys and the wherefores, impudent, loose-lipped, humourous), he did not know" (p. 176). And so, for all his apparent confidence that prostitution is not innate and that prostitution is society's fault, he is at a loss to think how legislative nurturing might overcome nature – for it seems to him to be an unredeemable nature that lies before him, "flung. . . on the earth, rid of all ties."

Clarissa makes a similar point about the intractability of this problem at the very beginning of the novel when explaining to herself why she loves "life; London; this moment of June": "Heaven only knows why one loves it so . . .; but the veriest frumps, the most dejected of miseries sitting on doorsteps (drink their downfall) do the same; can't be dealt with, she felt positive, by Acts of Parliament for that very reason: they love life" (p. 5). Although Clarissa believes that frumps and miseries share with her a love of life that is not answerable to reason or law, her association of alcoholism, vagrancy, unemployment, and prostitution with these fallen women implies that she regards feeblemindedness as the source of their love of life – and not the privileged wealth, leisure, and social position that are the precondition, if not the source itself, of her own love of life.

Woolf depicts this same question about whether prostitution is a hereditary or environmental problem in *Jacob's Room* (1922). The female narrator observes what may be three generations of a family conceived in prostitution, extending from the grandmother as prostitute to the grandchild as thief:

Long past sunset an old blind woman sat on a camp-stool with her back to the stone wall of the Union of London and Smith's Bank . . . singing out loud, not for coppers, no, from the depths of her gay wild heart – her sinful tanned heart – for the child who fetches her is the fruit of sin, and should have been in bed, curtained, asleep, instead of hearing in the lamplight her mother's wild song . . .

Home they went. The grey church spires received them; . . . as some believe, the city loves her prostitutes.

But few, it seems, are admitted to that degree. Of all the carriages that leave the arch of the Opera House, not one turns eastward, and when the little thief is caught in the empty market-place no one in black-and-white or rose-coloured evening dress blocks the way by pausing with a hand upon the carriage door to help or condemn – though Lady Charles, to do her justice, sighs sadly as she ascends her staircase, takes down Thomas à Kempis, and does not sleep till her mind has lost itself tunnelling into the complexity of things. "Why? Why? Why?" she sighs. On the whole it's best to walk back from the Opera House. Fatigue is the safest sleeping draught.[11]

The old prostitute is taken home by a daughter who may well be the mother of the little thief – so ambiguous is the narrative and so insidious is the effect of tainted germ plasm that the genealogy here is unclear. Yet whatever the relation, if any, between the prostitute's child and the thief, the sequence of the narrator's thoughts not only associates prostitution with daughters and little thieves out well past a proper bedtime, but also places the prostitute in an older generation in such a way that the narrator can be seen to be within the stream of a consciousness that associates the phenomenon of prostitution as a whole with the degeneration evident in the present generation of such daughters and such thieves.

Less advanced than Sally Seton, Richard Dalloway, and Clarissa Dalloway in thinking the problem through, Lady Charles has only just arrived – but arrived nonetheless – at the question of how the sins of the prostitute mother might be visited upon her children and her children's children. Unlike Woolf, who had decided what ought to be done with the degenerates she met by the canal in 1915, Lady Charles has not decided what her response to the problem of degeneration should be. Like the early Woolf, she would prefer not to confront either the problem or the people that constitute it: walking back from the opera will avoid the moral dilemma of what to do with the carriage door (that is, whether to impede or facilitate the arrest of the little thief, and whether to do either of these things openly or surreptitiously), and the very exercise of walking will make one too tired to dwell on such dilemmas in any event.

Yet however reluctant Lady Charles might be to think the matter through, the narrator of *Jacob's Room* implies that she herself has thought it through, and thinks what Clarissa thinks – thinks, that is, that the old prostitute sings "from the depths of her gay wild heart." The narrator, in other words, thinks that prostitutes sing from the gay wild heart of the feebleminded who by nature love life. The logic of association by which her narrative gaze shifts from the prostitute to the child of the prostitute to the little thief is implicitly eugenical.

The apparent assumptions of both Clarissa in *Mrs. Dalloway* and the narrator in *Jacob's Room* precisely parallel those of Mary Dendy, "one of Britain's leading workers with the mentally deficient in the decade before the First World War."[12] Dendy makes the same observation about the love of life that the feebleminded display when she responds to a conference paper, "On Insanity and Marriage," by none other than Sir George Savage: "Happiness was the normal condition of the feeble-minded; they had neither remorse for what they had done, nor any apprehension concerning what might happen in the future. . . Many such people belonged to the unemployed."[13] Clarissa, then, displays much more confidence than her husband that Acts of Parliament cannot avail against prostitution precisely because she possesses a special insight into the matter: happiness is the normal condition of the feebleminded – an insight grounded in Clarissa's eugenical assumptions.

Once again Woolf declines to indicate that she regards such eugenical assumptions as wrong. In the matter of the frumps, she certainly exposes the poverty of Clarissa's social conscience. Clarissa is implicitly criticized for her blindness to the miseries suffered by prostitutes. The complacency in the midst of privilege that enables such blindness is exposed as a version of the egoism that corrupts Bradshaw, Kilman, and Lady Bruton. She is explicitly indicted as "a snob" who, on the one hand, "hated frumps, fogies, failures" and, on the other, found that "Duchesses . . . stood for something real to her" (pp. 289, 115–16). Largely uncriticized, however, is her euge-nical belief that the prostitute's nature is not amenable to legislative reform – especially when the prostitute has also inherited the alcoholic's nature ("drink their downfall"). Furthermore, Sally Seton's environmental explanation of prostitution is undermined because it is located in 1890 and is therefore effectively a pre-eugenical idea. In fact, all of Sally's radical 1890s ideas are under-mined as old: Sally herself disavows them by the life she has led since; recalling the "argument . . . about women's rights" that led Sally to blame Hugh for "those poor girls in Piccadilly," Peter Walsh calls it "that antediluvian topic" (p. 110). By contrast, Clarissa's eugenical ideas at least seem up-to-date. Similarly, Woolf's silencing of Richard Dalloway on the practical matter of "what could be done for female vagrants" in some ways duplicates the silencing of Dr. Holt at the Eugenics Congress, thereby enforcing Clarissa's eugenical ruling early in the novel that such remedies as Acts of Parliament that would nurture development against the grain of a recalcitrant nature are out of order.

Woolf's most substantial contemplation of eugenical concerns in *Mrs. Dalloway*, however, occurs by means of references to Charles Darwin, Gregor Mendel, and the laws of inheritance.[14]

Woolf emphasizes the ubiquitousness of Darwin in the late nine-teenth century and early twentieth century. On the one hand, Clarissa's Aunt Helena "could not resist recalling what Charles Darwin had said about her little book on the orchids of Burma" in the 1860s (p. 272). On the other hand, Septimus is evidence of Darwin's impact on "one of those half-educated, self-educated men whose education is all learnt from books borrowed from public libraries . . . on the advice of well-known authors consulted by letter" (p. 127). His enthusiasm fired by the lecturing of Miss Isabel Pole, Septimus has been "devouring Shakespeare, Darwin, *The History of Civilization*, and Bernard Shaw" (p. 129). Like so many of his time (including Shaw), Septimus accepts Darwin's invitation to conceive life according to evolutionary theory's biological terms: "Why could he see through bodies, see into the future, when dogs will become men? It was the heat wave presumably, operating upon a brain made sensitive by eons of evolution" (p. 102). His musings on the truths that he must reveal to the Prime Minister again foreground Darwin: he marvels that he alone should be "called forth in advance of the mass of men to hear the truth, to learn the meaning, after all the toils of civilization – Greeks, Romans, Shakespeare, Darwin, and now himself . . ." (pp. 101–02).

It might seem to some a sign of an unbalanced mind that Septimus should rank Darwin's contribution to civilization with that of Shakespeare, the Romans, and the Greeks, but his list is actually an accurate sign of the times. That Darwin's prominence in such a list represents more than a madman's point of view is evident from the ruminations of Mr. Bentley, which introduce into the novel the Mendelian theory welcomed by biologists as an explanation of the mechanism by which natural selection works. Viewing an aeroplane overhead, Mr. Bentley regards it as "a symbol . . . of man's soul; of his determination . . . to get outside his body, beyond his house, by means of thought, Einstein, speculation, mathematics, the Mendelian theory" (p. 41).

Woolf thus shows that she knows the importance of the rediscovery at the turn of the century of Gregor Mendel's work on heredity. In the 1860s, Mendel's experiments with peas led him to theorize that characteristics were passed from generation to generation by means of paired units of heredity (today called chromosomes), one passed along by the father and the other by the mother. Ignored in its own time, Mendel's work was rediscovered in 1900, leading to widespread efforts in the early twentieth century to prove or disprove Mendelism. Mr. Bentley's grouping of the Mendelian theory with Einstein and mathematics suggests that Woolf was aware of the mathematical component of Mendelism, which claimed that units of heredity behaved predictably according to statistical laws.[15] This made Mendelism a challenge to Pearson's biometrics, the statistically based study of heredity that was favored in the Galton Eugenics Laboratory. As Kevles notes, however, Mendelism was generally accepted by the Eugenics Education Society, which especially embraced "the Mendelian heritability of mental defect."[16]

Woolf was familiar enough with Mendel's experiments to know that they involved charting inheritance patterns produced by hybridization. In *Night and Day*, for instance, she presents Cassandra Otway as an amateur Mendelian: "She had once trifled with the psychology of animals, and still knew something about inherited characteristics." Distracted by the prospect of romance, however, "[s]he forgot all about the psychology of animals, and the recurrence of blue eyes and brown . . ."[17] Woolf's interest in the Mendelian theory helps to make sense of a strange passage in *Mrs. Dalloway* in which Clarissa speculates that her daughter Elizabeth's unusual features may be the result of racial hybridization:

Was it that some Mongol had been wrecked on the coast of Norfolk (as Mrs. Hilbery said), had mixed with the Dalloway ladies, perhaps, a hundred years ago? For the Dalloways, in general, were fair-haired; blue-eyed; Elizabeth, on the contrary, was dark; had Chinese eyes in a pale face; an Oriental mystery; was gentle, considerate, still. (pp. 185–86)

The reference to Mrs. Hilbery recalls *Night and Day*, in which Mrs. Hilbery is Cassandra Otway's aunt. The aunt seems to have learned something from the niece about inherited characteristics, for she has offered the hypothesis of a dark-eyed, dark-haired forbear to account for Elizabeth's unusual combination of eye, hair, and skin color. By 1907, it had been demonstrated in Britain that human eye color obeyed Mendel's laws of inheritance, and the same was shown shortly thereafter for hair and skin color.[18]

Furthermore, Woolf lets us know that Clarissa's "favorite reading as a girl was Huxley" (p. 117). This explains her use of the word *Mongol* to represent both the particularity of Chinese features and the generality of Oriental features, for Huxley popularized the use of the word to denote "one of the five principal races of mankind."[19] Clarissa and Mrs. Hilbery, in short, speculate that miscegenation might explain Elizabeth's features. In doing so, they show that they are relatively up to date regarding contemporary thinking by euge-nists and anthropologists on the subject of race and heredity.

Miscegenation was certainly an issue that interested eugenists. The Whethams, for instance, like other eugenists and like many anthro-pologists, identified three principal races in the population of Europe. First, there is the Northern race: "tall and long-skulled; and, in its pure condition, blue eyed and fair haired. We find it in its greatest purity in the Scandinavian peninsulas and around the Dutch and English shores of the North Sea. We may recognize many of its characteristics, its vigor, its loyalty, its determination, its perseverance . . ."[20] The Dalloways are clearly Northern – geographically (they are from Norfolk), physically (they are "blue-eyed" and "fair-haired"), and temperamentally (Richard is a vigorous man of the stable, loyal to Clarissa, determined upon a number of social reforms, and nonetheless persevering in a career despite the fact that it is not likely to bring him a cabinet post).

Then there is the Mediterranean race: "short of stature, dark of complexion and hair, long skulled, vivacious, gregarious, and, one may perhaps add, at once restless and easy going – the typical Italian."[21] Woolf clearly embodies this stereotype in the "simple," "impulsive" Rezia from the Italian "streets crowded every evening with people walking, laughing out loud, not half alive like people" in England (*Mrs. Dalloway*, pp. 22, 34). The Mediterranean Rezia and the at least honorary – and perhaps actually – Mediterranean Sally Seton (she has "a sort of abandonment . . . much commoner in foreigners," "always said she had French blood in her veins," and has "a father or mother gambling at Monte Carlo") are notably interested in producing offspring : Sally has "five enormous boys" and Rezia "must have children" (pp. 48, 111, 261, 134). Similarly, in *To the Lighthouse*, the polyphiloprogenitiveness of Mrs. Ramsay seems to be explained in these racial terms by the Italian blood in her veins. All three women would be seen by the Whethams and other like-minded eugenists as testifying to the dysgenical threat represented by the Mediterranean race: "the apparent prepotency of the darker Mediterranean race, probably due to the Mendelian dominance of their characters, would gradually efface the northern characteristics as soon as intermarriage and unchecked social intercourse were permitted throughout the nation."[22] In *Mrs. Dalloway*, however, Rezia's potentially fatal fertility is neutralized by Septimus's impotence.

Finally, there is "the Alpine or Armenoid" race – "supposed to show tendencies suggesting an Oriental origin, and . . . usually believed to be the remains of a slow infiltration of population from Central Asia." Clarissa may not be able to distinguish between Armenians and Albanians (p. 182), but she can distinguish between the Armenoid and Northern elements in her daughter. Furthermore, Clarissa's sense of her daughter's "Oriental mystery," the narrator's reference to her "inscrutable mystery," and Woolf's leaving unanswered the question of Elizabeth's inscrutable future (will she become the professional that Kilman would like her to become, or will she follow her mother into the role of hostess?) all align Elizabeth with the eugenically inscrutable nature of the Armenoid or Alpine race as defined by eugenists like the Whethams: "The precise part played by the Alpine race in the civilization of modern Europe remains to be determined" (pp. 186, 199).[23] Eugenical discourse is very insidious indeed.

Yet the passage about Elizabeth's aberrant features also points to other questions about patterns of inheritance of more immediate concern to Woolf. For instance, Clarissa and Mrs. Hilbery (by no means competent Mendelians in their understanding of dominant and recessive hereditary units, however up-to-date their prejudices may be) assume that the male principle dominates in characteristics inherited by descendents. Why else rule out that Elizabeth's features might have come from the Parry side of the family? A common enough instance of the widespread (patriarchal) myth that in reproduction the male element is active and the female element passive, such an idea might well have been introduced to Woolf by Savage. Asked whether a person with a mental disorder should marry and have children, the latter responded with advice based on the same assumption that Clarissa and Mrs. Hilbery reveal: "Risk was involved by the slightest taint on either side; but if there was not a clear male element on both sides, the marriage should, if possible, be stopped."[24] His advising Woolf to marry in 1910 would have provided the occasion for Savage's sharing of this assumption with her, leaving her with a new and all-important criterion in the selection of a husband.

The sort of taint that Woolf was most concerned about is suggested by the attribution to Elizabeth of Mongoloid features – an attribution that might seem completely arbitrary. After all, her differences from the Dalloways could have been indicated in all sorts of ways other than the one that requires the hypothesis of a Mongol sailor. Against the background of the novel's question about the biological origin of such features, and against the background of Woolf's longstanding personal concern about the heritability of her own mental instability, however, this passage can also be seen as a freighted allusion to mongolism – a mysterious condition (today known as Down's Syndrome) that Woolf indirectly invokes as a figure for her eugenical anxieties about her own fertility.

In the early decades of the twentieth century, many eugenists certainly suspected that mongolism was heritable, so it would not be surprising if Woolf thought so, too. Interestingly, Woolf has Clarissa describe the ostensibly Mongolian Elizabeth in terms of the very characteristics that psychologists like Savage associated with mongolism. Clarissa tells us that Elizabeth is "gentle, considerate, still" (p. 186). In 1913, the researcher discussing mongolism in *The Journal of Nervous and Mental Disorders* uses essentially the same three terms: "Mentally, mongols are as a rule quiet, good tempered, and easily amused."[25] Savage's dinner table could easily have been the source of Woolf's apparent knowledge of mongolism. Yet it is also possible that while continuing to work on *Mrs. Dalloway* in 1924 Woolf noticed F. G. Cruikshank's "widely noted book" *The Mongol in our Midst* (1924), which hypothesized that mongolism could be explained as a reversion to an earlier human type – the Mongol – because of a recessive hereditary unit in the blood of certain Europeans.[26]

Of course this is not to suggest that Elizabeth Dalloway has Down's Syndrome in any literal way. Woolf presumably means to suggest simply that her features are sufficiently different from the features of her relatives to prompt idle comment. I suggest rather that Woolf's concern about the hereditary nature of mental defects is so great and so deep-seated that it wells up in this passage – unconsciously displacing anxiety about her own tainted germ plasm not only onto Clarissa's concern about the inheritance of quite other characteristics, but also onto a word (*Mongol*) that can express both Clarissa's descriptive purpose and Woolf's personal eugenical anxiety.

Not surprisingly, it is Woolf's depiction of Sir William Bradshaw that is the means of most directly associating insanity with heredity in *Mrs. Dalloway*. As we have seen, Bradshaw "made England prosper, secluded her lunatics, forbade childbirth" (p. 150). That he forbade childbirth on eugenical grounds is clear: "Sir William had a friend in Surrey where they taught . . . a sense of proportion. . . [T]he good of society, . . . he remarked very quietly, would take care, down in Surrey, that these unsocial impulses, bred more than anything by the lack of good blood, were held in control" (p. 154). Bradshaw's friend in Surrey is clearly Savage's friend in Sussex – Jean Thomas, whose views on the deformities that come of bad blood we have already reviewed. Yet however resentful the narrator (and presumably Woolf herself) may be in the face of Bradshaw's prescription for dealing with such bad blood (Woolf's contempt for doctors like Bradshaw and Holmes is clear), both the narrator and Woolf nonetheless share Bradshaw's interest in diagnosing its presence.

Bradshaw recognizes at a glance that Septimus has a mental

disorder: "He could see the first moment they came in the room . . .; he was certain directly he saw the man; it was a case of extreme gravity. It was a case of complete breakdown – complete physical and nervous breakdown" (p. 144). This glance detects a problem of breeding, which is for Bradshaw a problem of blood: "The fellow made a distasteful impression. For there was in Sir William . . . a natural respect for breeding and clothing which shabbiness nettled" (p. 147). Bradshaw is the physician of whom Max Nordau writes in *Degeneration*: one who "has devoted himself to the special study of nervous and mental maladies" and so can recognize "at a glance" both "degeneration . . . and hysteria."[27]

The narrator also expects to tell the presence of good or bad blood by a similar glance:

To look at, he might have been a clerk, but of the better sort; . . . his hands were educated; so, too, his profile – his angular, big-nosed, intelligent, sensitive profile; but not his lips altogether, for they were loose; and his eyes (as eyes tend to be), eyes merely; . . . so that he was, on the whole, a border case, neither one thing nor the other . . . (pp. 126–27)

One notes particularly the loose lips that betray the promise of other aspects of Septimus's profile, for he shares them with the prostitute. Richard Dalloway notes the latter's "loose-lipped" expression – an expression that speaks of bad blood (and the unredeemable nature that comes of it) both to Richard Dalloway and to the narrator alike. Similarly, the narrator of *Jacob's Room* associates national degeneration with the lips now seen at the opera:

Beauty, in its hothouse variety (which is none of the worst), flowered in box after box; and though nothing was said of profound importance, and though it is generally agreed that wit deserted beautiful lips about the time that Walpole died – at any rate when Victoria in her nightgown descended to meet her ministers, the lips (through an opera glass) remained red, adorable. (*Jacob's Room*, p. 67)

Betokening a breeding and beauty very much embodied, and embodied via the quasi-Mendelian "hothouse" of the aristocracy, these lips – to which the narrator's attention is drawn immediately after her contemplation of prostitutes, prostitutes' children, and little thieves – are the focus of a concern about a decline in national intelligence or native wit, what many a eugenist called mother wit. In *The Pargiters*, one of the things that makes the "grey leering face" of the imbecilic flasher so "horrible" is that he not only gibbers at Rose but also sucks his lips.[28] Narrators in all three novels diagnose a good deal by lips.

In reading Septimus's appearance, therefore, the narrator in *Mrs. Dalloway* – like Bradshaw – is reading his blood, and in reading his blood, the narrator – again like Bradshaw – has reduced him to a "case" for diagnosis. The difference between Bradshaw and the narrator (and perhaps the difference between Bradshaw and Woolf) seems to be that the former employs a "lightning skill" that leads to insensitivity and the outrage of "forcing your soul," whereas the latter demonstrates in her novel-long diagnosis of Septimus the actual qualities that Bradshaw is falsely reputed to have: "sympathy; tact; understanding of the human soul" (*Mrs. Dalloway*, pp. 144, 281, 144).

In effect, the diagnostic gazes of Richard Dalloway, Sir William Bradshaw, and the narrator herself reproduce Woolf's own diagnostic gaze in describing her "long line of imbeciles": there is the look ("The first was . . . just queer enough to look at twice"), and there is the same attention to profile, lips, and eyes ("every one [had] . . . no forehead, or no chin, & an imbecile grin, or a wild suspicious stare"). Woolf recalls this very experience in *Mrs. Dalloway* when Septimus observes a similar sight: "once a maimed file of lunatics being exercised or displayed for the diversion of the populace (who laughed aloud), ambled and nodded and grinned past him . . . each half apologetically, yet triumphantly, inflicting his hopeless woe" (p. 136). Once again, then, Woolf's contempt for Bradshaw should not be misread as a contempt also for his eugenics, for Woolf's own gaze seems to match not only that of her narrator, but that of Bradshaw.

In this diagnostic gaze, Woolf, her narrator, and her characters both reveal and perform the internalization of the cultural policing of criminality, insanity, and sexuality that Foucault hypothesizes as the mechanism of discipline and punishment that has most effectively extended the imperial sway of prevailing discourses of power since the eighteenth century. Bradshaw most notably functions as the overseer in the structure that Foucault, after Jeremy Bentham, calls the panopticon:

The principle was this. A perimeter building in the form of a ring. At the center of this, a tower, pierced by large windows opening on to the inner face of the ring. The outer building is divided into cells each of which traverses the whole thickness of the building. These cells have two windows, one opening on to the inside, facing the windows of the central tower, the other, outer one allowing daylight to pass through the whole cell. All that is then needed is to put an overseer in the tower and place in each of the cells a lunatic, a patient, a convict, a worker or a schoolboy. The back lighting enables one to pick out from the central tower the little captive silhouettes in the ring of cells. In short, the principle of the dungeon is reversed; daylight and the overseer's gaze capture the inmate more effectively than darkness, which afforded after all a sort of protection.[29]

This building and this system of surveillance become a structure of consciousness:

We are talking about two things here: the gaze, and interiorization. . . There is no need for arms, physical violence, material constraints. Just a gaze. An inspecting gaze, a gaze which each individual under its weight will end by interiorising to the point that he is his own overseer, each individual thus exercising this surveillance over, and against, himself.[30]

Because Septimus has threatened to kill himself, the law makes available to Bradshaw the Crown's power – precisely the arms, physical violence, and material constraint that Foucault calls "monarchical power." But Woolf emphasizes that Bradshaw prefers a more intimate exertion of power: according to Clarissa, Bradshaw enjoys "forcing your soul" (*Mrs. Dalloway*, p. 281). Clarissa senses that he will leave no privacy to the soul, and she senses that it is this privacy of the soul that Septimus has died defending. The narrator – seemingly indistinguishable from Woolf at this point – thus bitterly denounces Bradshaw's invasiveness of such privacy in the name of the goddesses Proportion and Conversion.

Yet as we have seen, this narrator's gaze is at times indistinguishable from Bradshaw's. No more than Bradshaw, furthermore, is she willing to leave dark spaces outside of the overseer's gaze. Just as she gazes upon Septimus, so she gazes upon Clarissa in her cell: "Like a nun withdrawing, or a child exploring a tower, she went upstairs . . . The sheets were clean, tight stretched in a broad white band from side to side. . . So the room was an attic; the bed narrow. . ." (p. 46). The narrator even allows Sally Seton to know something of the position in which she and the other characters have been placed by the narrator's gaze: "Are we not all prisoners? She had read a wonderful play about a man who scratched on the wall of his cell, and she had felt that was true of life – one scratched on the wall" (p. 293).

An omniscient narrator inevitably duplicates the role of the panopticon's overseer – enabling a fictional fantasy fulfillment of what Foucault calls "the formula of 'power through transparency,' subjection by 'illumination.'"[31] The psychological novel turns the gaze inward, and the stream-of-consciousness novel interiorizes it absolutely – power's fantasy completely fulfilled, it would seem. And so all the main characters in *Mrs. Dalloway* are in the same position as Septimus, Sally, and Clarissa, and how could it be otherwise given the novelistic technique that Woolf developed in writing this novel – the "tunnelling process, by which I tell the past by instalments, as I have need of it"?[32] Woolf tunnels in order to gain access to the caves in which her characters hide – betraying the same fear of darkness that Foucault finds in the Gothic novel:

Gothic novels develop a whole fantasy-world of stone walls, darkness, hideouts and dungeons which harbour, in significant complicity, brigands and aristocrats, monks and traitors. The landscapes of Ann Radcliffe's novels are composed of mountains and forests, caves, ruined castles and terrifyingly dark and silent convents. Now these imaginary spaces are like the negative of the transparency and visibility which it is aimed to establish.

The nun Clarissa in her convent, complete with tower, and the prisoner Sally, behind stone walls, are exposed to the light of the narrator's comprehensive gaze. The narrator exercises power "by virtue of the mere fact of things being known and people seen in a sort of immediate, collective and anonymous gaze."[33]

And so Bradshaw's vaunted self-control ("a curious exercise with the arms, which he shot out, brought sharply back to his hip, to prove . . . that Sir William was master of his own actions, which the patient was not") – the display of which reduces patients to tears and makes others challenge the imperatives of "bio-power" itself ("some weakly broke down; sobbed, submitted; others . . . called Sir William to his face a damnable humbug; questioned, even more impiously, life itself") – is something that Woolf simultaneously mocks and envies, rejects and duplicates (*Mrs. Dalloway*, p. 153). And she does so both in the novel and in her own life.

In 1926, she confesses to her diary that her childlessness is her "own fault": "a little more self control on my part, & we might have had a boy of 12, a girl of 10."[34] One wonders if this boy is the child that Lee speculates might have been due to be born in late 1913 or early 1914 – a child that would have been twelve in 1926. If so, Woolf's regrets about her lack of self-control range very widely indeed over the questions of childlessness, mental instability, and heritable taints. As Lee points out, "Woolf's reading of her own condition is greatly influenced by the idea of self-control. When she is writing to Vanessa or Leonard from nursing homes, she emphasizes, either pathetically or angrily, the need for control."[35] At times, the overseer is without; at times, the overseer is within. And whether within or without, at times, the overseer is an enemy, and, at times, the overseer is a friend.

As diagnosers of mental illness, therefore, Bradshaw, the narrator in *Mrs. Dalloway*, and Woolf herself are cut from the same cloth. They share the gaze of the panopticon's overseer, which makes everything a legitimate object of surveillance, and they reveal this surveillance interiorized. They can all judge people at a glance, including themselves. Even Septimus gazes upon the "maimed file of lunatics" in the same way that Bradshaw and Woolf do – summing up at a glance, and disapproving of himself insofar as he sees himself beginning to look like them: "would *he* go mad?" (p. 136). Just as Woolf both rejects and reproduces the overseer's gaze, so does Septimus. Indeed, Septimus's suicide is an ambiguous act that may signal either his resistance to the overseers, Bradshaw and Holmes, or his agreement with their diagnostic gaze. That is, his suicide can be seen as a version of Woolf's own suggestion in 1915 that death – not institutionalization – is the appropriate treatment for imbeciles and idiots. In this case, his disagreement with Bradshaw and Holmes is not about diagnosis, but about treatment: those who cannot interiorize the overseer's gaze must die, and so Septimus ironically escapes the monarchical power that would institutionalize him by arrogating its ultimate sanction – the power of death – to himself.

Although Greenslade suggests that "*Mrs. Dalloway* is both the first and the last fiction to deconstruct the fictions of degeneration" (Woolf delivers "the killer punch" in "her assault on the discursive practice of psychiatric medicine, . . . a direct attack on myths which she had lived with through her adult life"), I suggest that the diagnostic gaze in both *Mrs. Dalloway* and Woolf's diary is informed by an unchallenged pattern of eugenical values.[36] However damaged by such values, and however much damage she inflicts upon some of the holders of such values in her fiction, Woolf nonetheless continues discursively to circulate them. Septimus, Bradshaw, the narrator, and Woolf herself are all on the look-out for the biological criminal –

especially the loose-lipped outlaw. Loose lips can sink ships in any war – but this is especially true, in a completely different way, in the biological war: the ship of state could well sink under the tide of a fatally loose-lipped fertility.

CHAPTER 3

Body and biology in A Room of One's Own

Perhaps the most interesting and productive outcome of Woolf's engagement with eugenics is the eugenical logic of inheritance that enables important aspects of her conception of the woman-centered literary tradition outlined in *A Room of One's Own* (1928). In figuring the origin and development of such a tradition, Woolf adopts a thoroughly biological model of inheritance. The model is broadly evolutionary – sometimes drawing on Darwin, sometimes drawing on Lamarck, particularly in depicting a woman writer's literary inheritance of her forbears' acquired characteristics. Furthermore, Woolf focuses literally upon the question of biological inheritance by examining the relationship between the woman writer and genius – the question of the heritability of genius enduring into Woolf's time as an issue bequeathed to eugenists by Galton's ground-breaking study, *Hereditary Genius* (1869). Finally, Woolf's essay concludes by enjoining women writers to engage in eugenically responsible literary breeding: the proliferation of the literary germ plasm depends on it.

One can trace the inception of *A Room of One's Own*'s literary version of eugenical logic to a 1922 letter in which Woolf contemplates the literary and moral inheritance bequeathed her by friends and forbears like Shaw and the Webbs:

Leonard says we owe a great deal to Shaw. I say that he only influenced the outer fringe of morality . . . But don't you agree with me that the Edwardians, from 1895 to 1914, made a pretty poor show. . . We Georgians have our work cut out for us, you see . . . How does one come by one's morality? Surely by reading the poets. And we've got no poets . . . Consider the Webbs – That woman has the impertinence to say that I'm a-moral: the truth being that if Mrs Webb had been a good woman, Mrs Woolf would have been a better.[1]

The broad subject here is influence – literary and moral. As a group and as individuals, the Edwardians have influenced the Georgians –

particularly Woolf herself. Woolf conceives the mechanism by which such influence is disseminated in terms of a biological model of inheritance with which we are by now familiar. The Webbs are Woolf's Edwardian parents; Beatrice, her mother. For Beatrice Webb to say that Woolf is amoral is an "impertinence" because Woolf understands herself to have inherited her morality from her cultural precursors generally, and from her mother particularly. Her conception of inheritance, furthermore, is Lamarckian: she has inherited the acquired character of her Edwardian mother. And so, if Beatrice Webb had acquired more good character, Woolf would have inherited more good character. Finally, Woolf's evaluative frame of reference here is implicitly eugenical: the question is how to breed a "better" woman.

And so there is a further irony in this "like mother, like daughter" matter of the inheritance of acquired character. Woolf's vigilance on behalf of the "better woman" she might have been is itself mandated by mother Webb's eugenics: Woolf has inherited characteristics of the eugenics by which Webb herself set out to establish the conditions prerequisite to "the breeding of the right sort of man." However negligent in not making Woolf a better woman, Webb at least helps Woolf to the ideas in the light of which the two of them will be found lacking as mother and daughter, respectively.

The terms by which Woolf begins to explore the question of influence here are reproduced in *A Room of One's Own* a few years later. The simultaneously literary, moral, and biological question is how to produce the right sort of woman: Shakespeare's "wonderfully gifted sister."[2] As in the passage above, the biological model of literary inheritance prevails: "Drawing her life from the lives of the unknown who were her forerunners, as her brother did before her, she will be born." Again as in the passage above, the literary germ plasm is passed on in poetry: "The original impulse was to poetry" – the phrase "original impulse" recalling the "vital impulse" that Bergsonians located at the heart of creative evolution.[3] Similarly, her essay also focuses upon descent via women: "The 'supreme head of song' was a poetess" (*A Room of One's Own*, p. 67). Unlike Mrs. Dalloway and Mrs. Hilbery, Woolf conceives of influence as mainly heritable along the female line: "we think back through our mothers if we are women" (p. 76). She therefore discounts the importance of the male line of influence in the development of a woman's sentence: "It is useless to go to the great men writers for help . . . [They] never helped a woman yet, though she may have learned a few tricks of them and adapted them to her use" (76).

And again as in the letter above, the eugenical dimension of Woolf's ruminations about literary influence is evident in the Lamarckian conception of inheritance that she reveals. According to Woolf, to trace the woman-centered writing tradition that culminates in the just-published Mary Carmichael requires that one "consider her . . . as the descendent of all those other women whose circumstances [Woolf has] been glancing at and see what she inherits of their characteristics and restrictions" (p. 80). Jane Austen acquired a characteristic sentence: the question is whether or not Carmichael inherited it (p. 80). Given Mary Carmichael's limitations, Woolf recognizes that there is still some way to go before "Shakespeare's sister will put on the body which she has so often laid down," but the fact that she imagines that a woman will eventually acquire by inheritance sufficient character to be born Shakespeare's sister emphasizes the eugenical subtext of *A Room of One's Own* (p. 112). From this point of view, the essay can be read as an inquiry into the conditions prerequisite to both the literary and the literal breeding of the superwoman.

The language of inheritance is an important feature of Woolf's essay. Carmichael, unfortunately, writes "without the unconscious bearing of long descent," but Woolf is determined nonetheless to read her novel "as if it were the last volume in a fairly long series, continuing . . . Lady Winchelsea's poems and Aphra Behn's plays and the novels of the four great novelists. For books continue each other, in spite of our habit of judging them separately" (p. 92, 80). The journey to the enviable kind of unconsciousness that men writers display begins for women, paradoxically, with heightened consciousness of descent – the very consciousness that Woolf attempts to stimulate by means of *A Room of One's Own*.

The importance of this issue is announced in the first chapter when Woolf compares prewar and postwar luncheon parties at Oxbridge: "as I matched the two together I had no doubt that one was the descendent, the legitimate heir of the other" (p. 14). Yet whereas before the war, men were humming the love songs of Tennyson and women were humming the love songs of Christina Rossetti, they no longer do so. First, the relationship between men and women has changed, such that to hum such love songs now

seems "ludicrous," for "romance was killed" in the war; consequently, "Alfred ceased to sing" and "Christina ceased to respond"
(pp. 15–16). Second, poetry seems to have degenerated: "I went on
to wonder if honestly one could name two living poets now as great
as Tennyson and Christina Rossetti were then" (p. 16). People and
poetry are missing something. "Orphans is what we are – we
Georgians," says Woolf in her letter;[4] in *A Room of One's Own*, she
implies that postwar poets are orphans deprived of the "two living
poets" who might have been their parents. The thing missing is
figured as a missing inheritance – whether in the "descendent" and
"legitimate heir" of the earlier luncheon conversation, the present
generation of men and women who are bequeathed no romance, or
the poetic tradition that has lost contact with Tennyson and Rossetti.

The symbol of this matter of the missing inheritance is the "cat
without a tail" whose apparently fortuitous sighting by Woolf as she
flicks cigarette ash out a window leads to this overarching idea that
something is missing: "as I watched the Manx cat pause in the
middle of the lawn as if it too questioned the universe, something
seemed lacking" (p. 13). The cat is ultimately a trope for the main
subject of the essay: "the effect of tradition and of the lack of
tradition upon the mind of a writer" (p. 26). The language of
descent, of inheritance, and of degeneration in this first chapter thus
comes to a focus through the question that the Manx cat raises: "Was
he really born so, or had he lost his tail in an accident?" (p. 15). With
regard to the matter of literary inheritance, the tail symbolizes the
writing tradition; the tailless cat, the woman writer lacking such a
tradition. *A Room of One's Own* tells the tale of this missing tail – tells
how woman is absent in patriarchy's history, society, and writing.

Insofar as the tail represents the writing tradition, and insofar as
the writing tradition is man-centered, the woman writer is born
tailless – born without the phallus that constitutes the tradition.
Being born without such a tail is a good thing for a woman writer, for
the tradition in question is like a man's sentence, "unsuited for a
woman's use" (p. 77). But insofar as the tail represents the writing
tradition more generally, and insofar as a writing tradition can be
woman-centered, the woman writer has lost her tail in an accident –
the accident that is a patriarchal culture in which a woman's writing
tradition has not been preserved. From this point of view, "The
tailless cat . . . is a queer animal, quaint rather than beautiful," and
so being born without the tail that is a woman's writing tradition is a

misfortune: "It is strange what a difference a tail makes" (p. 15). Woolf's tale of the evolution of a woman's writing tradition from Lady Winchelsea to Mary Carmichael therefore attempts to restore the tail/tale that makes so much difference to cats and women writers.

The Manx cat is also the figure through which Woolf focuses some of her most important eugenical ideas. For instance, she contemplates the absence from the women's writing tradition of a founding figure like Shakespeare by asking what "if a woman in Shakespeare's day had had Shakespeare's genius" (p. 50)? Her answer to this question – "genius like Shakespeare's is not born among labouring, uneducated, servile people. It was not born in England among the Saxons and the Britons. It is not born today among the working classes. How, then, could it have been born among women . . .?" (p. 50) – takes her in the direction of eugenics. She betrays here Galton's classist assumption that genius appears most regularly in the upper classes and royalty. Yet her rhetorical question also shows that she accepts that genius could have been born in sixteenth-century women had society not conspired to abort it: "genius of a sort must have existed among women as it must have existed among the working classes. . . But certainly it never got itself on to paper" (p. 50). Woolf thus translates the question about the Manx cat's tail into a question about genius: is woman born without genius, or is the absence of genius the result of an accident?

These are the very terms in which the eugenical investigation of the heritability of genius was conducted at the turn of the century. At the Eugenics Congress of 1912, the American sociology professor Samuel G. Smith argued that "genius [is] the surprise of history": "There [is] not the slightest evidence that either talent or character, either intellectual or moral qualities were ever transmitted directly through the germ." Skeptical of eugenics, he argued that "the larger proportion of talented children" in the wealthy classes "was due to education and upbringing," concluding that the problem "is not how to bring better babies into the world, but how to take care of such as come."[5] Woolf implies a similar understanding of sixteenth-century genius: it was not nourished in the female babies born with it.

Smith's opinion, however, was an aberration at the Eugenics Congress. More prevalent was the classist language that Woolf displays. Saleeby, for instance, countered Smith's argument with the assertion that "[t]he inheritance of talent . . . might be more demonstrable than that of genius. The latter was probably due to a happy combination of a vast number of Mendelian units, which could only in the rarest cases be thrown into one or two germ-cells."[6] F. A. Woods reaffirmed the conclusions of *Hereditary Genius*: "Galton had shown that men of genius were related to each other to a very considerable extent." Woods himself "had investigated royal families," discovering that "[t]he percentage of geniuses . . . was between 50,000 and 100,000 times as great as among the masses," determining that this fact "was not due to environment or opportunity" but rather "was just what Mendelism led them to expect."[7]

Woolf also reflects awareness of the strategies of eugenical inquiry into the heritability of genius in other ways. In *The Family and the Nation* (1909), the Whethams set out (like Woods) to verify Galton's conclusions about genius. Whereas Galton had surveyed inherited eminence via "*Men of the Time*, . . . now represented by *Who's Who*," the Whethams surveyed inherited eminence via Leslie Stephen's *Dictionary of National Biography.*[8] Was Woolf aware of the eugenical service to which her father's work was being put? It is tempting to think so, given that Rachel Vinrace begins her search for a husband in *The Voyage Out* by pointedly consulting *Who's Who*, as though taking a eugenical cue from Galton and the Whethams.[9] The Whethams' contribution to Galton's investigation of the heritability of genius is to insist that it is necessary "[t]o examine the all-important problem of the effect of both parents on the inheritance of ability" – the problem being that women do not often appear in *The Dictionary of National Biography*, for "[t]he ability of women, naturally destined to be used in work even more honorable and important than that of men, makes less noise in the world, and very seldom gets noticed in public records."[10] From this point of view, regardless of Woolf's intentions, *A Room of One's Own* functions as a literary version of the women's eugenical supplement to *The Dictionary of National Biography* that the Whethams deemed necessary. By charting the inheritance of women's literary genius, Woolf effectively continues both her father's biographical work and the biological work to which it had been put by the Whethams.[11]

The Manx cat also functions as a figure for the dysgenic body, for its taillessness is indeed the result of genetic mutation preserved through selective breeding – a fact of which Woolf is presumably aware, since her question is whether the tailless cat that she has observed is genetically or accidentally tailless. Woolf calls it a "poor beast," "a queer animal," "a little absurd" (*A Room of One's Own*, p. 15). In this respect, the cat's body symbolizes Woolf's own body insofar as she was never comfortable with it – eventually coming to suspect an "inherited . . . ancestral dread" of the body.[12] More generally, the cat's appearance figures the equally queer and absurd impression made by a woman of genius who lacks a tradition for the expression of her genius: such a woman is "a witch . . . a woman possessed by devils . . . a wise woman selling herbs." The queerness and absurdity of this poor beast are a function of its body. Suicide, for instance, is one of the many queer results when genius like Shakespeare's is "caught and tangled in a woman's body." Because of her body, Shakespeare's sister would have been turned away by *any* law-abiding theater manager, and especially by the boor Woolf imagines: to him, the very image of "women acting" is as absurd as "poodles dancing" – an insult that Woolf makes all the more galling by putting it in the mouth of a dysgenically "loose-lipped" vulgarian (*A Room of One's Own*, p. 49).

Yet the possibility that the poor cat has lost its tail in an accident also marks its body as the site of an important potential, for the descendents of the cat whose tail has been bobbed will have their own tails. As Smith noted at the Eugenics Congress, "Nature [does] well in her transactions. The father might have one hand and the mother one eye, but the baby [has] two of each."[13] Woolf's implicit hope concerning the cat's tail becomes her explicit hope concerning a woman's writing tradition: it might be reacquired. Woolf's hopes for the bodies of cats and women are the hopes of eugenists for the bodies of the British people: over time, the body might be remade and redeemed.

This preoccupation in *A Room of One's Own* with the eugenical development of the body through time is also evident in Woolf's evolutionary language. In her dismissal of the influence of men writers – they "never helped a woman yet, though she may have learned a few tricks of them and adapted them to her use" – the language of adaptation turns Woolf's thoughts toward an evolutionary model of influence, leading her to add here the apparently gratuitous observation that "[t]he ape is too distant to be sedulous" (p. 76). The meaning of this sentence is obscure. The word "ape" may be an awkward denotation of "the thing to be aped" – the sentence itself meaning that aping a man's sentence is not worth while because it is too far removed from a woman writer's needs.

More interestingly, however, the sentence invokes the Darwinian idea that human beings descend from apes. Woolf thus depicts the man and his sentence as distant from the woman and her sentence in evolutionary terms: she is a human being and he is an ape; their bodies and their sentences are related, but too distantly for the woman to be sedulous in acknowledging the fact.

Similarly, looking to the future instead of the past, Woolf anticipates that the body will change just as dramatically. She envisions a time when it will not be the case that "a good dinner is of great importance to good talk," as it is now – "[t]he human frame being what it is, heart, body, and brain all mixed together, and not contained in separated compartments as they will be no doubt in another million years" (p. 20). Woolf even celebrates woman-centered aspects of Carmichael's novel as evolution in action. The scene in which "Chloe watched Olivia put a jar on the shelf" requires of the author so unprecedented a sensitivity to a woman's suspicion "of any interest that has not some obvious motive behind it" as to be representable only as an evolutionary breakthrough – both by the character Olivia and by the author herself:

The only way for you to do it . . . would be to talk of something else . . . and thus note . . . what happens when Olivia – this organism that has been under the shadow of the rock these million years – feels light fall on it, and sees coming her way a piece of strange food . . . And she reaches out for it . . . and has to develop some entirely new combination of her resources, so highly developed for their purposes, so as to absorb the new into the old without disturbing the infinitely intricate and elaborate balance of the whole. (p. 84)

The body is evolving – whether the body as a biological form, the body as a social form, or the body as a fictional form.

The idea of the eugenically evolved body is an important element in Woolf's confidence that the superwoman will come. In fact, she depicts the evolution of Shakespeare's sister in terms of progressive embodiment. The question is how to get Shakespeare's genius into his sister's body: she must be induced to "put on the body which she has so often laid down." In outlining the development of a woman's writing tradition from Lady Winchelsea forward, therefore, Woolf traces the progressive embodiment of genius in women:

Without . . . forerunners, Jane Austen and the Brontës and George Eliot could no more have written than Shakespeare could have written without Marlowe, or Marlowe without Chaucer, or Chaucer without those forgotten people who paced the ways and tamed the natural savagery of the tongue. For masterpieces are not single and solitary births; they are the outcome of many years of thinking in common, of thinking by the body of the people, so that the experience of the mass is behind the single voice. (p. 66)

The savage tongue in the savage body of the Saxon and Briton evolved into the refined tongue in the refined body of Chaucer, Marlowe, and Shakespeare. The tongue and body of woman have evolved similarly on the way from witch, devil-woman and wise woman to Austen, the Brontës, and Eliot. Her novel is no master-piece, so Carmichael has not yet adequately expressed the tongue and the body of woman – "I tried a sentence or two on my tongue. Soon it was obvious that something was not quite in order" – but even so she has "certain advantages which women of far greater gift lacked even half a century ago" (pp. 80, 91). Good Lamarckian eugenist that she is, Woolf credits each generation with a headstart courtesy of the good literary character it inherits from its precursors.

And so, evolution continues: "give her a room of her own and five hundred a year, let her speak her mind and leave out half that she now puts in, and she will write a better book one of these days. She will be a poet . . . in another hundred years' time" (p. 93). Further-more, when the poet fit to be Shakespeare's sister is born, she will find ready for her a literary form fit to embody the poetry in her. The novel will not be "rightly shaped for her use until it can serve as the vehicle of her poetry": "No doubt we shall find her knocking that into shape for herself when she has the free use of her limbs; and providing some new vehicle, not necessarily in verse, for the poetry in her. For it is the poetry that is still denied outlet" (pp. 77–78). In the end, the incorporation of woman's body and tongue into a writing tradition is the main project that Woolf prescribes for women's genius: "The book has somehow to be adapted to the body, and at a venture one would say that women's books should be shorter, more concentrated, than those of men" (p. 78). Such an elision of the body and the book might seem tongue-in-cheek were it not for Woolf's consistent application to literature of her biological model.

Woolf's commitment to this biological model leads her ultimately to qualify the lesbian implications of the radically woman-centered community that she depicts in her articulation of a woman's literary tradition. Until the final chapter, it seems that women writers can get on very well without men, for "the great men writers" are "useless" (p. 76). In particular, the man's sentence – symbolically, the phallus –

is "unsuited for a woman's use": "Charlotte Brontë . . . stumbled and fell with that clumsy weapon in her hands. . . George Eliot committed atrocities with it . . . Jane Austen looked at it and laughed at it . . ." (p. 77). Woolf imagines that the laugh of the emasculating woman motivates retaliation in both the misogynist professor who wrote *The Mental, Moral, and Physical Inferiority of Women* – "Had he been laughed at . . . in his cradle by a pretty girl?" (p. 33) – and contemporary novelists who show "an extraordinary desire for self-assertion" because "challenged . . . by a few women in black bonnets" during the "Suffrage campaign" (p. 98). Having thus argued both explicitly for the self-sufficiency of the body of women who constitute a woman's writing tradition and implicitly for the laughing self-sufficiency of woman's phallus-free body itself, Woolf somewhat surprisingly concludes her essay with a celebration of the true artist's "androgynous" mind (p. 97) – a concept that Elaine Showalter dismisses as a "myth that helped her evade confrontation with her own painful femaleness and enabled her to choke and repress her anger and ambition."[14]

Showalter may well be right, but the turn toward androgyny is also an expression of Woolf's eugenics. It represents the point at which Woolf's devotion to her biological model of influence leads her to define the ground of creativity in terms of heterosexual intercourse: "If one is a man, still the woman part of the brain must have effect; and a woman also must have intercourse with the man in her. Coleridge perhaps meant this when he said that a great mind is androgynous" (*A Room of One's Own*, p. 97). Whatever Coleridge meant, Woolf certainly means for us to understand the idea of androgynous intercourse between the internal woman and man in biological terms: "It is when this fusion takes place that the mind is fully fertilised and uses all its faculties. Perhaps a mind that is purely masculine cannot create, any more than a mind that is purely feminine" (p. 97). Writing as a woman exclusively, therefore, is fatal: "It is fatal for a woman to lay the least stress on any grievance; to plead even with justice any cause; in any way to speak consciously as a woman" (pp. 102–103). Fascist Italy betrays an opposite extreme of sex consciousness: "the sense of unmitigated masculinity." According to Woolf, the "self-assertive virility" of Italy will produce only monstrosities: "The Fascist poem, one may fear, will be a horrid little abortion such as one sees in a glass jar in the museum of some country town. Such monsters never live long, it is said; one has never

seen a prodigy of that sort cropping grass in a field. Two heads on
one body do not make for length of life" (pp. 101–02). And so: "[i]t is
fatal to be a man or woman pure and simple . . . And fatal is no
figure of speech; for anything written with that conscious bias is
doomed to death. It ceases to be fertilised. . . it must wither at
nightfall" (pp. 102–03). Women who announce their grievance or
plead their cause in novels – however justly – are refusing intercourse
with the male halves of their minds. Similarly, men who are
stimulated to a hyperconsciousness of their masculinity write with
only one half of their brains. The result is sterility, abortion, still-
birth, and short-lived monstrosities. Woolf implies that whether
biologically or literarily, homosexuality produces nothing stable or
enduring. Woolf's biological model of creativity is thus the Trojan
horse by which heterosexuality is let into the otherwise woman-
centered writing tradition that Woolf has been describing.

Woolf's scruple about the lesbian dimension of her conception of
woman-centered creativity parallels Clarissa Dalloway's scruple
about the lesbian dimension of her sexuality. Frigid and contracting
before Richard, Clarissa has "failed him . . . again and again": "She
could see what she lacked . . . something warm which broke up
surfaces and rippled the cold contact of man and woman." Clarissa
can, however, detect the "something warm which broke up surfaces
and rippled the cold contact . . . of women together. For *that* she could
dimly perceive. . . she could not resist sometimes yielding to the
charm of a woman." Yet she would resist this inclination, if she could:
"She resented it, had a scruple picked up Heaven knows where, or,
she felt, sent by Nature (who is invariably wise)" (*Mrs. Dalloway*, p. 46).
Faced with the alternative that her scruple about lesbianism is an
accident of her environment or something that she is born with,
Clarissa inclines toward the latter explanation. Her depiction of the
lesbian Kilman as a "monster" implies the same conclusion:
lesbianism is unnatural (p. 190). Nature has therefore given Kilman a
dysgenic body: "Heavy, ugly, commonplace," Kilman's body prevents
Clarissa from thinking about anything else, and it means for Kilman
"never meeting the opposite sex," for "[n]ever would she come first
with anyone" (pp. 190, 191, 195). Not surprisingly, Clarissa's "invariably wise" Nature proves to be eugenically wise.

Woolf's argument in *A Room of One's Own* follows a similar logic:
since biological creativity is heterosexual, and since nature is
"invariably" wise, literary creativity must be heterosexual. And so,

"[s]ome collaboration has to take place in the mind between the woman and the man before the act of creation can be accomplished. Some marriage of opposites has to be consummated" (*A Room of One's Own*, p. 103). Prospects for good literature in Italy are bleak because the model of creativity is unnatural: "it is doubtful whether poetry can come out of an incubator. Poetry ought to have a mother as well as a father" (p. 101). Men who would do without the womb and women who would do without the penis must be prepared, like Frankenstein, to entertain short-lived "monsters." Rentoul fulminates against "sexual perverts" in similar terms: "they have been created by the misdeeds of men and women – some great law of nature having been broken."[15] Woolf's respect for nature, like Clarissa's, is bound up with eugenical beliefs: anything against nature is monstrous, and monsters die young and without issue because of nature's eugenical wisdom.

From this point of view, the choice of Carmichael's book as the one by which to measure the contemporary woman writer's distance from the superwoman is not as random as it might seem. Carmichael is the pseudonym of Marie Stopes, the famous crusader for birth control and eugenics. Stopes participated in the Eugenics Congress of 1912, for instance, and her birth control clinics cooperated with the Eugenics Education Society in the dissemination of information.[16] By the late 1920s, however, eugenists like Blacker were criticizing Stopes: "Blacker had disliked Marie Stopes's tying contraception to the cause of women's sexual gratification and had been distressed that some birth control literature tended, so he thought, to the lascivious promotion of immorality."[17] Woolf presumably chooses *Life's Adventure* ("or some such title" – she has misremembered the title of Carmichael's 1928 novel *Love's Creation*) as a plausible test case for the argument that it is both possible and necessary for the woman with the obvious grievance and the just cause to lay them aside if she is to write a good novel (*A Room of One's Own*, p. 79). In short, the woman as activist (Stopes) has a grievance and cause: do they show up in the writing of the same woman as novelist (Carmichael)?

On the whole, Woolf judges Carmichael a successful novelist, for she "mastered the first great lesson; she wrote as a woman, but as a woman who has forgotten that she is a woman, so that her pages were full of that curious sexual quality which comes only when sex is unconscious of itself" (p. 92). Of course she was advantaged by a time and place that somewhat alleviated the "rage" that "deformed and twisted" Charlotte Brontë several generations before (p. 70). Nonetheless, some elements of Stopes's grievances against patriarchy are evident in Carmichael's novel: "Men were no longer to her 'the opposing faction'; she need not waste her time railing against them . . . Fear and hatred were almost gone, or traces of them showed only in a slight exaggeration of the joy of freedom, a tendency to the caustic and satirical, rather than to the romantic, in her treatment of the other sex" (pp. 91–92). Carmichael has "almost" set aside the grievances of Stopes – but "traces" remain. Since according to Woolf Carmichael's "books will no doubt be pulped by the publisher in ten years' time," one wonders whether even so mild an expression of grievance as the one Woolf documents here taints Carmichael with the shortened shelf-life that comes from Stopes's sex consciousness (91–92). After all, one notes that Woolf sees Carmichael's novel as an instance of the very death of romance between men and women that she ranges alongside the Manx cat, on the one hand, and the unheeded Tennyson and Rossetti, on the other, as evidence that something is missing in the modern world. However ameliorated by time and place, the debilitating taint of Brontë's rage has been passed on to Carmichael.

Woolf also seems to have chosen Carmichael's novel for review because of the focus that the figure of Stopes could bring to Woolf's eugenical concerns about literary descent, sexual activity, and biological inheritance. Like Blacker, Woolf was well aware of Stopes's impact on the sexual behavior of young people in the 1920s:

[T]he younger generation . . . are like crude hard green apples: no halo, mildew or blight. Seduced at 15, life has no holes and corners for them. I admire, but deplore. Such an old maid, they make me feel. "And how do you manage not- not- not- to have children?" I ask. "Oh, we read Mary Stopes of course." Figure to yourself . . . before taking their virginity, the young men of our time produce marked copies of Stopes! Astonishing![18]

Woolf as "old maid" in this letter is transposed into her contemporaneous novel *Mrs. Dalloway* as both the young Clarissa who turns "bright pink" at the news that a maid has had a baby out of wedlock and the old Clarissa who "could not dispel a virginity preserved through childbirth" (p. 89, 46). Woolf transposes her surprise at the change in the behavior of men and women in public onto Peter Walsh:

Those five years – 1918 to 1923 – had been . . . somehow very important. People looked different. . . this taking out a stick of rouge, or a powder-puff and making up in public. On board ship coming home there were lots of young men and girls . . . carrying on quite openly. . . The girl would stand still and powder her nose in front of everyone. And they weren't engaged; just having a good time; no feelings hurt on either side. As hard as nails she was . . . (*A Room of One's Own*, p. 108)

Whether Woolf sides with the "old maid" or the hard young women is no more clear in the novel than in the letter. Certainly the Woolf who strives in *A Room of One's Own* to free the woman writer from patriarchal constraint recognizes the importance of birth control: "You must, of course, go on bearing children, but, so they say, in twos and threes, not in tens and twelves" (p. 111). Yet there are two assumptions here: first, that women must continue to respect their biological function, and second, that women must respect what "they say" – "the economists are saying that Mrs. Seton has had too many children" (p. 111).[19]

And so there is another Woolf evident in these texts – a Woolf aware of the claims of the economists who urge birth control and eugenics as a means of industrial efficiency, and so a Woolf who is suspicious of young people who manage to have sexual intercourse and not to have children. Woolf's scruple is a moral one – and it is not simply the scruple of a prudish Victorian, but the scruple of a eugenist. In all three texts – Woolf's letter, *Mrs. Dalloway,* and *A Room of One's Own* – the thing to note is Woolf's interest in the relationship between sexual activity and procreation. The fact that in her letter Woolf offers a single question to explain the double aspect of her astonishment – "I admire, but I deplore" – is instructive. Her question has both a biological and a moral dimension: "how do you manage biologically not to have children?" and "how do you manage morally not to have children?" Woolf admires the technological sophistication but deplores the morality. The eugenical Woolf who would promote child-bearing by the daughters of educated men deplores the sterility of such behavior.

Woolf's ambivalence reflects her awareness that Stopes is the agent of both liberation and promiscuity. Woolf and Blacker, in short, share similar suspicions of Stopes – suspicions explained by their eugenical assumptions. Blacker's conservative understanding of sexual intercourse as having an exclusively procreative function was shared by many eugenists. Rentoul, for instance, argued that "sexual intercourse has for its sole purpose the begetting of healthy offspring."[20] At the 1912 Eugenics Congress, Mrs. Macoy Irvin argued that marriage "should be prohibited not only to the imbecile and the insane, but also to those who by lives of sensual indulgence had unfitted themselves for parenthood." She anticipated the concerns of Woolf and Blacker with her complaint that "marriage and maternity were not synonymous terms . . . But they ought to be. They had become divorced because of the prevalence of unwilling motherhood. The separation of these ideas in the mind of the young must inevitably lead to moral decay, as well as race-suicide."[21]

This fear of sexuality without issue was an extension of the fear of sexuality with bad issue, for the very pursuit of sexual gratification as an end in itself was taken as a sign of degeneracy. R. L. Dugdale, in his influential study of a family of criminals, *The Jukes*, concluded that "[h]arlotry may become a hereditary characteristic and be perpetuated without any specially favoring environment to call it into activity."[22] The Whethams noted "the prevalence of sexual immorality among the feeble-minded": "The lack of self-control which is noticeable among feeble-minded boys, and drives them ultimately into the prisons, sends the girls on to the streets . . . to increase and perpetuate the race of the feeble-minded."[23]

Against this background, Stopes seemed to be playing with a potentially dysgenical fire. And so, having by 1928 become a lightning rod in the debate about the nature of woman's sexuality and the naturalness of such sexualities as existed, the figure of Stopes can be found behind the anxiety in *A Room of One's Own* about any separation between sexual activity and procreation. In the essay's concluding chapter, the idea of sexual activity without issue becomes Woolf's figure for literary activity without issue. Whether in the bedroom or in the novel, such activity is evidence of degeneracy – moral and literary, respectively. According to the eugenical Woolf, then, romance is dead (and Tennyson and Rossetti have neither successors nor an audience) at least in part, it seems, because of Marie Stopes – that is, because of the threat to pure morality and pure literature that Woolf found in her birth control campaign's practical consequences in the lives of young women, on the one hand, and in the novels of women writers like Carmichael, on the other.

Not surprisingly, therefore, *A Room of One's Own* concludes with the injunction that women novelists should be careful to breed well. In an age of self-conscious virility – "men, that is to say, are now writing only with the male side of their brains" – the woman writer must be careful in selecting the men that she will read. The contemporary novelist "Mr. A" (presumably D. H. Lawrence) reveals the impotence that comes of having been made "stridently sex-conscious" by the woman's movement: the latter "must have roused in men an extraordinary desire for self-assertion" – a desire realized in "the dominance of the letter 'I' and the aridity, which, like the giant beech tree, it casts within its shade. Nothing will grow there" (pp. 97–99). Taking the poetry critic "Mr. B" in hand (presumably the "disso-ciated" T. S. Eliot), Woolf is disappointed: "the trouble was, that his feelings no longer communicated; his mind seemed separated into different chambers; not a sound carried from one to the other" (p. 100). Mr. B's writing on poetry is related to Woolf's image of the human frame of the future – "heart, body and brain . . . contained in separate compartments as they will be no doubt in another million years" (p. 20). Such an evolutionary freak can fertilize nothing here and now: "Thus, when one takes a sentence of Mr. B into the mind it falls plump to the ground – dead" (p. 100). Mr. B, it seems, cannot maintain an erection. Mr. A (a flasher) displays his phallic "I" "over and over . . . and over again" – "Mr. A, as the nurses say, does it on purpose" – but there is "some impediment of Mr. A's mind which block[s] the fountain of creative energy" (p. 99). Impotence and sterility prevail.

The woman writer must turn away, then, from "some of the finest works of our greatest living writers": "Do what she will a woman cannot find in them that fountain of perpetual life which the critics assure her is there" (p. 100). If she is to breed effectively and responsibly, the woman writer's only option is a somewhat necrophi-lial recourse to the dead – but admirably androgynous – Coleridge: "when one takes a sentence of Coleridge into the mind, it explodes and gives birth to all kinds of other ideas, and that is the only sort of writing of which one can say that it has the secret of perpetual life" (p. 100). Coleridge functions here as a literary sperm bank – a sperm bank similar to the Fascist incubator, and similarly suspect, for Woolf makes it clear that she chooses the past writer as father for her child only because the contemporary writers that she would prefer are impotent. Reduced to a "restless mood" by writers who "cannot penetrate" her mind, Woolf faces facts – the fact that Coleridge has the literary germ plasm that the woman writer should seek to combine with her own if Shakespeare's sister is to "put on the body which she has so often laid down," and the fact that since one's obligation is to the germ plasm, not to one's contemporaries, Coleridge it must be (pp. 101, 112). *A Room of One's Own*'s conception of the writer's responsibility thus duplicates the eugenist's conception of the biological parents' responsibility: "Their one sacred obligation to the immortal germ-plasm of which they are trustees is to see that they hand it on with its maximal possibilities undimmed by innutrition, poisons, or vice."[24]

I have often had to tease it out of Woolf's diaries, letters, essays, and novels – but the eugenics is there. Yet however "real" Woolf's participation in eugenical discourse, her eugenics generally might seem uninteresting from Foucault's point of view. One could argue that *Mrs. Dalloway*, her other novels, *Three Guineas*, her diaries, her letters, and her essays merely represent instances of the efflorescence of such a discourse in sites where it had appeared before: concerning reproduction by imbeciles, idiots, and the daughters of educated men; concerning the need to control feebleminded prostitutes; concerning the promotion of industrial efficiency; concerning emigration; concerning race; concerning mongolism, and so on. *A Room of One's Own*, however, represents an extension of the discourse of "bio-power" into a site where it had not been seen before – the site of women's imaginative creativity. In effect, Woolf's eugenics in *A Room of One's Own* foregrounds a biological model of woman's literary genius – especially in the equation between literary form and woman's body – that deploys in the realm of women's imagination what Foucault calls the "disciplines of the body and the regulations of the population . . . around which the organization of power over life was deployed."[25]

CHAPTER 4

Eliot on biology and birthrates

In *The Idea of a Christian Society* (1939), T. S. Eliot's recollection of the early years of the eugenics movement allows him to identify the permanent value of a "Liberalism" that he otherwise despises. Liberalism is a negative ideology, aspiring to negate abusive, obsolete, unreasonable restraints upon the individual. The problem is that "as its movement is controlled rather by its origin than by any goal, it loses its force after a series of rejections, and with nothing to destroy is left with nothing to uphold and with nowhere to go." Welcoming the passing of Liberalism, Eliot nevertheless warns against confusing the chaos that Liberalism causes with the "necessary negative element" that it represents. The danger is that the baby will be thrown out with the bathwater should Liberalism "come to signify for us only the disorder the fruits of which we inherit, and not the permanent value of the negative element." Thus "Out of Liberalism itself come philosophies which deny it," and so "Liberalism can prepare the way for that which is its own negation: the artificial, mechanised or brutalised control which is a desperate remedy for its chaos." Totalitarianism is one such control; eugenical legislation is another.

As an example of an intrusion upon "the preserves of 'private life'" that even those "most convinced of the necessity of *étatisme* as a control of some activities of life" would reject, Eliot describes the following scenario: "It is possible that a wave of terror of the consequences of depopulation might lead to legislation having the effect of compulsory breeding." He has eugenical breeding in mind. Yet he imagines such legislation issuing not so much from Nazi Germany as from the "authoritarian democracy" that might succeed Liberal democracy in "Britain, France, America and the Dominions."[1] Although the notoriety of Nazi Germany's eugenical racial policies accounts in 1939 for Eliot's musings about "compulsory

75

breeding," the hypothesis by which he makes such legislation
conceivable in democratic countries – the possibility of "a wave of
terror of the consequences of depopulation" – shows that Eliot
recalls here the passionate eugenical debates about depopulation and
birth control that he encountered during the Great War in such
journals as *The Egoist*, *The New Statesman*, *The Hibbert Journal*, *Shield*
(a "Review of Moral and Social Hygiene"), and *The Eugenics Review* –
debates about the effect of unregulated breeding upon everything
from the national birthrate to the state of the national germ plasm.
These debates for the first time made conceivable the possibility of
"legislation having the effect of compulsory breeding."

For Eliot, eugenics was a natural extension of the study of biology
and heredity. Employing the work of biologists from Lamarck and
Darwin to De Vries, Henri Bergson had introduced Eliot to an
intoxicating combination of biology, philosophy, and mysticism in
Creative Evolution (1907), inviting human beings to reclaim an intuitive
oneness with the Life Force that had been forsaken in the embrace of
practical intellect.[2] A few years later, in Josiah Royce's seminar at
Harvard (1913–14), Eliot encountered a more scientifically and
philosophically scrupulous discussion of biology and evolution. Inevitably, seminars included discussion of heredity and eugenics. The
class considered the work of Galton, Pearson, and Davenport,
questions of the relative influences of environment and heredity (they
discussed the infamous Jukes family), and the possibility of the
inheritance of acquired characteristics. One of the most regular
contributors to the seminar discussions on these topics was F. A.
Woods, who had already published *Mental and Moral Heredity in Royalty*
(1906).[3] At Harvard in 1915, Eliot took a course with the eugenist
William McDougall. As Robert Crawford notes, Eliot attended the
latter's "lectures on 'Mental Evolution' which dealt with primitive
man and the biological theories of Darwinian pangenesis, Weiss-
mann on germ-plasm, De Vries on mutation, and Mendel on
heredity."[4]

It is small wonder, then, that when invited in 1917 to review
"Recent British Periodical Literature in Ethics" for *The International
Journal of Ethics*, Eliot devoted several pages of his essay to articles in
The Eugenics Review. He focused in particular upon E. W. MacBride's
four-part essay "The Study of Heredity," commending it not only as
one of "the most valuable contributions" to its particular field, but

also as one of just two recent essays he judged to be of "exceptional importance" in the field of ethics as a whole.[5] Close attention to MacBride's essay in the pages that follow will show how extensive its influence upon Eliot was.

Eliot described "The Study of Heredity" as "in large part highly technical, although well written, and made as intelligible as possible to the uninitiated."[6] It is an account of the development of the science of eugenics from the discovery of cells in plants to contemporary investigation of the role of chromosomes and hormones in reproduction and heredity. In addition to supplementing his knowledge of the "Mendelization" of biology and eugenics acquired in Royce's seminar, it also acquainted him with the benefits of the internationalization of research activity:

> Published in a local journal with no very wide circulation, [Mendel's work] . . . remained entirely unnoticed by Mendel's contemporaries. In the year 1900, however, these results were unearthed by two botanists, De Vries and Correns, who repeated some of Mendel's experiments and confirmed his results. The matter was enthusiastically taken up . . . in England, and by many workers in America, and an enormous amount of research on similar lines has already been accomplished.[7]

De Vries, Correns, and the workers in England and America become Eliot's model for the minor poet and the minor critic: "there is much useful work done in science by men who are only clever enough and well enough educated to apply a method; and in literature there *ought* to be a place for persons of equivalent capacity."[8] Eliot thus acquires from MacBride both detailed knowledge of contemporary biology that he would subsequently flaunt and a more general scientific paradigm that would inform many of his discussions at this time of the nature of poetry and criticism.

Never shy to parade his learning, Eliot seems particularly to have enjoyed demonstrating his knowledge of biology. Later in 1918, advertising his own special knowledge of French literature and celebrating *The Egoist*'s awareness of "the importance of crossbreeding in poetry," Eliot explains the education of a poet in terms of the biological analogy that his allusion to Mendelian "crossbreeding" introduces:

> A poet, like a scientist, is contributing toward the organic development of culture: it is just as absurd for him not to know the work of his predecessors or of men writing in other languages as it would be for a biologist to be ignorant of Mendel or De Vries. It is exactly as wasteful for a poet to do

what has been done already, as for a biologist to rediscover Mendel's discoveries. . . To remain with Wordsworth is equivalent to ignoring the whole of science subsequent to Erasmus Darwin.[9]

Eliot shows off his relatively specialized knowledge: he knows of the importance of Mendel's work in crossbreeding peas; he knows that Mendel's discoveries went unnoticed for many years because science was not sufficiently internationalized when Mendel published his work; he knows that De Vries was one of the first to rediscover, corroborate, and publicize Mendel's work. Later the same year, Eliot applies his biological analogy to the situation of the literary critic: "Criticism, like creative art, is in various ways less developed than scientific research," but criticism will become more objective and less subjective "[i]f the critic has performed his laboratory work well." Like poetry, criticism must become "thoroughly internationalized" – "the results of any important experiment in one country . . . immediately taken up, tested and proceeded upon in every other." In biology, as opposed to poetry and criticism, "[a] vast improvement in this respect had taken place, for instance, since Mendel's time."[10]

Eliot was deeply impressed by MacBride's essay, and impressed not only by the account of biology's history and method, but also by the account of its modern achievement: eugenics. MacBride encouraged Eliot to regard eugenics as a natural extension of biology:

when one of a family survives because in some point it is a little better equipped than its brothers and sisters, it is tacitly assumed that some of the descendents of this survivor will exhibit this point in still stronger measure than did their progenitor. . . If these individual differences had the tremendous significance which Darwin . . . attributed to them, it was clearly of the first importance that they should be measured; and this step was taken by Sir Francis Galton, Darwin's cousin, who devised a scheme for the measurement of the inheritance of individual peculiarities among the human population.[11]

MacBride highlights Darwin's "tacit assumption" that advantageous characteristics can be inherited in stronger forms because such an assumption opens a space within Darwinism for eugenics. MacBride emphasizes that such characteristics can also become enfeebled, and so heredity can degrade a family: human "monsters . . . differ from the normal type, in the loss of some feature which the normal type possesses, and hence are to be looked on as defectives. . . [T]hese defectives act as Mendelian recessives . . . and cannot be entirely eliminated from the blood of a strain when once this has been infected by it."[12] According to MacBride, the story that begins with Darwin ends in eugenics: the laws of heredity assumed by Darwin and articulated by Galton and Mendel mean that human beings have a responsibility to breed carefully.

Eliot was especially interested in the eugenical conclusions that MacBride reached – calling them "conclusions of social import-ance." He approvingly summarizes MacBride's Darwinian justi-fication of eugenics: "in former times the struggle for existence was enough to keep down the defective element in the population; but under present conditions these people are protected and multiply."[13] MacBride's conclusion is that eugenical artificial selection can supplement Darwinian natural selection. His recommendation – endorsed by Eliot – is that "segregation and sterilization" of "defectives" is necessary "for the benefit of society." Although MacBride by no means introduced Eliot to Darwin – not only had Bergson, Royce, and McDougall already done that, but as an extension lecturer for the University of London in 1916 and 1917, Eliot lectured on Darwin and Darwinism – he showed him the way from Darwinism to eugenics.[14]

Eliot's acceptance of the naturalness of this connection is suggested later in 1918 in his review of *The Education of Henry Adams.* He lists many of Adams's disbeliefs – he could believe "neither in the sagacity of British statesmanship, nor in the perfection of the American form of government, nor in the New World, nor in the Old; not in Darwinism, or in Karl Pearson, or Ernst Mach, or in the wickedness of large issues of paper currency" – but it is Adams's skepticism about evolution that has caught Eliot's eye.[15] The elaborate negative rhetorical structure of Eliot's sentence about these disbeliefs derives from Adams's own sentence about his disbelief in evolution in particular – a sentence that Eliot quotes: "Neither in the *Limulus* nor in the *Terebratula*, nor in the *Cestraceon Philippi*, any more than the *Pteraspis*, could one conceive an ancestor, but, if one must, the choice mattered little."[16] Furthermore, given that his list of Adams's disbeliefs is designed to illustrate the pervasiveness of Adams's skepticism by providing examples of perfectly believable ideas, Eliot implies his own belief – that not to believe in Darwin and Pearson is rather extraordinary.

The continuing influence of MacBride's discussion of evolution is also indicated by Eliot's 1923 essay "The Beating of a Drum": "The inquiries of Darwin appear to have made no more impression on literary criticism than that recorded by the misleading title of Ferdinand Brunetière, 'L'évolution des genres.'" Eliot is frustrated that scholars should continue merely to "trace the external chronicle of some 'form.'" Such a "chronicle, once recounted, is a preface to be forgotten, unnecessary for the 'appreciation' of the finished product – appreciation for which, as a rule, ignorant sensibility is the chief qualification."[17] For Eliot, the scholarly chronicle represents the efflorescence in literary criticism of the value-neutral time philosophies of the likes of Bergson – ignorant appreciation in literary criticism paralleling the flux of values in a Bergsonian world where "everything may be admired, because nothing is permanent."[18] Through Darwin, however, Eliot has learned that "the *nature* of the finished product ('finished,' of course, is relative) is essentially present in the crude forerunner" – a lesson taught by MacBride, who argues that many forms of life contain within their life cycles evidence of their cruder forerunners, such that their "life history 'recapitulates' the history of the race."[19] From this lesson Eliot draws the literary conclusion that "literature cannot be understood without going to the sources: sources which are often remote, difficult, and unintelligible unless one transcends the prejudices of ordinary literary taste." Like the evolutionary biologist, the literary critic must become the "anthropologist" of form, rather than its "chronicler" – a fact that would become obvious "If literary critics, instead of perpetually perusing the writings of other critics, would study the contents and criticize the methods of such books as 'The Origin of Species' itself. . ."[20]

Eliot is exercised by the same shortcoming in Adams: the latter's understanding of Darwin is as flawed as the contemporary literary critic's. The sentence about how "little" the choice of an evolutionary ancestor matters to Adams actually anticipates Eliot's complaint in "The Beating of a Drum" that the chroniclers of literary form do not understand the importance of determining "the ancestry" of literary form.[21] Eliot quotes Adams's cavalier attitude about evolutionary choices as prelude to his observation about how "little" questions of *moral* choice matter to Adams. Adams writes that "[h]e was a Darwinian for fun": "he really did not care whether truth was, or was not, true" (*Education*, pp. 231–32). Eliot complains that "Wherever this man stepped, the ground did not simply give way, it flew into particles" (361–62). Adams – "seeking for education, with the wings of a beautiful but ineffectual conscience beating vainly in a vacuum jar" (362) – is Eliot's version of Arnold's "beautiful *and ineffectual*" Shelley: "a vision of beauty and radiance, indeed, but availing nothing, effecting nothing."[22]

The inconsequentiality of moral choice for Adams makes *The Education of Henry Adams* a mere chronicle. Eliot therefore makes his review an anthropological exercise in which he suggests why Adams could not make moral choices and why his conscience was without effect. He notes, for instance, that pragmatism and what he calls the "dissolvent" "Boston doubt" work "with and against conscience" in Adams.[23] Eliot's list of Adams's disbeliefs – Darwinism, Karl Pearson, Ernst Mach – is an index of factors working "with and against" Adams's "beautiful" conscience. Darwin, it turns out, works with this conscience; Mach works against it; Pearson works with it and against it simultaneously.

That Eliot should have paid attention to Adams's treatment of Pearson is not surprising. On the one hand, Pearson is initially presented as someone sympathetic to Adams. According to Adams, a friend had suggested that he read Pearson as an answer to his general questions about "race and sex" (*Education*, p. 449). He subsequently read Pearson's *Grammar of Science*, but "never found out what it could have taught" his friend (p. 449). This friend presumably recommended Pearson to Adams because of the latter's fixation upon the biological foundations of modern American society: upon the birthrate, upon the possibility of Census questions about whether young women "wanted children, and how many," and upon related "vital statistics" bearing on "the foundation of a serious society in the future" (p. 447). Pearson's *Grammar of Science* encouraged the very statistical quantification of biology that appealed to Adams. On the other hand, Pearson seems to be a figure interesting to Eliot in his own right, for Eliot shared with Pearson a distrust of sentimental biological enthusiasms. Eliot dismissed the Life Force as a "ju-ju" and "gross superstition."[24] Pearson, as Kevles notes, aspired to remove from biology "speculative concepts – 'species,' 'germ plasm,' and a variety of life 'forces' – that purported to explain vital phenomena yet were beyond operational test," preferring "to deal only with directly observable quantities, to give measurable operational meaning to evolutionary change" – an aspiration subsequently realized in "biometrics," his eugenical combination of biology and statistical analysis.[25]

The questions about race and sex that led Adams to read Pearson

are broadly evolutionary and eugenical, focusing ultimately upon
fears about depopulation. Adams believes that "[r]ace classifie[s]
thought" and therefore asks whether a race that opposes America
can be "overcome without destroying the race in order to reconstruct
it" (*Education*, p. 441). But his deeper question concerns the threat to
the future of the American "race" itself represented by the New
Woman. On the one hand, "[w]hatever else stops, the woman must
go on reproducing, as she did in the Siluria of Pteraspis; sex is a vital
condition, and race only a local one" (p. 441). On the other hand,
"woman had been set free" (p. 444). Women could be seen "taking
themselves seriously"; "they were not content" (p. 445). If woman's
"force were to be diverted from its axis, it must find a new field, and
the family must pay for it. So far as she has succeeded, she must
become sexless like the bees. . . [T]he American woman ha[s] . . .
nothing to rebel against, except her own maternity" (p. 446). Adams
makes his opinion of the woman's movement clear: "Inertia of sex
could not be overcome without extinguishing the race, yet an
immense force, doubling every few years, was working irresistibly to
overcome it. One gazed mute before this ocean of darkest ignorance
that had already engulfed society" (p. 448). Disbelieving that Pteraspis is his ancestor, Adams nonetheless warns woman against
betraying her evolutionary inheritance from Pteraspis: her biology is
her destiny. Adams's evolutionary "disbeliefs" thus do not prevent
the emergence of a broadly eugenical belief: that the emancipation of
woman may lead to race suicide.

Here is the supreme test of Adams's "beautiful" conscience, for he
is faced with another biological choice – not a choice about
ancestors, but a choice about descendents. Does one encourage the
New Woman – and perhaps race suicide – or not? Yet he remains
"mute" in the face of rebellion against maternity – not because he
does not care, but because he is a historian who claims as his sole
value the chronicling of change, and to chronicle purely must
preempt choice:

No honest historian can take part with – or against – the forces he has to
study. To him even the extinction of the human race should be merely a fact
to be grouped with other vital statistics. . . An elderly man . . . could not
compel the Superintendent of the Census to ask every woman whether she
wanted children, and how many; he could not even require of an
octogenarian Senate the passage of a law obliging every woman, married or
not, to bear one baby – at the expense of the Treasury – before she was

thirty years old, under penalty of solitary confinement for life . . . He could draw no conclusions whatever except from the birth-rate. . . He could suggest nothing. (p. 457)

Adams is not mute; he cannot maintain his equanimity at the prospect of the extinction of the human race. He cares deeply about the declining birthrate. Furthermore, in a sentence that pretends to explain why as historian he cannot offer such advice, he promotes a Census question about childbearing intentions and a Senate bill enforcing compulsory breeding. As Adams himself explains, "though his will be of iron, he cannot help now and then resuming his humanity or simianity in face of a fear" (p. 457).

Darwin and Pearson are the flapping wings of Adams's conscience here, beating vainly in the vacuum jar of his professional detachment. When push comes to shove, Adams's conscience is sufficiently Darwinian to claim a simian ancestor and sufficiently Pearsonian to contemplate laws on compulsory breeding. Eliot noticed this conscience and the flap it made about depopulation. This fear in the face of a declining US birthrate is an instance of the turn-of-the-century "wave of terror of the consequences of depopulation" that Eliot recalls twenty years later in *The Idea of a Christian Society*. Similarly, Adams's proposals for the Senate amount to "legislation having the effect of compulsory breeding" – the thing that Eliot anticipates for "Britain, France, America and the Dominions" as another world war begins.

Adams has been deprived of an *effective* belief in evolution and eugenics by relativism. Sought out as an answer to questions about race and sex, Pearson instead serves as the focus of a chapter about Adams's skepticism about science. Eliot concludes his list of Adams's disbeliefs by referring to Ernst Mach and, later in the review, to Jules Henri Poincaré to emphasize that because of the "speculations" of these relativistic philosophers of science, science itself "disappeared entirely" for Adams.[26] According to Adams, Pearson sees scientific order as a fiction: "Chaos was the law of nature" (p. 451); Mach "admitted but two processes in nature – change of place and interconversion of forms. Matter was Motion – Motion was Matter – the thing moved" (p. 453); Poincaré, with a touch "more destructive . . . than the heaviest-handed brutality of Englishmen or Germans, . . . went on to upset relative truth itself" (p. 455). Pearson is thus a transitional figure in Eliot's anthropological list, linking Darwin the preeminent scientist and Mach the preeminent philosopher of scientific relativism: Pearson's eugenics descends from Darwin's theory of evolution; his skepticism about scientific order leads to Adams's disappearing faith in science. For Adams, the science that grounds evolution and eugenics, which in turn ground the conscience he displays, is but another occasion for the disbelief that works against conscience. Eliot's *anthropology* discovers the beating wings of an ineffectual conscience in a way that Adams's own *chronicle* cannot. Eliot shares this conscience, but not the equanimity in the face of its ineffectuality.

As a philosophy student in 1911, Eliot had already encountered one discourse on evolution in the work of Bergson – a discourse that he criticized philosophically. MacBride's essay, however, encouraged him to renew his criticism of Bergson's creative evolution from a biological perspective. In fact, in his depiction of Adams as a believer in change with no ground or goal, Eliot rehearses his criticism of philosophies like Bergson's creative evolution and H. G. Wells's evolutionism. According to Eliot, "the Bergsonian time doctrine . . . reaches the point of a *fatalism* which is wholly destructive. It is a pure naturalism. What is true for one age is not true for another, and there is no external standard." The "Bergsonian stream flows so rapidly and turgidly" that those who cannot accept the values of their age need merely stand mutely with Adams and wait for change: "In a Bergsonian world, we may hope that these [values] will in turn be replaced by something else." For Adams and Bergson alike, human choices become irrelevant in a "fluid world": "everything may be admired, because nothing is permanent. There is therefore no place in it for the human will."[27] Wells reveals a similarly "deterministic conception of history" in a "superficial philosophy [that] has had an extensive influence":

Mr. Wells seems to propagate a strange false humility of evolutionism: as the higher apes are to us, he says in effect, so are we to the men of the future; and as we regard our animal ancestors, whether apes, lemurs or opossums, so will they of the future regard us. This is, of course, the quite natural corollary of a naif faith in perpetual evolution, combined with a denial of any sharp dividing line between the human and the animal: that is, a denial of the human soul.[28]

Eliot confesses that he "cannot see why we should take such pains to produce a race of men, millenia hence, who will only look down upon *us* as apes, lemurs or opossums. It seems a thankless labor" (p. 19).

Such eugenical labor would not be thankless, however, were we to look at the race of the future, and were the race of the future to look at us, through a proper understanding of evolution. According to Eliot, Wells, Adams, and Bergson believe in evolution without sufficient respect for the science that grounds the theory. Wells's "faith in perpetual evolution" is naive; Adams is a skeptic for whom science disappears; Bergson is simply a bad scientist – a confused amateur: "Bergson makes use of science – biology and psychology – and this use sometimes conceals the incoherence of a multiplicity of points of view."[29] Eliot goes so far as to call Bergsonism a "folly" and "stupidity" because it mixes genres, confusing philosophy, imagination, and science.[30] Eliot's respect for biology is so great that he will not countenance such sloppiness. Life Forcers like Wells and Shaw "all hold curious amateur religions based apparently upon amateur or second-hand biology."[31] The danger is that "the numberless crowd of sentimentally religious people who are incapable of following any argument to a conclusion . . . will be misled until they can be made to understand that the potent ju-ju of the Life Force is a gross superstition."[32]

In this matter, Eliot follows MacBride in distinguishing between evolution as "a strictly biological hypothesis" and evolution as "an affair for the metaphysicians." MacBride complains that "Darwin's theory of evolution is often confused in the popular mind with other theories of evolution" – such as Herbert Spencer's. Whereas "Darwin's theory. . . is a strictly biological hypothesis," "Spencer's theory of evolution was a philosophical doctrine, which sought to comprehend under one formula all the activities of the universe, from the formation of planets to that of men."[33] Bergson's creative evolution and Shaw's Life Force (deriving secondhand from Samuel Butler's biology) are similarly ambitious philosophical doctrines.

The problem that Adams, Bergson, Spencer, Wells, and Shaw demonstrate is a general one: people do not understand the biology that underlies the theory of evolution. Eliot calls Shaw's explanation of the Life Force in the Preface to *Back to Methuselah* a "farrago of Mr Shaw's conversation about economics, politics, biology, dramatic and art criticism." Shaw represents for Eliot the undisciplined Edwardian mind: "we shall demand from our next leaders a purer intellect, more scientific, more logical, more rigorous." Shaw's *Back to Methuselah* is "the last word of a century" in which "it was biology that influenced the imagination of non-scientific people. Darwin is

the representative of those years." By 1921, however, "[c]reative
evolution is a phrase that has lost its stimulant and sedative
virtues."[34]

The all-encompassing philosophies of such amateur biologists
struck Eliot as an unfortunate displacement of the religious sensibility. John Middleton Murry's book *God*, for instance, defines a
philosophy called "metabiology" which locates the ultimate Value in
the universe in perpetually creative organic process. To Eliot,

Metabiology seems . . . to be a philosophy which employs terms which
appeal to the biological imagination. And I cannot believe that the
biological imagination is as permanent as the religious one, or that Mr.
Murry's philosophy is more than a variant of that philosophy of our time of
which we have other "significant variations" in Bergson, Driesch, White-
head or Eddington or Lloyd Morgan.

The biological imagination is doubly unreliable. On the one hand,
biological knowledge changes and develops; on the other hand, such
biology as the nonscientific person appropriates is imperfectly understood. In the case of Murry's philosophy of metabiology, Eliot is
confident neither that Murry's biology is up-to-date nor that he
actually understands the biology that he pretends to know:

In order to swallow his philosophy, I suspect that I should have had to
swallow a number of other things first, so as to accept a number of terms
without requiring definition of them. Words like *emergent, organism, biological unity
of life*, simply do not rouse the right "response" in my breast. They are terms
which may have definite meanings within the restricted field of biology; but
a philosophy based upon biological knowledge is a different thing from
biology. To call it *metabiology* seems to me a verbal trick; playing on the
useful pun of "physics" and "metaphysics."

One detects an echo here of MacBride's distinction between biology
and metaphysics and Pearson's distrust of the tendency to explain
biology by means of special "forces." Eliot is "out of tune" with
Murry's terms, "which tend to command popular assent," not
because Murry is ahead of his time, but because Murry – like Shaw –
is mired in "the philosophy of our time," which is based upon an
amateur and secondhand biology that MacBride allowed Eliot to
transcend.[35]

One might accuse Eliot of overestimating his own knowledge of
biology, but he did not overestimate the importance of biology itself.
Biology and evolution (understood as a strictly biological hypothesis)
have to do with but one part of human being – its physical dimension.

It is here, according to Foucault, that power over life has evolved – and it has done so in two basic ways:

One . . . centered on the body as machine: its disciplining, the optimization of its capabilities, the extortion of its forces, the parallel increase of its usefulness and its docility, its integration into systems of efficient and economic controls . . . The second focused on the species body, the body imbued with the mechanics of life and serving as the basis of the biological processes: propagation, births and mortality, the level of health, life expectancy and longevity. . . .[36]

Accepting that the species *body* is imbued with the mechanics of life in this way, Eliot refuses to accept that the species *spirit* can be understood in the same terms.

Shaw is Eliot's whippingboy on this score: "He was interested in the comparatively transient things, in anything that can or should be changed; but he was not interested in, was rather impatient of, the things which always have been and always will be the same." The virtue of Shaw's *Back to Methuselah* is that "[h]is creative evolution proceeds so far that the process ceases to be progress, and progress ceases to have any meaning. Even the author appears to be conscious of the question whether the beginning and the end are not the same."[37] This sense of the endlessness of the physical process of what Eliot calls in *Sweeney Agonistes* "Birth, and copulation, and death" is reflected at the beginning of *East Coker*, where – against the background of "the coupling of man and woman" in "daunsinge" and "matrimonie," depicted as movement "Round and round," "joined in circles" of "Feet rising and falling. / Eating and drinking. Dung and death." – Eliot makes a similar observation: "In my beginning is my end" (*CPP* pp. 122, 177–78). Shaw "has not realized that at the end he has only approached a beginning, that his end is only the starting point towards the knowledge of life."[38] Eliot rewords this observation in *East Coker*: "In my end is my beginning" (*CPP* p. 183). In each case, biology or evolution is only the beginning of knowledge of life.

Eliot's point in his comments about Shaw (1921) is the same as his point in *East Coker* (1939): human being is incomplete in a way that no biological development can overcome. Tongue in cheek, Eliot pretends that

It is possible . . . that evolution will bring the human race to such a point of perfection that thinking will no longer be necessary. Thinking is painful and requires toil, and is a mark of human incompleteness. Theology will no doubt become obsolete . . . But in this painful "meanwhile," as Mr. Wells would say, . . . a great many theological works are being published, and presumably being read by somebody.[39]

Of course Eliot does not accept Wells's time philosophy: the human condition reveals an incompleteness that is not a biological "meanwhile" in an evolution towards completeness but rather a spiritual *all the while* – world without end. Eliot thus flags his willingness to contemplate eugenical solutions to problems evident in the temporal aspect of the human condition as quite provisional: he is perfectly prepared to accept that in the fullness of time such painful thinking will be exposed as another proof of our human incompleteness.

Yet although biology is not all-important, it is certainly important. The physical dimension of human being cannot be ignored, however true it may be that ultimate value is spiritual rather than metabiological. Eliot accepts that questions about the improvement or the deterioration of the germ plasm, for instance, cannot be ignored. Accepting "[t]hat in former times the struggle for existence was enough to keep down the defective element in the population; but under present conditions these people are protected and multiply," Eliot frequently reveals in his literary criticism his fear that the unregulated proliferation of the masses threatens to cause national degeneration. In his 1918 "Observations" for *The Egoist* he suggests that "the forces of deterioration are a large crawling mass, and the forces of development half a dozen men." His topic is the fate of the English language, but his hyperbolic rhetoric expands the topic to include the fate of the Anglo-Saxon race. Eliot paraphrases Ford Hueffer's "remarks upon journalese":

that flail of the Anglo-Saxon race, that infinite corruptor of the Anglo-Saxon mind, that destined and ultimate cause of the downfall of Anglo-Saxon empires, since the race that cannot either in allegories or in direct speech think clearly is doomed to fall before nations who can, and Japan is ever on the threshold with the tendrils twining round its well-ropes. . .[40]

Hueffer and Eliot clearly reflect the turn-of-the-century British fear of "the yellow menace": the perception of the threat to empire represented by rising Asian nations like Japan. The assumption was that the fittest nation would survive; therefore, Britain must see to its fitness. Furthermore, from his reading in *The Eugenics Review* for his 1918 *The International Journal of Ethics* (*IJE*) essay, Eliot was also aware of eugenists' fears that the vigor of the Anglo-Saxon race would be sapped by the loss of so much eugenically valuable blood in the war.[41] And so, although "not sure of the imminent ascendency of Japan," Eliot accepts that Britain suffers from "degeneracy" and suggests that "Mr. Hueffer's warning is certainly just, and could perhaps be stated in more general terms." These more general terms, however, remain eugenical: "What we want is to disturb and alarm the public:. . . To point out that every generation, every turn of time when the work of four or five men who count has reached middle age, is a *crisis*. Also that the intelligence of a nation must go on developing, or it will deteriorate."[42] The topic is national language and intelligence, but the paradigm is eugenical. Just as biology provides a paradigm for explaining the nature of poetry and criticism, so eugenics provides a paradigm for improving language and intelligence: beware "the crawling mass."

Ten years later, contemplation of the fate of the English language again serves as an opportunity for Eliot to express his eugenical concerns about the proliferation of the masses. An odd "Commentary" in *The Criterion* yokes together two apparently unrelated topics: the debasement of the English language in newspapers and the proposed demolition of slum houses. Eliot's reflections on language are familiar:

A minor consequence of the doctrine of evolution – or rather, of the "time philosophy" based upon it – is an attitude of unconscious fatalism which we adopt toward many processes. We are accustomed, for instance, to the belief that the English language deteriorates, and that it must deteriorate. We like to think that this deterioration began somewhere near the bottom . . . and that it is working its way slowly and inevitably towards the top.

We know this resentment of the fatalism at the heart of evolutionary time philosophies. And we have seen this fear of the masses before, yet Eliot surprisingly suggests that "[a]s a matter of fact, the language is probably in a healthier condition among the lower classes of society . . . than it is among the middle and upper classes." The threat represented by the lower classes resides elsewhere – geographically, in the slums; biologically, in their numbers. Eliot notes that "more 'slums' of small houses in various parts of London are to be demolished." His response is that "[s]uch wholesale hygiene always calls for scrutiny." Eliot is interested to determine whether social hygiene will lead to racial hygiene: "If the families who now sleep three or four in a room are to have habitations with a room apiece, there is everything to be said for the readjustment. But will they?. . . [O]ne would like to know whether the London workman can be

given enough room for all his family, at a rent that he can pay? or will
he merely increase his family?" The language may be healthier
among the lower classes than elsewhere; the living conditions of the
lower classes may be made healthier than they now are; but it is
doubtful that a change in the location or an increase in the numbers
of the lower classes will make for a healthier city: demolishing slums
"is certain to make London more hideous; and if it merely drives the
present population to seek new slums, or if it leaves them just as
crowded as ever, then London will have been disfigured for
nothing."[43] Concern about London's disfigurement veils thinly a
concern about the simultaneous disfigurement of the race.

Eliot is not so complacent as to resign all hope for improvement in
this world in favor of a faith that justice will be achieved in the next:
"What we can do towards the greatest material well-being of the
greatest number is indeed of the utmost importance." In fact, "[w]e
must believe . . . that [the human race] can improve both its material
well-being and its spiritual capacities. We must also have a conception of a perfect society attainable on earth." He accepts that "the
human race can, if it will, improve indefinitely" – "by social and
economic reorganization, by eugenics, and by any other external
means possible to the science of intellect." Of course Eliot argues
that however much a person is improved by these means, he or she
"will still be only the *natural* man, at an infinite remove from
perfection," but the prominence of eugenics in Eliot's list of means of
improving the human being's material well-being is nonetheless
noteworthy: eugenics is as important as social and economic reorganization – the only other means of improving material well-being
that comes to Eliot's mind.[44]

Not surprisingly, one finds that Eliot regards a knowledge of
eugenics as an important furnishing in the mind of anyone who
wishes to be considered up-to-date: he writes of the futurist John
Rodker that he "is up-to-the-minute, if anyone is; we feel sure that he
knows all about hormones, W. H. R. Rivers, and the Mongol in our
midst."[45] MacBride introduced Eliot to the importance of hormones,
speculating that they might be the mechanism responsible for the
inheritance of acquired characteristics;[46] Rivers was a Cambridge
anthropologist, neurophysiologist, and Freudian psychologist whose
Essays on the Depopulation of Melanesia Eliot read as a warning of
imminent depopulation on a global scale ("the 'Civilization' forced
upon them has deprived them of all interest in life. They are dying

from pure boredom. . . [W]hen applied science has done everything possible with the materials on this earth to make life as interesting as possible, it will not be surprising if the population of the entire civilized world rapidly follows the fate of the Melanesians");[47] *The Mongol in our Midst* was F. G. Cruikshank's famous book arguing that imbecility derived from a recessive element in the vestige of primitive Mongol blood that still flowed in the veins of many a Briton.[48] In each case, Eliot implies that our future – insofar as our material well-being is concerned – depends to a large extent upon eugenics.

Of course Eliot's knowledge of biology was not quite what it was cracked up to be. He could disdain Shaw's "ideas" in "his master-piece . . . *Man and Superman*" as no "more than the residue of the great Victorian labors of Darwin, and Huxley, and Cobden" – so much for Shaw's mix of creative evolution and Fabian socialism – and yet accept MacBride's Lamarckism (itself the residue of the great Victorian labors of Lamarck, and Butler, and Shaw himself) as though it were the latest word in evolutionary biology and eugenics.[49]

In fact, by 1917 MacBride was one of the few scientists who took Lamarckism seriously. At issue was the question of the origin of species via adaptation to environment – the "problem which it was the object of Darwin's work to elucidate – . . . *the* problem of organic nature." According to MacBride, since to convert one species into another "would require an indefinite number of 'internal accidents,'" and since differences between species and genera seem to be adaptive, "the conviction arises in our mind that they can only be adequately explained by the existence of some force which moulds the organism to its surroundings." What is the nature of this force? MacBride does not accept Darwin's "theory of the frequent appear-ance of small inherited mutations, all tending in the same direction," suggesting that "the evidence at present available does not favor" such an explanation. Instead, he introduces Lamarck's hypothesis as an alternative. Given that "most animals are able in the course of their individual lives to adapt themselves somewhat to their sur-roundings. . . It was an obvious assumption to make that these changes, which may be termed *reactions to the environment*, were inheritable." Noting that "[t]his theory of the inheritable character of functional reaction . . . was put forward by Lamarck long before the days of Darwin, and [that] it has been generally rejected by biologists," MacBride vigorously promotes it in "The Study of

Heredity," arguing that chemicals like recently discovered hormones can "act on the growing germ-cells . . . and become stored up in them" should an "organ be stimulated by the environment to extraordinary growth . . . and give off a chemical emanation into the blood different in quantity and, perhaps, in quality, to that which it had given off before." An adaptation to environment would thus become inheritable, for "[w]hen these germ-cells develop this chemical will affect the growing tissues and tend to produce in them the same changes as were in the first instance produced by the environment."[50]

Eliot takes particular note of this Lamarckism, in part because it gives rise to one of MacBride's "conclusions of social importance." MacBride's Lamarckism allows him to urge a positive eugenics alongside the negative eugenics of "segregation and sterilization" for defectives, for, as Eliot himself notes in his summary of MacBride's conclusions, "The transmissibility of acquired characters makes the problem of education of the highest importance: we must adopt such a system of education that 'the next generation may start at a very slightly higher level of capacity than their fathers.'" Eliot also reports on MacBride's further development of this argument in *The New Statesman* later in 1917 (service above and beyond what was called for in his *IJE* essay), particularly as regards Lamarckism and eugenics:

Professor MacBride points out . . . that the inheritance of acquired characters is not taken as proved, but only as rendered highly probable. . . [H]e says that while racial improvement by any means must be a very slow process, the harm done by the propagation of the defective is very quickly felt. Furthermore, he insists upon the importance of the responsibility of the parents: "there is no system of state subvention," he says very justly, "which will not break down if parental responsibility be removed and reckless reproduction encouraged."[51]

Alive to the controversial nature of MacBride's Lamarckism, Eliot is sufficiently impressed by his science in general to accept both his Lamarckism and the eugenics that derives from it.

The impact of these reflections about the eugenical importance of the family and the Lamarckian conception of heredity is evident as late as *Notes towards the Definition of Culture* (1948). We have seen already Eliot's fear that improved housing for the lower classes may only encourage reckless reproduction; in *Notes towards the Definition of Culture*, he suggests that "we have arrived at a stage of civilization at which the family is irresponsible, or incompetent, or helpless; at which parents cannot be expected to train their children properly; at which many parents cannot afford to feed them properly, and would not know how, even if they had the means."[52] MacBride's observations on "parental responsibility" in 1917 were developed further in studies on nutrition in the 1920s and 1930s – studies that promulgated eugenical assumptions about the correlation between class and nutrition. E. P. Cathcart and A. M. T. Murray reported that the lower classes tended to comprise the least fit members of society in general and, so far as nutrition was concerned, people who were parentally inefficient: "We believe it is essential to recognise that a physical segregation has taken place. The weaker and less effective members of society do and must gravitate to the bottom of the economic scale."[53] They argued that parental inefficiency was hereditary: the feeblemindedness and mental inefficiency of the lower classes led to bad domestic management and poor nutrition. Eliot echoes these assumptions in his assertion that parents not only cannot afford to feed children properly, but also "would not know how, even if they had the means."[54]

Eliot's discussions of the role of family and class in the development and maintenance of culture imply similar assumptions about the role of heredity in society. He reveals in a talk broadcast in Germany in 1946 that he contemplates culture "as a student of social biology."[55] He thus situates himself within the discourse of the social hygienists, who promoted the need for general awareness of the relationship between biology and social life, proposing in particular to align nineteenth-century interest in environmental reform with twentieth-century interest in heredity and control of human reproduction.[56] Contemplating "the stratification of England by sects," he acknowledges that a historian might trace "the tendencies to religious fission" to

ineradicable differences between the culture of the several tribes, races and languages which from time to time held sway or contested for supremacy. He might, furthermore, take the view that cultural mixture does not necessarily follow the same course as biological mixture; and that, even if we assumed every person of purely English descent to have the blood of all the successive invaders mingled in his veins in exactly the same proportions, it need not follow that cultural fusion ensued.

Despite Eliot's explanation that "[s]uch speculations . . . lie outside [his] scope" and that, in any event, he is "too unlearned to support or oppose" them, it is clear that he understands biology to have an important role in social criticism. The assumption here is that culture often shows the impact of biology (it is understood that "blood" is a significant variable in the development of culture); the question is whether "cultural mixture . . . *necessarily* follow[s] the same course as biological mixture."[57]

In *After Strange Gods* (1934), Eliot implies that culture does indeed follow biology when he defines "tradition" as involving "all those habitual actions, habits and customs . . . which represent the blood kinship of 'the same people living in the same place.'"[58] Early in *Notes towards the Definition of Culture*, he specifies "advantages of birth" as one of the "essential conditions for the growth and for the survival of culture." Another of these conditions is "organic (not merely planned, but growing) structure, such as will foster the hereditary transmission of culture." Against the background of Eliot's "social biology" and the hereditarian assumptions of many in the social hygiene movement, phrases like "blood kinship," "advantages of birth," "organic structure," and "hereditary transmission" resonate with a biological significance that one might otherwise overlook, even though Eliot includes the biological definition of "culture" in his search for the meaning of this term: "When the term 'culture' is applied to the manipulation of lower organisms – to the work of the bacteriologist or the *agri*culturalist – the meaning is clear enough . . . When it is applied to the improvement of the human mind and spirit, we are less likely to agree as to what culture is." In the end, Eliot does not foreground his biological assumptions in his inquiry into the nature of culture, but he is sufficiently aware of them to warn readers that "there may be deeper levels than that upon which the enquiry is being conducted."[59]

At such a deeper level, for instance, Eliot's paradigm when explaining the development of class is not only biological, but Lamarckian. Whereas MacBride advances the "theory of the inheritable character of functional reaction, or, as it is more commonly termed, the effects of use and disuse," Eliot argues that "the functions of individuals become hereditary, and hereditary function hardens into class or caste distinction."[60] Eliot's explanation of the origin of classes echoes MacBride's explanation of the origin of species:

As a society develops towards functional complexity and differentiation, we may expect the emergence of several cultural levels: in short, the culture of the class or group will present itself. . . [T]here must be these different levels. . . [T]he difference of opinion turns on whether the transmission of group culture must be by inheritance – whether each cultural level must propagate itself – or whether it can be hoped that some mechanism of selection will be found . . .[61]

If a new species is to originate and propagate itself, according to MacBride, its acquired character must become inheritable. Other-wise, the environment will stimulate functional reactions in discrete individuals whose acquired character will die with them because it is not transmissible. Eliot finds that the same holds true of class, implying that the choice is between a still-to-be-developed "mech-anism of selection" and a tried-and-true natural selection. Of course Eliot could mean by his discussion of inherited functions simply that individuals inherit their jobs from their parents and that in time this passing-on of jobs creates distinct groups of people in society. Yet it would be a mistake to read Eliot's biologically inflected language as exclusively metaphorical; there is a sense in which his study of class is literally a "social biology": use and disuse of human abilities streams individuals into classes whose acquired characters become inheritable via the biological means that Lamarck and MacBride hypothesize.

As important as MacBride's essay was in consolidating Eliot's knowledge of contemporary biology and eugenics, it was but one of the factors persuading him that a biological crisis was at hand. The "wave of terror of the consequences of depopulation" to which he alludes in *The Idea of a Christian Society* was a very real phenomenon in certain quarters before, during, and after World War I. The "terror" before the war concerned the prospect of a nation weakened by depopulation when on the verge of armed conflict with rival European imperial powers. As Angus McLaren notes, sociologists, demographers, and census takers had identified a real phenomenon: "marriages of the late 1860s, when they lasted twenty years or more, produced an average of 6.16 births; the marriages of the 1870s, 5.8; those of the 1880s, 5.3; those of the 1890s, 4.13, and those of 1915, 2.43."[62] During the war, as Leonard Darwin reveals, the potential dangers and advantages of depopulation were debated:

A general increase in the population has been advocated, both on account of our future military needs and in order to fill up the gaps made by the war in the ranks of industry; whilst, on the other hand, the poverty expected to result from the war has been adduced as an additional argument in favor of the promotion of a general decrease in the birth-rate.[63]

In reviewing the report of the National Birth-Rate Commission, which was appointed "before war was declared or generally anticipated," A. K. Chalmers suggests that "the war has added an importance to the work which cannot readily be over-estimated."[64]

The depopulation phenomenon particularly worried eugenists. They agreed with the statisticians – the population was declining – but focused attention more on the question of quality than on the question of quantity. In *On the Diminishing Birth Rate* (1904), John W. Taylor complained that the large family of the nineteenth century was being replaced by "the so-called family of three or two or one" and that responsibility for even *this* so-called family was being resigned to "the lower classes of our population and to the Hebrew and the alien."[65] As Taylor reveals, of special concern was the differential birthrate – the lower classes were reproducing at a higher rate than the middle and upper classes – and the consequent depopulation of the fittest class relative to the less fit classes.

When the National Birth-Rate Commission's report was finally published in 1917 as *The Declining Birth-Rate: its Causes and Effects*, Eliot complimented Chalmers for his "able article [in *The Eugenics Review*] on the report of the National Birth-Rate Commission." He also applauded the journal *Shield*'s "useful service in reprinting the report of the Birth-Rate Commission in England."[66] Chalmers summarizes the Commission's official mandate:

The object of the inquiry. . . was to inquire into the extent and character of the decline in the birth-rate; its relation to infant mortality; its distribution, topographically and according to income, occupation, and religious profession of the parents; the relation of sterile to fruitful marriages; the alleged causes of decline, whether physiological (age at marriage, effect of town life, etc.), or prudential; the effect of the decline on the children, on their parents, and on home life; and its economic and national aspects.

He also acknowledges an unofficial mandate – to consider the contribution of the differential birthrate to race suicide: "Were we to accept the teaching that the economically unsuccessful in life are always and only reckless people, so reckless in fact that they had proposed, and were proceeding to supply 50 per cent. of the next generation, then the resulting moral degeneration added to physical unfitness would complete the ruin of the race." Acknowledging the "surface" logic of such a claim, Chalmers argues that "[i]n grim earnestness the answer has come from the trenches that we are neither morally degenerate nor physically unfit." Yet he also argues that although "the greater part of class inferiority is probably due to bad surroundings and example," rather than inheritance, "the Legislature must recognise that 'any form of State relief which favors the reckless at the expense of the provident, will, in itself, have the effect of multiplying the former and diminishing the latter.'"[67]

Among the propositions that the Commission considered to be "definitely established" were the following: "the birth-rate has declined to the extent of approximately one-third within the last thirty-five years," and "on the whole the decline has been more marked in the more prosperous classes."[68] Accepting that the birth-rate problem has this double nature (the quantity *and* the quality of offspring are declining), Chalmers approvingly quotes advice to the Commission as to how to increase the birthrate among the more prosperous classes: "If you allowed a man to write off in his income-tax paper the expenses of education as he does his life insurance, it is possible you would have a good many more babies than you have."[69] Having reviewed the Commission's report and Chalmers's summary of it, Eliot agrees that there is indeed what he calls a "birth-rate problem."[70]

That he regards this "problem" as a matter not just of declining quantity but also of declining quality is clear from his comments on Leonard Darwin's *Eugenics Review* essay "Quality *Not* Quantity," with which he introduces the first of his references to the Birth-Rate Commission's report. According to Leonard Darwin,

all who believe in selection as a main agent in evolution, and all who have learnt from Galton how greatly men differ from each other in inborn qualities, will accept . . . that average excessive poverty must be accepted in this country in some degree as a test of the average unfitness of a class, and, moreover, that destitution is likely to become a more and more reliable criterion of innate inferiority as time goes on.[71]

Darwin concludes, therefore, that "any relative increase in the rate of multiplication of the class in question must be dysgenic, whilst the opposite would be true of a richer class." Noting this aspect of the essay in particular – "Darwin . . . discusses methods for encouraging reproduction on the part of the best classes in the community, and for discouraging reproduction on the part of the incompetent, thriftless and pauper element" – Eliot assures readers that Darwin's "articles always deserve attention."[72]

In fact, Eliot paid sufficient attention to Darwin's views on working-class reproductive tendencies to echo them in his own views on slums and working-class reproduction ten years later. According to Darwin:

The man who requires and obtains a considerable amount of extraneous help to enable him to maintain his children with decency is likely . . . to perceive that an addition to his family will bring with it further State or charitable assistance, and he will be even less likely than now to limit the number of his progeny. The many efforts which have been made in the past to reduce the numbers of those living an utterly degraded life . . . may have continually been defeated by dregs of society being thus made to multiply more rapidly . . . Can it be said that a study of the worst slum areas of our great cities makes it at all improbable that this is a true picture of what is now actually taking place?[73]

As we have seen, Eliot fears that working-class families, given more space in which to house their families, will simply have more children to fill the space available: "one would like to know whether the London workman can be given enough room for all his family . . . or will he merely increase his family?"[74] Chalmers, Darwin, and Eliot alike fear the differential birthrate: at the very least it disfigures London and the country's great cities; at worst it disfigures the race and threatens race suicide.

CHAPTER 5

To breed or not to breed: the Eliots' question

Eliot's close attention to MacBride's "Study of Heredity" and his survey of issues in eugenics in general through his reading of the 1916–17 issues of *The Eugenics Review* and *Shield* coincided with events in his personal life that made him extremely conscious of his eugenic responsibilities and reinforced his sense of what Foucault identifies as late nineteenth-century bourgeois obligations to safeguard family blood:

The concern with genealogy became a preoccupation with heredity; but included in bourgeois marriages were not only economic imperatives and rules of social homogeneity, not only the promises of inheritance, but the menaces of heredity; families wore and concealed a sort of reversed and somber escutcheon whose defamatory quarters were the diseases or defects of the group of relatives – the grandfather's general paralysis, the mother's neurasthenia, the youngest child's phthisis, the hysterical or erotomaniac aunts, the cousins with bad morals.[1]

Perhaps Eliot's poetic scrutiny of Aunt Helen, Cousin Harriet, and Cousin Nancy ironically acknowledges the menaces of heredity. Certainly his own marriage forced him to acknowledge this menace. On the one hand, his marriage to Vivien Haigh-Wood forced him to confront the possibility that her various health problems were heritable. On the other hand, his medical classification as "unfit" when applying to join the US navy forced him to contemplate defects in his own physical constitution at a time when the valiant soldier was being celebrated as eugenically ideal stock. The potentially dysgenical dimension of both his own and his wife's health problems seems to have led him to question whether or not they should have children.

Eliot married Vivien Haigh-Wood on 26 June 1915 after an acquaintance and courtship of less than three months. He first refers to her in a letter of 24 April 1915 as one of "several English girls" that he has met in Oxford at the "large hotels [that] have dances on Saturday nights." Haigh-Wood and the other English girls were a revelation to him: "As they are emancipated Londoners I have been out to tea or dinner with them several times, and find them quite different from anything I have known at home or here. . . They are charmingly sophisticated (even 'disillusioned') without being hardened; and I confess to taking great pleasure in seeing women smoke . . ."[2] More obliquely, the same theme appears in a letter to Pound about events ten days earlier: "Something might be said . . . about the Evil Influence of Virginity on American Civilization. . . The Degradation of Women in American Society. . . Pardon these ravings: I am suffering from the effects of a debauch . . ."[3] I suspect that Haigh-Wood made one of the company at the "debauch" in question and that she was the English girl in particular who gave rise to Eliot's reflections on virginity, for (as we shall see) he ever after associates her with his post-debauch observations about the different valuations of virginity by American and European women. Furthermore, in fiction that she later wrote for *The Criterion*, Vivien Eliot implies that she was from the beginning aware of the contrast that Tom Eliot was drawing between the chaste morality of American women and the looser morality of European women. In "A Diary of the Rive Gauche," Fanny Marlow (a name Vivien Eliot used as pseudonym) shares with her diary reflections prompted by her encounter with a young American:

[W]hy do Americans insist that all European women are *au courant* with every form of vice (to them all pleasure or amusement really means vice, so far as I can see) – whereas they insinuate that the female of their own species is supremely innocent and unsullied. They actually appear to be trying to protect their own women from *us*! Why? Because they cannot cope with European women. Ha! they can't cope with us![4]

She implies also that she was from the beginning aware of the disapproval latent in his observation. And so, taught by his father that sex was "nastiness," but nonetheless longing to lose his virginity ("I should be better off, I sometimes think, if I had disposed of my virginity and shyness several years ago: and indeed I still think sometimes that it would be well to do so before marriage"), the American Tom regarded the European Viv as an incitement to sexuality.[5]

Accounts of their early relationship are sketchy, but the sexual element in it is often remarked upon. According to Aldous Huxley, the relationship between them was "almost entirely a sexual nexus . . . [O]ne sees it in the way he looks at her . . . [S]he's an incarnate provocation."[6] Vivien Eliot herself told Bertrand Russell that "she married him to stimulate him"; Russell opined that "[o]bviously he [Tom] married in order to be stimulated."[7] Tradition has it that they met while punting on the Thames at Oxford. According to Lyndall Gordon, "[d]uring the Trinity term of 1915 Eliot went punting with another American, Scofield Thayer. The party included Thayer's sister, Lucy, and an English girlfriend, Vivienne Haigh-Wood."[8] Stephen Spender reveals that Vivien Eliot "was known among Eliot's social friends . . . as 'the river girl'" – perhaps because of the occasion of their first meeting.[9] And so, it may be that both the geographical origin of the courtship on the Thames and its emotional origin in an encounter with a girl on a river are remembered in Part III of *The Waste Land,* where the "Thames daughter" "Supine on the floor of a narrow canoe" raises her knees and participates with a man in an "event" that causes him to weep and promise "a new start." However we read this passage biographically – whether as a reference to the actual event in which Eliot finally lost his virginity or simply as a type of the sexual failure that troubled Tom and Viv – the thing to note is the woman's casualness about "the event." Whether or not the sexual event was physically consummated is not clear, but that the man should have "wept" and "promised a new start" suggests that the event was devastatingly unfulfilling for him. For the woman, however, the event, the weeping, and the promise evoke "no comment." She invests so little significance in the event that she cannot react to its failure: "What should I resent?" (*CPP* p. 70).[10]

Here again Eliot charges his Vivien-figure with the English woman's sexual sophistication and disillusionment, the European woman's un-American casualness about lost virginity, yet this characterization marks her as more than the bearer of a non-American tradition; it also marks her as the bearer of an inherited defect: "moral insanity."

During their courtship Vivien kept Eliot in the dark about her history of health problems. Peter Ackroyd notes that since childhood "she had suffered from tuberculosis of the left hand"; she experienced "from the age of twelve an irregular and over-frequent menstrual cycle"; she suffered from headaches and cramps and "was given morphine-based depressants to control her moods."[11] Gordon notes that "[i]n 1914 Vivienne mentions a liver complaint, neuralgia, fainting."[12] According to Ackroyd, Eliot "did not know . . . that she had a history of illness from her earliest years," a fact that "he did not discover until after the marriage." What he learned upon meeting the Haigh-Woods just a week after his marriage was that Vivien's mother Rose "was always fearful that [Vivien] had inherited what was then known as moral insanity."[13]

As McKim explains, the moral idiot or the moral imbecile is "one who has less than the normal capacity – or perhaps no rudiment of it – for appreciating the distinctions between right and wrong . . .; for exercising self-restraint; and for cherishing an ideal of virtue under any form."[14] The American eugenist Henry H. Goddard explained this phenomenon as an instance of feeblemindedness, which involved a lack of "one or the other of the factors essential to a moral life – an understanding of right and wrong, and the power of control." According to Goddard, feeblemindedness was carried by a Mende-lian hereditary unit, producing "a condition of mind or brain which is transmitted as regularly and surely as color of hair or eyes."[15] Debate about whether there was such a condition as moral insanity and whether any such condition was heritable had no more been settled during Vivien Haigh-Wood's childhood than at the time of her marriage, yet Rose Haigh-Wood clearly accepted that there was such a thing as moral insanity and that it was a hereditary condition.[16] Ackroyd reveals that because of her fear that her daughter had inherited this defect, Rose Haigh-Wood "had been instrumental in the breaking up of the relationship between Vivien and Charles Buckle" – just months before Tom and Viv married.[17] If her mother's fears, and her mother's actions in consequence of such fears, were known to Vivien Haigh-Wood, one can understand her keeping her marriage a secret from her mother, and her mother a secret from her future husband.

Rose Haigh-Wood may have had another reason for fearing that her daughter was liable to moral insanity: her tuberculosis (or consumption, or phthisis) of the hand. In *Race Culture; or, Race Suicide*, Rentoul argues that "[s]ome diseases, such as consumption, cause intense sexual desire; hence the early marriage and amorous nature of these physical deteriorants. Hysteria and nymphomania are but a name for the symptoms."[18] Associated with moral insanity, tuber-culosis was itself thought by many eugenists to be heritable – even after the discovery of the tubercle bacillus. In his 1912 Galton Laboratory Lecture "Tuberculosis, Heredity and Environment,"

Pearson argues that tuberculosis cannot be explained merely as the result of infection; it is also hereditary: "the intensity of parental resemblance with regard to phthisis is absolutely similar to what we find for insanity or deaf-mutism . . . and is of the same order as we know occurs in the case of the chief physical characters in man."[19] Such arguments about the heritability of tuberculosis and its role in moral insanity may have contributed to Rose Haigh-Wood's fears about her daughter's inherited defects.

Rentoul's assumption of a connection between hysteria and the morally defective mind was common. According to McKim, a congenital structural abnormality of the brain may lead to moral idiocy, whereas injury to the brain may lead to moral insanity:

The cause of moral *idiocy* is almost invariably an inherited defect of brain, due most frequently to ancestral insanity, drunkenness, or epilepsy. Moral *insanity* may be induced in a person apparently normal through injuries and such degenerative processes of brain as apoplexy, senile involution, paralytic dementia, drunkenness, and the graver neuroses, as epilepsy and hysteria.[20]

The connection between hysteria and moral insanity that both McKim and Rentoul assume makes Eliot's prose poem "Hysteria" especially interesting, for the poem seems to be about Tom and Viv, and it seems to have been written shortly after Eliot learned about Rose Haigh-Wood's fear that her daughter might have inherited moral insanity.[21]

In this poem, Eliot pathologizes his new wife's behavior as hysteria – a diagnosis as interesting etymologically as eugenically. Perhaps at risk of an attack of hysteria himself, a man tries to cope with the hysterical laughter of his female companion as a waiter suggests they move to the restaurant garden where they will present less of a spectacle. The woman displays the "short gasps" and "laughter" characteristic of hysteria. Furthermore, faithful to the Greek root of the word (*hyster* means "uterus" or "womb") and faithful also to the ancient presumption that hysterical constriction of the throat was caused by the womb's wandering upward from its proper position, Eliot depicts his speaker as devoured by displaced vagina and womb – "lost finally in the dark caverns of her throat, bruised by the ripple of unseen muscles" (*CPP* p. 32).

The poem depicts Eliot's fear of woman's sexuality in general, yet it also reveals his particular fear of Vivien's sexuality – his fear of her womb. In depicting the suffocating effect of Vivien's wandering womb, the new husband presumably knows now of Vivien's "irregular and over-frequent menstrual cycle." It seems to be acknowledged in the middle verse of the later poem that recalls their "Tortured" wedding night, "Ode" (1918). In the Eliots' case, menstrual blood is as likely as a ruptured hymen to have produced the "blood upon the bed" from the "Succuba eviscerate" of this poem.[22] On the one hand, Vivien's hymen was not necessarily intact at the time of her marriage. On the other hand, as Ackroyd notes, the appearance of "blood upon the bed" because of Vivien's frequent and irregular menstrual cycles was itself a frequent enough occurrence to have led to her "obsessive habit of washing her own bed linen even if she was staying in an hotel."[23] The appearance of menstrual blood on the bed sheets would explain the apparently premature end of wedding-night intercourse, for the bridegroom looks at the "blood upon the bed" "Indignant / At the cheap extinction of his taking-off."[24] "Ode"'s bed linen may even be anticipated in "Hysteria"'s table linen – the "pink and white checked cloth" functioning as a displaced version of the more disturbing image.

Vivien's menstruation problem certainly seems to have preoccupied him, as is evident from his near approach to telling his squeamish father about the situation: he reveals that "when she worries she bleeds internally" – but he obscures his meaning by explaining that he means this "in a metaphorical sense."[25] He approached the subject more nearly and more graphically several years later in correspondence with Aiken. Determined to disparage the latter's effusive praise of *Poems 1909–1925*, Eliot sent him a page torn out of the *Midwives Gazette* that instructed nurses with regard to correct responses to various questions likely to be faced on exams for nursing certificates. As Aiken explains, "[a]t the top, T. S. E. had underlined the words *Model Answers*. Under this was a column descriptive of various forms of vaginal discharge, normal and abnormal. Here the words *blood, mucous,* and *shreds of mucous* had been underlined with a pen, and lower down also the phrase *purulent offensive discharge.* Otherwise no comment." Aiken replied, "Have you tried Kotex for it? Manufactured by the Dupont Powder Co. Absorbent, Deodorant, Antiseptic . . ." Eliot apparently responded to this letter by telephone: "a little flustered and embarrassed, a little at a disadvantage, but excessively friendly. There was no reference to his communication to me, and only a passing reference by me to my suggestion of Kotex, a suggestion for which he thanked me."[26]

Victor Li suggests that Eliot here either rebukes Aiken for his excessive verbal outpouring in his review of *Poems 1909–1925* or characterizes *Poems 1909–1925* itself as just such an excessive verbal outpouring – each message relying on "the overdetermined figure, used by both Eliot and Aiken, of the female body and its reproductive functions as analogues or images of linguistic offenses and disorder." Li further concludes that "Eliot's sheepish thanks to Aiken's suggestion reveals that he understood Aiken's point about his (Eliot's) own hysterical language, his 'offensive' verbal discharge and of the need for some kind of discipline or order for which Kotex becomes the unlikely symbol."[27] Brilliant as it is, Li's reading overlooks the simpler possibility that Eliot is sheepish because he realizes that Aiken – long aware of the couple's sexual misadventures – has divined that Eliot's reading in the *Midwive's Gazette* reflects his very real concern about Vivien's menstruation problems.[28] It is entirely possible that Aiken's jesting reference to Kotex also represents genuine advice – or at least genuine concern – for the couple, for which Eliot genuinely thanks him.

In poems about his new wife and her uncontrollable womb, then, Eliot seems to agree with Rentoul and McKim: hysteria is associated with a variety of disorders, ranging from excessive vaginal discharge to moral insanity. According to the eugenic logic implicit in this poetry, the wandering womb of the Vivien-figure in "Hysteria" produces in "Ode" a "succuba" – a prostitute or whore. In *The Waste Land*, the Vivien-figure's still wandering womb leads her to threaten to "rush out" from her bedroom and "walk the street / With [her] hair down": she remains the succuba in search of a sexual partner (*CPP* p. 65). This wandering womb, furthermore, is potentially fatal to both woman and man: in "Hysteria," it threatens to choke her and to swallow him; in "Ode," its irregular and over-frequent discharge of blood threatens to "eviscerate" her and to extinguish him.

Emerging from this poetry and from this logic are a Viv-figure and a Tom-figure – a neurotic, promiscuous woman and an ascetic, ineffectual man, respectively. Prostitutes and ascetics in Eliot's poetry are certainly more than aspects of Tom and Viv, but I suggest that wherever one encounters prostitutes and ascetics in this poetry one also encounters – in addition to the many other concerns that the overdetermined images of prostitutes and ascetics represent for Eliot – a variety of displaced eugenical concerns that continuously preoccupied the couple.

Note in "Ode," for instance, the speaker's symbolic defense against the Viv-figure's womb. Embedded in the very image that leaves him "Tortured" is the image of Vivien as "Succuba eviscerate" – an image that constitutes a fantasy of Vivien disemboweled, womb removed. This fantastic defense against the threat of a woman's indiscriminate sexuality had by the twentieth century been transformed into medical practice and eugenical advice. On the one hand, removal of the ovaries and uterus was urged by some eugenists as a way of addressing the problem of moral insanity. Rentoul, for instance, argues that for those suffering from diseases that cause intense sexual desire – "such as consumption" – "the removal of the ovaries or uterus often gives marked relief."[29] On the other hand, eugenical sterilization laws designed to prevent the feebleminded from breeding allowed removal of the ovaries and uterus as one means of sterilization.[30] State-enforced sterilization was legal in many jurisdictions in the United States well before Eliot left in 1914 to take up residence in Britain. By 1911, six states had passed laws allowing compulsory sterilization of the unfit. Furthermore, as Kevles points out, "[i]n the United States, a strong consensus in favor of sterilization – supporters ranged from Margaret Sanger to Theodore Roosevelt – grew among eugenists."[31] In Britain, there was much less support for such legislation – as Jones notes, "[t]he Royal Commission on the Care and Control of the Feebleminded in 1908 reported that only 3 out of 21 witnesses who mentioned sterilization as a solution to mental deficiency spoke in its favor" – but the debate about the benefits of sterilization was nonetheless vigorous.[32] McLaren observes that in Britain's "population debate at the turn of the century. . . the question of the forcible sterilization of the unfit was widely discussed."[33] And discussion continued into Eliot's first years in Britain. Cambridge's Arthur Balfour Professor of Genetics, R. C. Punnett, published "Eliminating Feeblemindedness" in 1917, accepting "that most desirable goal of a world rid of the feebleminded" and asking "[a]t what rate can we hope to free a population of an undesirable recessive character by isolating, or otherwise sterilizing those individuals which exhibit the character?"[34] Against this background, "Ode"'s "Succuba eviscerate" can be read as a wish-fulfillment fantasy (of Vivien neutered and her sexual threat neutralized) that is enabled by eugenical discourse about sterilization and hysterectomy.

Like "Hysteria" and "Ode," "Burbank with a Baedecker: Bleistein with a Cigar" also reveals Eliot's suspicion that Vivien is morally insane. In this poem, he inflicts Vivien's tuberculosis of the hand upon Princess Volupine, who "extends / A meagre, blue-nailed, phthisic hand" (*CPP* p. 41). In Princess Volupine's entertaining of both Burbank and Sir Ferdinand Klein, he also attributes to her the indiscriminate sexuality of the consumptive and morally insane type, as defined by eugenists like Rentoul and McKim. Regarding Princess Volupine as symbolic of "prostituted Venice," Anthony Julius reads the poem as Eliot's indictment of the "courtesan's degraded impartiality toward her clients": she is "either extending hospitality to Jew and Gentile alike, or else submitting to a specifically Jewish pimping."[35] Eliot's anti-Semitism all the more foregrounds his imputation of moral insanity to the sinisterly phthisic Vivien-figure.

The prostitution of the Vivien-figure's wandering womb to American Gentile and British Jew alike involves her in Eliot's eugenical fears about the birthrate. Eugenists worried that the Anglo-Saxon race was about to be overwhelmed by Jews and Irish Catholics; so did Eliot. Given the decline in the birthrate, Sidney Webb warned that "national deterioration" would be the result of the unregulated birth in Britain of "Irish Roman Catholics and the Polish, Russian, and German Jews."[36] Taylor worried about the high birthrate of "the Hebrew and the alien." Noting that the birthrate in London's "poorest" boroughs was 50 percent greater than the birthrate in its "rich" ones, the Whethams warned that "the 'poor' boroughs contain not only the highest number of Irish Roman Catholics, but also the largest proportion of foreigners and Jews."[37] The National Birth-Rate Commission acted on these prejudices – noting the rise in the birthrate of Jews in London's East End at a time when the birthrate fell in London as a whole, and noting that the birthrate in Catholic Connaught (Ireland) "has been rising in the last few years with even greater rapidity than it has been declining in this country."[38] The Jew and the Catholic in Eliot's poems of 1918 and 1919 figure this eugenical racism.

The anonymous "Jew" in "Gerontion" and the Jewish Bleistein in "Burbank with a Baedecker: Bleistein with a Cigar" are figured as primitive life forms reproducing on the margins of the human community – the one "[s]pawned in some estaminet of Antwerp," the other merely projecting itself toward the rudimentary cell division implied as "[a] lustreless protrusive eye / Stares from the protozoic slime" (*CPP* pp. 37, 40). B. C. Southam suggests that in

"Burbank with a Baedecker: Bleistein with a Cigar," the name "Burbank" may be an allusion to "Luther Burbank (1849–1926), a famous American botanist," but he does not note the eugenical significance of such an allusion.[39] Crawford, however, remarks that Burbank was "a much-discussed figure" by Eliot's Harvard days, someone "hailed by the *Nation* as 'the most ingenious and successful of all hybridizers.'" Crawford regards the poem as "pointedly about the hybridization of the human plant 'Chicago Semite Viennese,'" suggesting that the science represented by Burbank allows Eliot "a biologically vast sweep over the gaze which at once uneasily connects and uneasily separates the aboriginally primitive from the sophisticatedly civilized painter of the elaborate city, when crude eye in 'protozoic slime' stares at Canaletto's perspective."[40] Having argued in *The Training of the Human Plant* (1907)[41] that selective mating could breed a superior race in the United States, Burbank is a point by which the degeneration represented by Princess Volupine and Bleistein can be measured. Indeed, that Burbank himself "fell" before Princess Volupine is proof of "Time's ruins" as "The smoky candle end of time / Declines": degeneration prevails (*CPP* pp. 40–41).

In "Gerontion," Juan Leon notes a similar eugenical theme. Reading in the poem an allusion to the biological consequences of the influenza epidemic that ravaged the world in 1918 and 1919, he notes that just as the very old and the very young were often untouched by the influenza, so an old man and a young boy are prominent survivors of the blighted world in Eliot's poem. Thus, "[t]he old man's decayed 'house' and 'dry brain' represent a wasted race and an enfeebled stock. . . [T]he Jew emerges as the unfit usurper of whom Webb has warned. It is the degenerate who have inherited here."[42]

The other usurping, debasing inheritor of the modern world is Sweeney. As Leon notes, "the emphasis falls repeatedly upon Sweeney's brute physiognomy, sexuality, and sensibility. Straddled in the sun, he is both an atavism and the monster of future history. This character, like the Jew, augurs the dysgenic flood."[43] This reading of the Sweeney figure is quite accurate. Although Eliot confesses in a 1915 letter that acquaintance with two "very agreeable" Irishmen has "rather raised [his] opinion of that race," it clearly did not raise his opinion very much.[44] His racist characterization of the Irish as the archetype of the prolifically unfit is ubiquitous.

In "Mr. Eliot's Sunday Morning Service," for instance, Sweeney is an Irish baby dropped into his bathwater by his "polyphiloprogenitive" race. The first word of the poem, "polyphiloprogenitive," is invented by Eliot, but Southam notes that Arnold's use of a similar word in *Culture and Anarchy* may have been his inspiration: "It is a little unjust, perhaps, to attribute to the Divinity exclusively . . . philoprogenitiveness, which the British Philistine, and the poorer class of Irish, may certainly claim to share with him."[45] Southam suggests that the passage "could well have been in Eliot's mind at this time since he was lecturing on Arnold in spring and autumn 1917."[46] The passage seems even more likely to have been remarked by Eliot given not only its reinforcement of his general prejudices against the Irish, but also its reinforcement of his particular eugenical fears about the role of the Irish in the population "problem." Recall that Eliot paid especially close attention to the reports of the National Birth-Rate Commission's work in the issues of *The Eugenics Review* and *Shield* that he was reading at the end of 1917. In the context of Eliot's eugenical concerns about the birthrate, the image of the physical, animal, and Irish Sweeney appropriately concludes a poem that begins with an amplification of Arnold's word for the power that God and the Irish share. Sweeney is the culmination of a poem preoccupied with polyphiloprogenitiveness: the divine creativity that produces three gods in One through "superfetation"; the theological creativity that "at the mensual turn of time / Produced enervate Origen"; nature's creativity when "the bees / With hairy bellies pass between / The staminate and pistillate" (*CPP* pp. 54–55). Polyphiloprogenitive himself, the Irishman of the Sweeney poems incarnates fertility – particularly when measured against figures like the castrato Origen and other reproductively enervated figures such as "the dead men" in *The Waste Land* who have "lost their bones" (*CPP* p. 65).

Note, furthermore, that Sweeney is indiscriminate in his sexual behavior. He consorts regularly with the equally promiscuous Vivien-figure, who appears in "Sweeney Erect" as the "Succuba eviscerate" of "Ode" become the "withered root of knots and hair / Slitted below and gashed with eyes," and as the woman with the toothed genitalia and wandering womb in "Hysteria" become "This oval O cropped out with teeth" (*CPP* pp. 42, 32, 42). They are both degenerate – in moral and evolutionary terms: her "Gesture of orang-outang / Rises from the sheets in steam"; Sweeney is "Apeneck" in "Sweeney Among the Nightingales" (*CPP* pp. 42, 56). Eliot has reached the same conclusion as Mary Dendy: "the weaker the *Intellect* . . . the greater appears to be the strength of the reproductive faculties. It is as though where the higher faculties have dwindled the lower, or merely animal, take command."[47]

And so Eliot betrays both the eugenist's general fear that the Anglo-Saxon race is about to be swamped by Irish Catholics and Jews *and* his own particular eugenical fear that the phthisic and hysterical Vivien is morally insane – and therefore as fatal in her fertility as Irishman and Jew. Her tuberculosis of the left hand was cause enough for eugenical concern in its own right. Pearson argued that "the bulk of the tuberculous belong to stocks which we want *ab initio* to discourage."[48] Leonard Darwin, in an issue of *The Eugenics Review* that Eliot read (recall that his "articles always deserve attention"), noted that returning soldiers contained "large numbers of consumptives" and argued that "we ought not to take any steps especially designed to encourage to become parents those who are likely to be endowed with a heritable tendency to this disease. This is a very real eugenic danger which cannot be neglected."[49] Add to the mix of Irishman and Jew the morally insane consumptive – who cannot tell a eugenically good relationship from a bad one, and who lacks restraint in any event – and the result will be race suicide.

How did Eliot understand his own eugenical responsibility in the face of such fatal fertility? Never mind Irishman or Jew, was he himself fit to father children – by Vivien or any other woman? As it turns out, Eliot was led to reflect upon this question as a consequence of his attempt to enlist in the US armed forces.

Pleased by the United States' entry into the war in April of 1917, he was in no hurry to enlist. Although Vivien suspected that "he would almost like to [fight]," he explained to his mother: "I certainly do not feel in a position to go until 'called out' . . . I should go then, but not till then."[50] Eliot would not enlist voluntarily because he did not wish to leave Vivien on her own, describing her as an "invalid." Furthermore, he believed that because she was "entirely dependent" upon him he was unlikely to be "called out."[51] To his father, he explained further the qualifications he attached to his patriotic spirit: "To me all this war *enthusiasm* seems a bit unreal, because of the mixture of motives. But I see the war partly through the eyes of men who have been and returned, and who view it, even when convinced of the rightness of the cause, in a very different way: as something very sordid and disagreeable which must be put through. That would be my spirit."[52] He also anticipated that physical disability would prevent his being accepted for active service. Apparently responding to a question from his mother on this point, he wrote: "I daresay the hernia might make a difference, though there is no indication of its still being open."[53]

Circumstances ultimately forced Eliot to attempt to enlist. Ackroyd suggests that "the Allied misfortunes of early 1918 seem to have persuaded Eliot that it was his duty to join the American army."[54] It is more likely, however, that Eliot decided to seek a commission because he feared that he was liable to be "conscripted as a private" and knew that he would "suffer very badly on a private's pay."[55] In July of 1918, the British and French governments were pressuring the American government to commit to the raising of 5,000,000 further troops by July of 1919.[56] These developments seem to have been announced to Eliot in a letter from his mother, who appears to have made the information a pretext for a question about the likelihood of his being conscripted; only Eliot's reply survives: "I have not seen anything about the Treaty you refer to. Please keep me posted if you see anything but put it on a separate sheet of paper, writing to the Bank. Vivien worries a great deal about me (and I about her, and also about the *financial aspect* of it)."[57] On 26 July 1918, President Wilson approved the raising of 3,360,000 new troops in less than a year. Eliot began trying for a commission in the navy's Intelligence Service at "the end of July"[58] – presumably anticipating conscription after hearing confirmation of the new commitments that the US had made.

As he had expected, enlistment was complicated by his hernia. To his brother he explained that he had been "passed fit for *limited* service (hernia)"; to the literary patron John Quinn he explained that he had been "graded unfit for *active* service (fighting) on account of a hernia"; to his father he revealed two "physical disabilities (hernia and tachycardia)," which he hoped "would not disqualify" him from the Intelligence Service.[59] After ten weeks of frustration – "[e]verything turned to red tape in my hands" – Eliot gave up hope of getting the position he sought in the Intelligence Service, deciding that his "only course [was] to appeal for exemption [from service] on the ground of a dependent wife, and being partially unfit physically."[60] Lloyd's Bank signed this appeal for his exemption from service just two days before the Armistice was signed.[61]

Having to declare himself "partially unfit physically" scarred Eliot. To have been "graded unfit for *active* service" might have protected him from being tarred for cowardice with the white feather, but it could not protect him from his own concerns about his eugenical unfitness. His reading in *The Eugenics Review* of 1916–17 acquainted him with agitation by the Eugenics Society for recognition of the eugenical superiority as breeders of those who achieved distinction for active service during the war. Leonard Darwin argued that

the sailors and soldiers, who have actually fought in this war, constitute a class above average in civic worth. . . In the early days of the war all who enlisted were volunteers, in itself a guarantee that they possessed certain high qualities. . . [T]hose with the strongest sense of duty generally forced their way into the fighting line. . . [C]an it be denied that the men who have served in the trenches form a selected class of the community, both in many physical and in some mental qualities?

For a long time a non-volunteer, never a combatant, and in the end not even a soldier, Eliot also found himself eugenically suspect because he did not pass his medical examination. Darwin implies that rejection at enlistment and being "retained in England as unequal to service" *after* enlistment together constitute a eugenical pre-selection by which the unfit are prevented from going abroad. He lumps together as unfit "those defective in body and obviously defective in mind, and, of course, all those confined or resident in prisons, lunatic asylums, homes for imbeciles, hospitals, and other institutions." For Darwin, being graded unfit by the army was tantamount to being graded unfit for parenthood: "As to the men who stopped home, we know that no adequate steps are being taken to prevent even those of them who are lunatics, imbeciles, drunkards and criminals from parenthood, let alone the host of the other unfit."[62]

Could Eliot really have seen himself as one of "the host" of the eugenically unfit, or even have worried that he would be seen by others as such? On the one hand, his own doctor informed him that his hernia was a heritable physical disability: "The doctor told me at the time that there was usually a family predisposition in such cases." Accepting that a predisposition to hernia is inherited in his family, Eliot confidently assures his mother that this fact means that his brother Henry is unlikely to be accepted for the army: "I don't believe that Henry would be accepted for anything."[63] On the other hand, he shows great concern about how others will react to his having "stopped at home." To Quinn, he writes: "the armistice came, and I was very glad – anyway, it was not my fault that I had not been able to make myself useful to the country." To his mother, he suggests that with the armistice signed "it is really all for the best that I did not get into the Navy. One may be very useful, but it is not the same thing after the fighting has ceased . . . Anyway, no one can say that I did not try my best to get into Army or Navy."[64]

Eliot is clearly concerned about how his not having served will be perceived. Perhaps he remembers the white feather campaign when women publicly humiliated young men not in uniform by handing them the white feather of cowardice. Perhaps he protests too much, feeling guilty at his lack of war "enthusiasm." It is likely, however, that the eugenical aspersions cast upon noncombatants by Darwin in the issues of *The Eugenics Review* that Eliot read at the end of 1917 and beginning of 1918 play a part in this sensitivity about how his own non-combatant role will be perceived. His reaction to his brother-in-law's having volunteered for the US army and having been assigned to assist engineers at a South Boston army base is instructive:

I am distressed about George [Lawrence Smith, his brother-in-law]. His action seems to me quite irresponsible. A man well over forty, with two children, ought to know better. Even at the most excited period here no one would have expected a man in such a position to enlist. I can't see what good it will do him; no one will give him work for being "patriotic," as he is not going into the firing line . . .[65]

Once again Eliot reveals his sensitivity about his own refusal to volunteer (the arguments that condemn the brother-in-law's action simultaneously explain and justify his own inaction), but more interesting is the evidence here of Darwin's influence. This letter was written 22 December 1917, presumably when Eliot was reading *The Eugenics Review* for his January *IJE* essay. As for Darwin, so for Eliot: service at the front is what counts. Advocated by Darwin on eugenical grounds, and accepted by Eliot as a likely consequence of the war, are programs after the war to find jobs for soldiers who served at the front:

With regard to the return to civil life of all soldiers [returning from the front], damaged or undamaged, all other questions in fact shrink into insignificance compared with that of getting them back to work . . . [T]he re-establishment in civil life of the sailor and soldier may be assisted by putting them in the way of finding jobs in their old lines of work, by training them for new employments, or by giving them necessary employment under the State . . .[66]

Accepting Darwin's distinction between those at the front and those stopping at home, Eliot is concerned that his brother-in-law will not benefit from any such programs. Darwin's eugenics, in short, seems to have contributed to Eliot's high valuation of the front, "the firing line," and "fighting."

The insecurity caused by being graded unfit both by the army medical examiners and by the distinguished president of the Eugenics Society is evident in Eliot's poetry. Gerontion, for instance, emphasizes three times in four lines that he has "Not fought" (*CPP* p. 37). And so Eliot places Gerontion the noncombatant (in this respect, a figure for Eliot himself) alongside the anonymous "boy" and the anonymous "Jew" as another of the dysgenic inheritors of the postwar world. They have all survived, but at what cost to the race?

In the context of the eugenical question that the poem implies, Gerontion's solution is to retreat from sexual activity. The cryptic fifth stanza in this most cryptic poem, that is, can be read as a declaration of celibacy by a dysgenic Tom-figure to a dysgenic Viv-figure. The dysgenic prostitute of contemporaneous poems reappears here as the inhabitant of the "rented house" (the "rented house" may even be her body) where Gerontion seems to "Stiffen" in erection. Gerontion's claim that they "have not reached conclusion" in this sexual act is none other than Eliot's constant refrain that life is more than biology. Gerontion makes the same point by suggesting that his erection ("this show") is misleading (a mere "show"): it is not a function of the old passion (that would be to concite the past toward which Dante's devils symbolically retreat by looking behind themselves and walking backwards), but rather a function of a physiological reflex.[67] In short, an erection is less than love. Gerontion is remote from the woman's heart, remote from her beauty, and remote from his own passion – and he wishes to remain so. His fear that his passion will "be adulterated" through sexual intercourse suggests both the aspiration toward a purely spiritual passion that is evident elsewhere in the poem *and* the eugenical concern about the adulteration of the Anglo-Saxon germ plasm by similar adulterations evident in contemporaneous poems. The phthisical, hysterical, morally insane prostitute ought not to engage in sexual intercourse with the herniated, tachycardial noncombatant for fear of the adulterated offspring they might produce.

Not surprisingly, both Tom and Viv invoke the image of children as a figure for the sexual frustration and failure at the heart of their married life. The assumption that they would have children vexed the Eliots from the beginning. As Eliot explained to Conrad Aiken, friends and acquaintances made it clear that they were expecting news of pregnancy from the newly married couple by their assumptions about the cause of Vivien's illness during her first year of marriage: "You know that my wife has been very ill all the winter. She has been getting gradually better, but very slowly. . . [I]t was a great anxiety all winter and spring, as she kept having incidental troubles like teeth which set her back. I may say that this was not a case of maternity in any degree. Most people imagine so unless I explain."[68] Five years later Vivien contributed to *The Waste Land* the line, "What you get married for if you don't want to have children?" (*WLF* p. 15). Vivien presumably recognizes that Lil's situation is similar to her own. Like Vivien, Lil is ill (after an aborted pregnancy as opposed to a pregnancy merely assumed by others), and like Vivien, Lil is the subject of gossip about her health and married life. No doubt Vivien herself, like Tom, felt the sting of the rhetorical question with which Lil is flailed.

Eliot's frustration at the knowing assumptions of "[m]ost people" is clear, but the basis of his confidence that Vivien's bad health "was not a case of maternity in *any* degree" (emphasis added) is not clear. He could not have known what he so confidently asserts – that Vivien had *never* been pregnant (even if only for several weeks and then spontaneously aborted a fetus) – unless it had been determined that one or the other was infertile, or unless they had taken reliable precautions against pregnancy – and perhaps the most reliable precaution of all: abstinence. As his information on the matter of Vivien's certain non-pregnancy is offered to the friend to whom he earlier confessed his desire to lose his virginity, one might read the letter in question as a confession of continuing sexual frustration: "I can assure you that Vivien has never been pregnant because she has been so ill that sexual relations have been impossible." Whatever the case, it is clear that from the beginning the question of offspring and the question of Vivien's health are bound up together in Tom's mind.

Vivien provides a hint as to the tensions that childlessness caused by requesting that Tom remove from *The Waste Land* the line, "The ivory men make company between us" (*WLF* p. 13). The removal of the line occurs very late in the composition process. Vivien had not suggested this revision when marking her other suggestions on an early draft of the poem. In fact, she writes "Yes" beside this very line. The line seems not to have been criticized on aesthetic grounds: Vivien lets it stand; Pound lets it stand; Eliot himself never even tinkers with it – either in *The Waste Land* drafts or in "The Death of the Duchess," where it also appears. In fact, Eliot's confidence in the line survives a lapse of almost forty years during which the poem never appears with this line in it, for "[t]he author restored it, from memory, when he made a fair copy of the poem for the sale in aid of the London Library in June 1960."[69] One of the last lines to be omitted; the only line of all those omitted to be restored (and after forty years!) – Tom and Viv agree that it is a very important line.

What does it mean? Occurring at the end of a one-sided conversation between an angry, vituperative woman and a lethargic, disdainful man, the line represents the man's apparently unspoken conclusion that the couple needs company – that the relationship between the man and the woman lacks something. The same suggestion is made in "The Death of the Duchess" where this line appears alongside "it is terrible to be alone with another person" and "If it is terrible alone, it is sordid with one more" (*i.e.* the charwoman) (*WLF* p. 105). Appearing in a section of the poem that their friends were going to read autobiographically, Tom's expression of his unhappiness in marriage may have displeased Vivien.[70] (More explicit in articulating the same message, "The Death of the Duchess" was certainly never published.) Yet why focus on this line alone? Vivien called "WONDERFUL" the equally revealing depiction of the Vivien-figure as a nervous, sex-starved, and hectoring neurotic and of the Tom-figure as an unexcitable, sexually-uninterested, unresponsive accidic (*WLF* p. 11). If she had hoped that suppressing the line would hide their unhappiness, then the revision was not worth the effort: this whole section of the poem is about a couple's unhappiness. Presumably she was reacting to something else.

I suggest that Vivien recognized that the line was not only a complaint about loneliness but also a complaint about childlessness. That Eliot diagnosed childlessness as an important element – perhaps the most important element – in a couple's loneliness is evident in *The Family Reunion* where Harry's father and mother are remembered as

> A man and a woman
> Married, alone in a lonely country house together,
> For three years childless, learning the meaning
> Of loneliness.   (*CPP* p. 332)

Like so much of the play, these lines seem autobiographical – a recollection of the early years of the marriage between Tom and Viv. That Eliot's regret at their childlessness is not a late phenomenon but rather a phenomenon of the early years of marriage is suggested by the history of the image by which he expresses this regret: children hidden, invisible, remote – their small voices singing or laughing in the distance. In *The Family Reunion*, Agatha recalls the vision by which she knew her own regret at her childlessness: "I . . . looked through the little door / When the sun was shining on the rose-garden: / And heard in the distance tiny voices" (*CPP* pp. 334–35). In a similar garden in *Burnt Norton*, Eliot uses the same image to depict a nostalgia for the children that might have come of marriage to Emily Hale: "the leaves were full of children, / Hidden excitedly, containing laughter" (*CPP* p. 172).[71] In *The Waste Land* the unclean daughter of Sweeney and the prostitute Mrs. Porter is contrasted with another version of these distant "*enfants, chantant dans la coupole*" (*CPP* p. 67). Before this, however, we meet the same image in "Ode," where "[c]hildren singing in the orchard" represent the same nostalgia for children never to be born.

Mayer suggests that "[t]he children singing in the orchard is a festive image evoking innocence, joy, and fruitfulness in marriage and in nature" and that Eliot evokes this image "to purge sex of what Eliot's father called 'nastiness' and to 'eviscerate' (rob of its power) the image of his bride as a succuba."[72] Yet the image also suggests that children will not come of this particular marriage. As in the contemporary poem "Gerontion," Eliot announces his withdrawal from a sexual relationship with Vivien: his hair now "smoothed," the morning "already late," this man will no longer be discomposed and retarded, for he will not return to the marriage bed – a fact acknowledged indirectly by the poem's typescript title: "Ode on Independence Day, July 4th, 1918." This man is now independent of this woman. The title situates the poem three years and one week after the Eliots' marriage, anticipating the later reference to the Monchenseys' three years of childlessness. In each relationship, three years marks a watershed: in the one, Harry Monchensey is conceived; in the other, childlessness is chosen. The "Children singing in the orchard" are thus continuous with the children in subsequent poems who will not be born. What Mayer calls "the classical wedding cry of fertility" – "Io Hymen Hymenaee" celebrates the Greek and Roman god of marriage – is thus reduced to parenthesis, an ironic memory of wedding night promise betrayed by the succubine reality that has replaced it in the course of three years of marriage.[73]

The child that Tom feared that he and Viv might produce is imagined in the early drafts of *The Waste Land*: "The infant hydrocephalous, who sat / At a bridge end, by a dried-up water course / And fiddled (with a knot tied in one string)" (*WLF* p. 75). As Leon points out, "[t]he infant, its head abnormally enlarged by excessive liquid about the brain, constitutes . . . an example of the hydrocephalic type that was frequently the subject of eugenicists' attention."[74] The child's fiddling and its string link it to its mother: "A woman drew her long black hair out tight / And fiddled whisper music on those strings" (*WLF* p. 75). In still another draft of this section of the poem, this woman is accompanied by "[a] man, one withered by some mental blight" (*WLF* p. 113). Leon therefore finds here "the degenerate couple of the eugenicist's fears" – and their child.

I suggest that this couple is the Eliots; the infant, the child that Eliot feared. The woman in Part v who draws "her long black hair out tight" is continuous with the Vivien-figure in Part ii whose "hair" – "under the brush" – "Spread out in fiery points" (*CPP* pp. 64–65). The man "withered by some mental blight" is "Yet of abnormal powers" – surely a figure for Eliot himself, the self-styled literary authority withered by accidie and mental breakdown at the time of the poem's composition, but still writing. The "infant hydrocephalous" belongs in *The Waste Land*, Leon notes, as an instance of "a horrific 'death by water,'" but it belongs to the Eliots in particular, I suggest, because the acute form of hydrocephaly that causes death by water (on the brain) was called tubercular meningitis.[75] Eliot's fevered eugenical imagination combines Vivien's tuberculous inheritance with his own withering mental blight to produce the tubercular brain of the "infant hydrocephalous."

That the choice of childlessness was Tom's and not Viv's is suggested by Vivien's interventions in *The Waste Land*. Her line "What you get married for if you don't want to have children" can be read as her projection upon the working-class couple of the kind of assumption that the Eliots themselves encountered in the early years of their marriage: marriage brings children; it is no surprise when they are born; it is a matter for comment if they are not. The line would thus serve as a joke upon themselves that the couple can indulge because they both have experienced the social pressures that such assumptions exert. Yet assuming that Eliot had announced to Vivien as early as 1918 that he would not be the father of her children, the line can also be read as directed against Tom by Viv: "What you get married for if you don't want to have children?"

Of course Vivien's line is a perfect addition to a section of the poem that betrays Eliot's continuing concern at the prolific reproduction rate of the working class: Vivien recognizes that the issue in this part of the poem is fertility. That she recognized that the issue was the fatal fertility of the working class is suggested in a later diary entry: horrified by the menace of women rattling prams behind her in the street, Vivien speculates that they are "dying to propagate their own loathsomeness."[76] Her resentment is explicitly eugenical and implicitly autobiographical. She makes the same point as Tom in *The Waste Land*: the irresponsible Alberts and Lils of the world can go on having children, heedless of the consequences, but the responsible Toms and Vivs cannot.

It would seem, then, that both Tom and Viv wanted to have children, but that Tom did not want to have children with Viv. To expose the question of childlessness via her own line is relatively innocuous. No one would read Albert and Lil as Tom and Viv. The joke upon themselves and the jab at Tom would remain private. It was clear, however, that many of their friends were going to see the Eliots in the bedroom couple. In this context, the problem with "The ivory men make company between us" is that it functions as a complaint by the Tom-figure against the Viv-figure. He would suffice as company for her; she will never suffice as company for him. Since the complaint is articulated by the man, the assumption will be either that the woman does not want children or that she cannot have them because she is barren. If indeed Tom has determined that the couple will not have children, Vivien has reason to resent the line as a laying of blame against her. She would not have wanted their friends to have taken this message from the poem, and since Mary Hutchinson was already assuring Virginia Woolf that the poem was Tom's disguised autobiography, she had reason to be vigilant about this matter. In the end, Eliot seems to have acknowledged that he had not only a eugenical obligation to the unborn, but also a civil obligation to his wife – sparing Vivien the blame for their child-lessness so long as she was living, reasserting his complaint only after she was dead.

CHAPTER 6

Fatal fertility in The Waste Land

That *The Waste Land* is about fertility is not news. Eliot himself pointed to the studies of fertility rituals that inspired him – "Jessie L. Weston's book on the Grail legend: *From Ritual to Romance* . . . [and] another work of anthropology . . . *The Golden Bough*; I have used especially the two volumes *Adonis, Attis, Osiris*. Anyone who is acquainted with these works will immediately recognise in the poem certain references to vegetation ceremonies" (*CPP* p. 76). From the beginning, critics saw fertility as an important theme. In an early review, Edmund Wilson describes Eliot's waste land as "a desolate and sterile country, ruled over by an impotent king, in which not only have the crops ceased to grow and the animals to reproduce their kind, but the very human inhabitants have become unable to bear children."[1] In *New Bearings in English Poetry* (1932), F. R. Leavis reads the references to "Vegetation cults" and "fertility ritual" as a reminder of the "remoteness" of modern "human culture" from "natural rhythms": "Sex here is sterile, breeding not life and fulfilment but disgust, accidia, and unanswerable questions."[2] Cleanth Brooks reads infertility as a symbol of the decline of Christianity's influence: for Eliot "Christian terminology is . . . a mass of clichés," and so, since he cannot deal with the Christian material directly, "[t]he theme of resurrection is made on the surface in terms of the fertility rituals."[3] Similarly, Northrop Frye suggests that inhabitants of the waste land "live the 'buried life' of seeds in winter: they await the spring rains resentfully, for real life would be their death. . . Physical death is the final judgement between the seeds who can understand the commands of the thunder and die to new life, and those who merely die and are rejected, as the sterile seed is rejected by nature."[4] Stephen Spender finds in the focus upon infertility the essence of Eliot's "method" of conflating public and private spheres: "The key idea is that the private failure of the sacrifice and sacrament, which is ritual between bride and bridegroom, is the result of the public failure of creativity within the civilization."[5]

More recent and more adventurous critics continue to focus upon the question of fertility. James E. Miller suspects that the poem's anxieties about fertility are related to Eliot's repression of homosexual desire for his dead university friend Jean Verdenal: Eliot himself is "the fisher-king suffering the sexual wound (loss of Verdenal) that has rendered him impotent in his marriage like the fisher-king of the waste land legend."[6] Sandra Gilbert and Susan Gubar read Eliot's "mysteriously sterile Fisher King" as an instance of the modern man emasculated by the war's dehumanization of the soldier, on the one hand, and its empowerment of women in various ways, on the other: "the gloomily bruised modernist antiheroes churned out by the war suffer specifically from *sexual* wounds, as if . . . all have become not just no-men, nobodies, but *not* men, *un*men."[7] Even in Harriet Davidson's reading of the poem as an expression of a hermeneutic philosophy, fertility figures prominently as a symbol of meaningful being-in-the-world: "By the end of the poem, the spring rain will undergo an interpretive metamorphosis from a cruel to a saving release, as generation and interpretation are chosen over sterility and rigidity."[8]

Nearly everyone agrees that *The Waste Land*'s interest in the question of fertility symbolizes important themes, but only Crawford and Leon have suggested that we might take the poem's concern about fertility literally – that is, as a eugenical concern about biological fertility. Crawford notes that the poem begins with the "Burbankian theme of plant breeding" and proceeds to contemplate Mr. Eugenides as "the antithesis of the good breeding his name pronounces" and the horror of the "emotionless lovemaking of clerk and typist."[9] Leon identifies eugenical anxiety not just in the image of the "infant hydrocephalous" of the early drafts, but also in much more familiar images in the published poem. The "cockney woman" Lil has had five children and so "has manifested a dangerous fertility." He finds "eugenic terror" in "the attention to insanity, doleful and perverted maternity, and whelming human throngs" in the last section of the poem. Leon links Mr. Eugenides, anything but "well born," with Lil: they are both threats because of their sexual activity, and their sexual activity is in each case eugenically neutralized – the one has induced an abortion and the other is gay. Leon concludes that in *The Waste Land* "[t]he dysgenic flood is both recognized and staved off."[10]

The poem's preoccupation with eugenics, however, is both more general and more particular than Crawford and Leon suggest. The prostitutes that appear in the poem from beginning to end are continuous with the hysterical, epileptic, and morally insane women of the earlier poems, yet they also reflect Eliot's reading about eugenics and prostitution in *Shield*. They make his eugenical point – not that the modern world is infertile, but rather that it is irresponsibly and dangerously fertile.

Of course Eliot was long fascinated by prostitutes, walking the streets of "one-night cheap hotels" during his student days in Cambridge, Paris, and London (*CPP* p. 13). "Rhapsody on a Windy Night" depicts an encounter with a prostitute on such a walk: a woman leans out a door, dress "torn and stained with sand," enticing the speaker to enter (*CPP* p. 24). Eliot understood these walks to be the result of "nervous sexual attacks" that he suffered "when alone in a city": "One walks about the streets with one's desires, and one's refinement rises up like a wall whenever opportunity approaches."[11] As Vivien divined, this sexual repression led him to see European women as a type of the prostitute – from whose example American women needed to be protected. And as we have seen, his imagination transformed Vivien into this prostitute-figure in poems written shortly after his third-anniversary review of their wedding night: she becomes the "Succuba eviscerate," the phthisic Princess Volupine, and the epileptic, hysterical partner of Sweeney.

By 1918, the prostitute of Eliot's imagination has become invested with eugenical significance. On the one hand, she represents a recognized subset of the morally insane – a fact that Eliot acknowledges in "Sweeney Erect," where he attributes to the "epileptic" prostitute subject to "hysteria" two of the characteristics identified by eugenists as triggers of the inherited predisposition to moral insanity (*CPP* p. 43). Many eugenists believed not only that moral insanity was heritable, but also that a tendency toward prostitution itself was heritable. Charles B. Davenport defined prostitutes as "feebly inhibited," having inherited an abnormally enlarged erotic center.[12] In the original drafts of *The Waste Land*, such an inheritance explains how Fresca (she of the "hysteric fits") could have been either "A meek and weeping Magdalene" or "The lazy laughing Jenny of the bard," for "The same eternal and consuming itch / Can make a martyr, or plain simple bitch." It is only because "By fate misbred" that she has become "a sort of can-can salonnière" instead of a "strolling slattern in a tawdry gown" (*WLF* p. 27). Environmental factors disguise the biological inheritance that would otherwise have seen her "consuming" (consumptive?) itch satisfied through prostitution. From this point of view, the prostitute is a dysgenic threat to the germ plasm.

On the other hand, the prostitute conveys venereal disease not just to her client, but also to her children and so – according to Shaw – "the diseases that follow prostitution . . . avenge the prostitute to the third and fourth generation of them that buy her."[13] Similarly, at the Eugenics Congress of 1912 it was observed that venereal diseases "tended to die out in three or four generations, but meantime caused great mischief."[14] The mischief that could die out in a few generations was bacterial. As McLaren notes, "[t]he realization at the end of the nineteenth century that syphilis could be carried even to the unborn spread fear and panic throughout society."[15] One of the doctors attending the Eugenics Congress argued that of the instances of "ante-natal mortality" not caused by "wilful" abortion, "most of the deaths were due to syphilis."[16] And so, McLaren observes that "eugenists used the concept of bacterial infection to support the idea that prostitutes had to be controlled". [17] The eugenical assumption was that one "could not get a good race unless this disease was extirpated."[18]

Prostitutes therefore not only polluted the germ plasm; they also infected the breeding stock bacterially. Social hygienists concerned to control venereal disease by controlling prostitution thus found themselves allied with racial hygienists – a fact that Eliot remarks upon in reviewing the essays in *Shield*. He notes both that *Shield*'s "activities intersect with those of the *Eugenics Review*, but it is occupied with the social aspect of eugenics exclusively," *and* that "it devotes much of its space to the subject of prostitution." In the October issue of 1916 and the March issue of 1917 that Eliot reviews, *Shield*'s "social" eugenics is to be found in "statistics, notes, reports, and . . . reviews." Here, Eliot explains, rather than in the "articles . . . of various merit," "this quarterly performs excellent work."[19] For instance, *Shield* publishes an "important" – and eugenical – addition to the Report by the National Birth-Rate Commission recommending that the nation seek "not only to increase but also to improve the population" and that "the natural functions of parenthood should be exercised under the control of affection, reason, conscience and racial obligation."[20] It reprints a manifesto urging eugenical considerations as a reason for compulsory notification of authorities of cases of venereal disease:

the disease is now very largely spread by girls of between 15 and 18 years of age. Can we wait while these mere children . . . become the mothers of the future generation and give birth to children more miserable than themselves?. . . Only through legislation can the whole community be really educated and imbued with a full sense of responsibility towards the race.[21]

Disagreeing with this campaign for compulsory notification, *Shield's* editor Alison Neilans nonetheless accepts that eugenics is important, suggesting in an editorial (*Shield's* "editorials," Eliot writes, "are usually written in a sensible and moderate tone") that a soldier's "sense of duty. . . to his race" may be effective in subordinating the "sexual instinct" that creates the demand for prostitution.[22]

Eliot's sense of the bacterial threat represented by prostitution is evident in *The Waste Land*, where prostitution and disease always go together. In the original drafts, Myrtle is concerned to preserve the reputation her house has for being free of disease: "I've kept a clean house for twenty years, she says, / And the gents from the Buckingham Club know they're safe here" (*WLF* p. 5). Not every house is so clean, and not every client is as careful as the members of the Buckingham Club. The "nice guy – but rough" and "too drunk" in Part I is symbolically equivalent to "the drunken ruffian" in Part IV, but whereas the former tries to get into "Myrtle's place," the clean house, the latter seems to be the one leaving "Marm Brown's joint" in Part IV, a relatively unclean house (*WLF* pp. 5, 55, 5, 59). That is, the "drunken ruffian who descends / Illicit backstreet stairs, to reappear / . . . limping with a comic gonorrhea" seems to issue from Marm Brown's: the sailors who later laugh at the thought of "Marm Brown's joint, and the girls and gin," presumably laugh at the recollection of this diseased ruffian's "comic" plight (*WLF* pp. 55, 59). At Marm Brown's joint, clients can pick up a venereal disease as easily as they can pick up a girl.

In 1921, to refer to gonorrhea as "comic" is pointedly ironic. According to Shaw, such an attitude represents the medical ignorance of the late-Victorian male: gonorrhea, "admittedly very common, was considered transient, easily curable, harmless to future generations, and, to everyone but the sufferer, dismissible as a ludicrous incident." Writing in 1909, Shaw argues that gonorrhea can no longer be dismissed so lightly. It "is said to be the commonest cause of blindness: it is transmitted from father to mother, from mother to child, from child to nurse, producing evils from which the individual attacked never securely gets free."[23] In fact, Shaw ranks venereal diseases alongside intentional sterility and criminal abortion as the gravest of threats to national well-being.

From this point of view, the most dangerous of *The Waste Land*'s prostitutes is the one who survives the revisions: Mrs. Porter. She comes from "one of the less bawdy versions" of a song that "was popular among Australian troops in World War I."[24] Eliot's note to his lines about Mrs. Porter confirms the Australian provenance of the song. C. M. Bowra agrees that Eliot quotes "the song in an inevitably bowdlerized form," yet he finds that Eliot nonetheless "shows how fit a companion Mrs. Porter is for Sweeney."[25] Sweeney, in short, is once again in the company of a prostitute, for, as Bowra explains, Mrs. Porter "kept a bawdy-house in Cairo" where she "was a legendary figure" among the Australian troops awaiting embarkation for Gallipoli. She was "legendary" in that she symbolized for these troops the venereal disease that was rife in the prostitution houses of Cairo. Indeed, the first casualties returned to Australia during World War I were troops sent home from Cairo with venereal disease.[26]

Eliot draws attention to Mrs. Porter's disease by his reference to the prostitutes' feet: "They wash their feet in soda water" (*CPP* p. 67). The song from which he quotes explains that they "oughter" do this "To keep them clean." The soldiers' concern was not with unclean feet, but with unclean sexual organs. Their interest in "clean" feet is the same as Myrtle's interest in a "clean" house. The song's "soda water" may even be a nickname for the chemical recently introduced as a treatment for venereal disease. Although syphilis was treated in the early years of the century with salvarsan and mercury, just before the war, Dr. H. Hallopeau, a eugenist and a Professor of Medicine at Paris, recommended at the Eugenics Congress that syphilis be treated with a chemical with the jaw-breaking name of benzosulpho-paraaminophenylarsenate of soda.[27]

The Australian army was severely traumatized by its Cairo encounter with Mrs. Porter and venereal disease, and Eliot knew of these matters via reports on them in the pages of *Shield*:

we believe we are correct in saying that the licensed houses in Cairo and elsewhere were the source of a very serious flood of venereal disease in some of its worst forms. It is common talk that the women used to flaunt their medical certificates about amongst the soldiers . . . The fact is that no doctor in the world could guarantee safety in sexual acts with promiscuous women. If this had been explained to the men, and if simultaneously the houses had been placed out of bounds, then the authorities would at least not be open to the reproach that Australian mothers now bring against them, namely, that they let their boys loose in a land of licensed vice and allowed them to think it was safe.[28]

Shield also complained about the Australian army's attempt to deal with the prostitution problem that its troops faced in London by allegedly providing "prophylactic kits": "We have received information . . . that when Australian troops are going up to London on leave the authorities serve out to them a regular outfit of preventive appliances and medicinal preparations for the prevention of venereal infections; further, that the army medical officers specially instruct the men in the use of these outfits."[29] Mrs. Porter having shown the need for both prophylactic *and* moral instruction, *Shield* bemoaned the fact that the army saw fit to provide the one but not the other.

Whether or not Eliot continued to follow *Shield*'s discussion of these matters in its next issue is not clear. He ends his survey of *Shield*'s essays with the last entry in *IJE*'s March issue. In the next issue, he would have found an article from Sydney, Australia, complaining about the impact of Cairo's bawdyhouses on the Australian army: "We have learned that a tremendous number of Australian troops were more or less incapacitated through venereal disease, and that, had these men been available, the history of the Dardenelles campaign might have been very different."[30] Eliot's note in *The Waste Land* suggests that he may well have read this article, for he claims that the song about Mrs. Porter "was reported to [him] from Sydney, Australia" (*WL* p. 77). The song itself is not discussed in the article, but the subject it broaches certainly is.

In any event, Eliot had read enough about Mrs. Porter to conclude that she was compromising troop health and morality – if not the war effort itself. From a eugenical point of view, she was also having a negative impact on the future of the race. If responsible for military defeats, she would also be responsible for dysgenic postwar consequences, for – according to Leonard Darwin – the nation was deprived by battlefield deaths of some of the best breeders of the next generation. Eliot seems to agree insofar as "The sound of horns and motors" in the postwar world brings "Sweeney to Mrs. Porter in the spring": the polyphiloprogenitive Irishman is, like her, one of the dysgenic survivors left to breed a new generation (*CPP* p. 67). Similarly, to the extent that she is responsible for the proliferation of venereal disease, Mrs. Porter's dysgenic impact is beyond doubt. Hallopeau suggested to the Eugenics Congress that "if the modern term 'eugenic' is to take a permanent place in the international vocabulary, the opposite term 'dysgenic' might well describe this disease."[31] Eliot again seems to agree, for Mrs. Porter has bequeathed to her daughter both her profession and her disease. Mrs. Porter's "daughter" is both her symbolic daughter – as employee, the Cairo prostitutes who work in her bawdyhouses – and her actual daughter – as child of her loins, the offspring of the prostitute and the Sweeney-type. Mrs. Porter thus reaps what she and Sweeney have sown: they perpetuate moral insanity in their daughter genetically (she has inherited the same moral insanity), and they perpetuate venereal disease in her bacterially (she has to use the same soda water).

Other children in *The Waste Land* are also the diseased and deformed offspring of prostitutes. The "infant hydrocephalous" is one such. Leon suggests that the infant is implicitly the child of Sweeney and the prostitute in "Sweeney Erect" because "the knot of string the infant fiddles with is also a knot of hair"[32] – thus linking it to the hair in "Sweeney Erect," where the prostitute is a "withered root of knots of hair / Slitted below and gashed with eyes" (*CPP* p. 42). Furthermore, the infant's mother in Part v – the woman who draws "her long black hair out tight" – is related to the woman in Part ii – "under the brush, her hair / Spread out in little fiery points of will" – who threatens to "walk the street / With my hair down, so" (*WLF* pp. 75, 17, 19). They are latently if not actually streetwalkers. In the original drafts, the "infant hydrocephalus" is thus the imagined offspring of a potential prostitute. In the published poem, the same figure produces the "bats with baby faces" in Part v's monstrous parody of motherhood (*CPP* p. 73). As mother, the prostitute is at least as much of a danger as she is in her role as streetwalker.

Against the background of *The Waste Land*'s preoccupation with prostitution and disease, Agatha's observation in *The Family Reunion* that "A curse comes to being / As a child is formed" needs to be scrutinized. The word *curse* here is an allusion to original sin, but it also connotes disease. The language at this point in the play is both mystical (Agatha recalls *The Cloud of Unknowing* in her reference to "accident / In a cloud of unknowing") and physical – even biological in its imagery of children and curses being conceived, being born, and growing to maturity (*CPP* p. 336–37). This ambiguity is no surprise, for Eliot calls for human perfection and imperfection to be understood in both spiritual and physical terms. Despite its theological connotations, then, the word *curse* retains its sense of "blight" or "blast" – as in William Blake's use of the term: "the youthful Harlot's curse / Blasts the new-born Infant's tear, / And blights with plagues the Marriage hearse."[33]

In fact, Eliot hints that he regards the curse of which Agatha speaks as this very "harlot's curse": venereal disease. In assuring the "child" (or "curse") that it will "be fulfilled," Agatha notes that "The knot shall be unknotted / And the crooked made straight" (*CPP* pp. 336–37). On the one hand, the words "knot" and "crooked" recall prostitutes in early poems – the prostitute with the "knots of hair" in "Sweeney Erect" and the prostitute whose "eye / Twists like a crooked pin" in "Rhapsody on a Windy Night" (*CPP* pp. 42, 24). On the other hand, Eliot explains Harry Monchensey's psychology in sufficiently autobiographical terms for us to recognize a description of his own psychology during the early years of his marriage: "The effect of his married life upon him was one of such horror as to leave him for the time at least in a state that may be called one of being psychologically partially desexed: or rather, it has given him a horror of women as of unclean creatures." Harry "is aware of the past only as *pollution*, and he does not dissociate the pollution of his wife's life from that of her death."[34] Eliot and Harry both see their wives – and women in general – as polluted and polluting prostitutes.

Yet Eliot was also aware that one could characterize the man who patronized the prostitute as the real eugenical menace. Frances Swiney suggested that race degeneration was caused by poisonous semen containing "sexual germs" spread by the incontinence of men.[35] As Greenslade notes, "[f]or the feminist writers of the nineties the syphilitic male became a primary target."[36] In Showalter's words, such feminists saw the syphilitic male as a "carrier of contamination and madness, and a threat to the spiritual evolution of the race."[37] Yet as McLaren notes of these feminist eugenists, "whereas the eugenists used the concept of bacterial infection to support the idea that prostitutes had to be controlled, the feminists used it to call for control of males. . . The man could be a 'carrier' of 'poisoned germ plasm' and the wife therefore had the duty and right to take whatever means necessary to protect herself and her children."[38] McLaren implies an opposition between eugenists and feminists, but it would be more accurate to characterize the opposition as between patriarchal eugenists and feminist eugenists, for feminists like Swiney remain eugenists.

The feminist position was also advanced in a non-eugenical form. According to Christabel Pankhurst, the problem was that the artificial cultivation of male "sexual instinct" led to depravity.[39] *Shield*'s feminism often takes this form, explaining the prostitution problem in terms of environment: "Public opinion on the whole does believe that we must expect a certain amount of promiscuity from most men before marriage; it further believes that the strictest chastity must be required from the woman who is to be married. The obvious result of these two ideas is that the civilised world is divided into three sorts of people – men, women, and prostitutes."[40] Eliot makes the same point when he ends his review by congratulating the Burmese "for the absence of prostitution" in their society: "the primitive Shan tribes are undoubtedly more civilized than ourselves."[41] The editor urges public opinion to "condemn the double standard of morals" according to which "when a woman solicits a man it is depravity, but when a man yields to the solicitation it is merely human nature."[42] She asserts the man's complicity in the prostitution problem in general – "Why don't we have Rescue Homes for men?" – and the venereal disease problem in particular: "What about the diseased soldier's promiscuous mode of life? That, we are given to understand, is human nature; *but, even so, it is quite as effective in spreading venereal disease.*"[43] Eliot again agrees: "The Editor . . . rightly deprecates the agitation for the protection of soldiers from 'harpies,' and points out that much of the 'protection' is merely weakening the soldier's sense of personal responsibility and self-control. . ."[44]

Neilans and Eliot agree that the men and the women involved in this debased sexuality are equally vile. Eliot is no admirer of Tereus, who "so rudely forc'd" Philomel, or "the young man carbuncular," who "assaults" the typist (*CPP* p. 68). Neilans and Eliot also agree that promiscuous men are both a genetic and a bacterial danger. In *The Waste Land*, the men are as diseased as the women and just as much a threat to pass pollution on. As we have seen, the putative father of the "infant hydrocephalous" suffers from "some mental blight" – a blight symbolically if not actually bequeathed to his child

(*WLF* p. 113). The man that Myrtle turns away is turned away because of "the reputation the place gets off a few bar-flies" like him: in other words, he is the kind of guy who carries the venereal disease that will earn her house a reputation as unclean (*WLF* p. 5). Similarly, the man leaving Marm Brown's joint has gonorrhea. These men are dangerous. As noted in *Shield*'s discussion of "The Campaign for Compulsory Notification of Venereal Disease" (which Eliot read with close attention), "[i]t is not only women who spread disease. Every woman was infected by some man, and it is usually men who carry disease into families, who infect wives and children."[45] *The Waste Land*'s leaving, limping version of the Fisher-King is on his way elsewhere – carrying his disease to others. He is the demobbed Albert who "wants a good time" and is on his way home to the reluctant Lil and the "Other women" who will "give it him" (*WLF* p. 19). He is "the young man carbuncular" visiting the typist's flat – one who, like Tiresias, has foresuffered elsewhere (and who knows where?) "all / Enacted on this same divan or bed" (*CPP* p. 69). Given that "[t]he number of persons made blind by gonorrhoea" was "one of the great subjects of social purity speakers" (in fact, "one of their trump cards against 'vice'"), the "blind" everyman Tiresias may have the sexual disease that Christabel Pankhurst believed every man was likely to have (*CPP* p. 68).[46]

"Preventive checks" are no solution. From the point of view of conventional sexual morality, prophylaxis helps maintain health but also facilitates vice. In considering ways of preventing venereal disease, Eliot suggests that "[p]rudence and morals are both good things, and can be brought to support each other, but they should not be confused."[47] From a feminist point of view, prophylaxis would encourage men to overindulge – either with their wives or with other women – the very sexual instinct that Christabel Pankhurst sought to reeducate. Furthermore, the use of preventive checks might enslave women. In *The Freewoman*, feminists argued that a man's use of preventive checks would deprive the wife of her reproductive power and thereby reduce her to the role of prostitute. Isabel Leatham called the use of such prophylactics "a gross outrage on the aesthetic sensibilities of women."[48] Shaw warned that husbands who insisted on using prophylactics would reduce their wives to "a barren bodily slavery."[49] As McLaren explains, male contraception struck many feminists "as an unnatural practice employed for the benefit of men."[50]

Shield shares this assumption. Prophylactic kits – "preventive appliances and medicinal preparations for the prevention of venereal infection" – are "Wrong Methods of Prophylaxis."[51] Distribution of the kits and instruction in their use encourage men to continue in vice and thereby perpetuate the exploitation of women. The editor recommends that the soldier subordinate his vaunted "sexual instinct" to an ideal – "religious principle, chivalry, loyalty to his wife or to his future wife, a sense of duty to his regiment or to his race."[52] Chastity is the best prophylaxis, and reeducation is the key: "The present state of the streets is the direct expression of our own wrong beliefs. We have the morality we deserve."[53]

In the wake of this reading, Eliot seems to have entertained the possibility that the solution to the problems in the streets and the problems in his own marriage was the same: early marriage, easy divorce, and chastity. He concludes his essay on "Recent British Periodical Literature in Ethics" with a review of the Bhikku Silacara's essay in *Shield*, "Sex-Morality in Burma," summarizing the author's "reasons for the absence of prostitution and irregularity" among the Shan tribes: "he adduces the lack of a pastoral clergy (marriages are civil and can easily be dissolved on reasonable grounds, even on the ground of incompatibility), the example of the Bhikkus, or monks (who apparently practice without preaching), and the simplicity and low cost of living, which render early marriages possible."[54] Eliot accepts that early marriage makes prostitution unnecessary by making early satisfaction of the "sex instinct" possible; recall that he had wandered the streets longing to lose his virginity before marriage. He accepts that easy divorce makes prostitution unnecessary by making remarriage to a compatible mate possible; in 1917, however, Eliot wrote of "the struggle between the desire for happiness and the fact of marriage," declaring the latter "something more than merely a Christian dogma."[55] By 1918, then, Eliot found that only one of these means to a married life beyond "prostitution and irregularity" remained for him: chastity – the chastity modeled by the "celibate" Bhikku.[56]

The abstinence recommended by feminists like Pankhurst and the celibacy practised and preached by the Bhikku Silacara are part of the asceticism introduced by allusions to Augustine and the Buddha at the conclusion of Part III of *The Waste Land*. According to Eliot, "[t]he collocation of these two representatives of eastern and western asceticism . . . is not an accident"; neither is the collocation of themes regarding eugenics, prostitution, venereal disease, celibacy, and asceticism (*CPP* p. 79). They are all part of the complex response to the turn-of-the-century perception of the fatality latent in irresponsible behavior with regard to human fertility.

Correspondence about chastity and venereal disease in *The Egoist* (the just renamed *Freewoman*) reveals the inter-implication of these issues in 1914. Dora Marsden reviews Christabel Pankhurst's *The Great Scourge*, complaining that her "disease-story is overdone": "there is more danger to 'health' to be awaited from the misery of renunciation and the dull heats of virginity than from the ills of syphilis and gonorrhoea." To Pankhurst's claim that "[t]here can be no mating between the spiritually-developed women of this new day and the men who in thought or in conduct with regard to sex affairs are their inferiors," Marsden rejoins that mating is a question of the power of attraction: "the vision of 'suitors' with aspect as wholesome as sound field-turnips each having a doctor's certificate in his pockets is powerfully unalluring."[57] A correspondent agrees: "Let us continue to treat men and women as human beings and not as steam rollers, sewing machines, or problems in Algebra."[58]

Marsden expresses the Bergsonian optimism that "[t]here *can* be no disease of 'matter'. . . There can only be such a breaking down of the spiritual unitary stream as to render it incapable of penetrating the material which it has assimilated and organised into a body."[59] Others simply assume that "we will some day outgrow syphilis."[60] In each case, optimism is founded on the expectation that attitudes and behavior can be changed. Beebon and Noel Teulon Porter argue that acknowledgment by both sexes of a woman's sexual desires will "reduce that huge army of married men who seek for that physical passion in the street which they cannot find at home," and will thereby reduce the cases of "post-nuptial syphilis in men, from whom their wives to-day receive the contagion, and from whom in turn their children inherit or receive it."[61] Alternatively, a tough-minded eugenical perspective might allow us to outgrow our fear of prostitution. As one correspondent argues, since the desire of the unfit to mate with the fit is presently contained within the institution of prostitution, freer access to prostitution would mean that the unfit "would hardly have any children."[62]

Others agreed with Marsden that one ought not to confuse health and morality: "Miss Pankhurst's book is remarkable for the fact that she scarcely alleges any motive for chastity except the avoidance of venereal disease."[63] A correspondent from British Columbia writes to observe that Pankhurst "has vulgarised chastity" and "managed to bring the whole subject into a mundane and utilitarian atmosphere."[64] This is Eliot's point: prudence ought not to be confused with morality.

Yet utilitarian chastity had its defenders. One correspondent objects to Marsden's depiction of "married women [as] being on the level of prostitutes": "My knowledge of married women leads me to believe that they attach a great deal less importance to the sexual act than the freewoman does. . . The women who seriously object to the sexual act or to preventive measures generally contrive, after they have had a child or two, to live in married celibacy; there are quantities who do." The "real fondness and loyalty for their husbands" that these women have means that they are not prostitutes.[65] The Teulon Porters celebrate "asceticism and chastity, and their beneficial functions in life."[66] A correspondent argues that "a portion of humanity has arrived at that stage in which the spiritual part of them rules and limits those bodily desires in question . . . The vital powers of the body. . . are capable of being utilised for the good of the body, by a process of will-power." Although prostitution will remain "until men cease to demand the satisfaction of animal appetite at the expense of a woman's body and soul," women undoubtedly "possess powers of love infinitely greater than a man's, that can turn them into nobly-striving women, worthy to perpetuate their kind." Only when this latent power is "thwarted or sunk" do women "sink from occasional animal satisfactions into complete prostitution."[67] Expressed as chastity, willpower can eugenically elevate the vital powers of the species.

The impact of popular debates like this one on the understanding of asceticism's eugenical role in the modern world is evident in Jane Harrison's conception of asceticism as a modern religion in *Epilegomena to the Study of Greek Religion* (1921). Assuming the same Bergsonism evident in Marsden's criticism of chastity, Harrison argues that theology in general and asceticism in particular have a "biological function":

The function of theology is to keep the conflict that would be submerged in the sphere of the conscious and prevent its development into a mischievous subliminal complex. . . Probably but for its aid man long before he developed sufficient reason to adapt himself to his environment must have gone under. . . Physical life once secured by civilization and the general advance of science, religion turns not to the impulsion of life but to its betterment, and the betterment of life involves asceticism.

Harrison regards asceticism as "the setting of the will towards what Bergson calls the 'ascending wave' of the *élan vital* against the descending wave which he calls matter." As for Eliot, so for Harrison – the body is not as important as the soul ("Asceticism is the setting out of the soul towards the higher value"), but neither is it to be neglected (asceticism is "not the mortification of the flesh," but "the attuning of an instrument"): asceticism includes eugenics.[68]

The asceticism of Part III of *The Waste Land* is thus part of a much wider story of potentially fatal fertility. As we have noted, this story includes Eliot's declarations of celibacy in "Ode" and "Gerontion." In *The Waste Land*, this celibacy is performed by the Tom-figure "in rat's alley" who declines all invitations to sexual intimacy by his female partner, the Viv-figure. Depicting a man's determined withdrawal from conjugal relations after suggesting that "still the world pursues" sexual violence against women, Eliot presents the man as to some extent a version of the ascetic feminist hero.

McLaren presents "[f]eminist demands for an ascetic if not celibate life" and feminist "suspicions of and hostility toward artificial means of fertility control" as "a logical if extreme response to the outrageous demands made for women's compliance to the sexual inclinations of men and the manipulative manner with which fertility was discussed by the eugenically-minded."[69] According to Ellis Ethelmer, asceticism is the only solution to the problems that arise from man's having "rudely forced" women – menstruation being the most noticeable "sign of his misdeed." Assuming a Lamarckian perspective, Ethelmer argues that menstruation is "an acquired painful consequence" of "forced sexual abuse"; a "last abhorrent trace" of woman's subjection to man, menstruation will disappear in the "rectification or reduction to pristine normality" that the cessation of "*masculine* excess or abuse" will entail.[70]

From a feminist point of view such as Ethelmer's, Eliot's "Succuba" has been eviscerated by her partner and Mrs. Porter has been infected by a limping man. The man who has lost his interest in sex is infinitely preferable. In terms of the copular genealogy implied in the first verse paragraph of Part II of *The Waste Land*, such a man is no Tereus, forcing himself upon Philomel; no Adam, for whom Eve is created; no Aeneas, for whom Dido is a distraction on his way to found Rome. The speaker declares such narratives the "withered stumps of time" – anticipating the man's declaration of emasculation in "rat's alley / Where the dead men lost their bones" (*CPP* pp. 64–65). This man is so far from an Albert imposing his "sexual instinct" upon Lil that he creates – albeit by neglect – the sexual preconditions for his partner's emancipation. Whether because she is morally insane or because she is culturally conditioned by the stories "told upon the walls" about how "the world pursues" women, however, this particular woman so prefers her role as prostitute that she threatens to "walk the street" (*CPP* pp. 64–65). No more than Albert or Lil's gossiping friend can she comprehend the recommendation of Augustine, the Buddha, the Bhikku Silacara, and a whole host of feminists that the way forward is through asceticism.

The eugenical dimension of such asceticism is depicted in Lil. She is as much of an ascetic as the Tom-figure who refuses intimacy with his partner – as much of an ascetic as the initial speaker in the poem who resists the world's call to regeneration, as the man in the hyacinth garden who glimpses the "heart of light" through failure to respond to the sexual allure of "the hyacinth girl," and as the Augustine–Buddha figure who believes that the Lord plucks him out of this world. Like them, she refuses to participate in the burning world of regeneration (inducing an abortion with "them pills"), she refuses to make herself "a bit smart" and thereby make Albert burn with desire for her, and she refuses all the other demands of the burning world put to her by her gossiping friend.

On the one hand, this pragmatic asceticism is a version of the strategic "frigidity" by which Victorian women achieved periods of abstinence within a marriage regarded by the husband (and society itself) as a mandate for sexual license ("What you get married for if you don't want children?") (*CPP* p. 66).[71] Lil's asceticism is perhaps a feminist attempt to take control of her own fertility. On the other hand, her asceticism is set in a context fraught with eugenical significance. As a breeder, the Cockney Lil is prolific – "She's had five already" – and as such is typical of her class, according to eugenists. The Alberts and Lils of the world are responsible for the differential birthrate that will lead to national degeneration. Ironically, however, Lil also represents another national danger, for the abortion that she induces is also typical of her class – and as such it threatens an industrial nation with the depopulation of its working class.

The Report of the National Birth-Rate Commission alerted Eliot to the "problem" of abortion amongst the working class: "there is good reason to think that, in addition to other means of limitation, the illegal induction of abortion frequently occurs among the industrial population." Eliot even finds "them pills" in the Report, which notes "the injurious effect of lead compounds . . . used to procure abortion" and "recommends they should be scheduled as poisons and only dispensed on a medical prescription."[72] Concerned to arrest the decline in the birthrate, the Commission met "a deputation of manufacturers to discuss the best means of checking the sale of a widely-known abortificient."[73]

From the Commission's point of view, Lil is wrong to have contributed to the decline in the birthrate. Eliot, however, regards quality as more important than quantity. Apparently interested like Darwin in "encouraging reproduction on the part of the best classes in the community, and . . . discouraging reproduction on the part of the incompetent, thriftless and pauper element," he implies that Lil has had enough children (she "nearly died of young George") and that she is right to have determined to have no more (whether or not her chosen means of birth control is proper).

Sympathetic to Lil, Eliot is not nearly so understanding of the middle-class couple introduced at the beginning of Part ii. The Commission notes that "[c]onscious limitation of fertility is widely practiced among the middle and upper classes."[74] The "gossip of the market- place" was that this "volitional and deliberative act" was in part the result of a desire that "the parents would have more freedom, more 'enjoyment of life.'"[75] Eliot implies disapproval. If the couple in question has chosen childlessness out of a selfish desire for more "enjoyment of life," they have made a mistake, for they have achieved only boredom: "What shall we do tomorrow? / What shall we ever do?" (*CPP* p. 65).

This boredom is a greater threat to the nation than either the differential birthrate or abortion. Later in the poem, the boredom that is a *consequence* of childlessness is reintroduced as a *cause* of childlessness. The sexual relationship between the typist and "young man carbuncular" is a function of such boredom. Because "she is bored," the typist does not defend herself against the young man's sexual "assault." She is "the human engine," "Like a taxi throbbing waiting" for the young man. "Hardly aware," with but "one half-formed thought," she is the automaton, who "smoothes her hair with automatic hand, / And puts a record on the gramophone" (*CPP* p. 68–69). Her "squalid food," cramped quarters, and "false / Japanese print" identify the typist as a member of the lower class aspiring toward the middle class (*WLF* p. 45). In an essay written at the same time as *The Waste Land*, Eliot glosses the question of class and eugenics that this scene in the poem veils:

The lower classes still exist; but perhaps they will not exist for long. . . With the dwindling of the music-hall, by the encouragement of the cheap and rapid-breeding cinema, the lower classes will tend to drop into the same state of amorphous protoplasm as the bourgeoisie. The working-man . . . will now go to the cinema, where his mind is lulled by continuous senseless music and continuous action too rapid for the brain to act upon, and he will receive, without giving, in that same listless apathy with which the middle and upper classes regard any entertainment of the nature of art. He will also have lost some of his interest in life. Perhaps this is the only solution.[76]

The "solution" to which Eliot refers is at the very least massive depopulation – perhaps race suicide:

In . . . *Essays on the Depopulation of Melanesia* the great psychologist W. H. R. Rivers adduces evidence which has led him to believe that the natives of that unfortunate archipelago are dying out principally for the reason that the "Civilization" forced upon them has deprived them of all interest in life. They are dying from pure boredom. When every theatre has been replaced by 100 cinemas, when every musical instrument has been replaced by 100 gramophones, when every horse has been replaced by 100 cheap motor cars, . . .when applied science has done everything possible with the materials on this earth to make life as interesting as possible, it will not be surprising if the population of the entire civilized world rapidly follows the fate of the Melanesians.[77]

Eliot's image of the typist as an apathetic, bored "Taxi" awaiting her passenger confirms that she is presented as evidence of this threat to the lower classes – "that part of the English nation which has perhaps the greatest vitality and interest" but which is now on the verge of succumbing to the depopulating threat represented by the hegemony of the middle class.[78]

The typist's profession is also a sign of depopulation, for Bertrand Russell's eugenical essay "Marriage and the Population Question" – an essay Eliot is likely to have read, for it appeared in *The International Journal of Ethics* shortly after he became a contributor to this journal and it was immediately reviewed in an issue of *The Eugenics Review* that he read – defines typists as typical of the childless women that the combination of woman's emancipation and old-fashioned morality was ostensibly creating.[79] On the one hand, "[m]ore and more, women find motherhood unsatisfying, not what their needs demand." On the other hand, the moral code's disapproval of sexual intercourse outside of marriage imposes "clandestine and childless" relations upon unmarried women: "These women, though not debarred in practice from relations with men, are debarred by the code from having children. In this class are to be found an enormous and increasing number of women who earn their own living as typists, in shops, or otherwise." The result is a "sterilizing of the best parts of the population." The note about the typist in Pierre Leyris's French translation of *The Waste Land* (Eliot, John Hayward, and Leyris cooperated in the production of the translation and new notes) implies a similar conclusion in describing the intercourse between the typist and the young man as an example of "*L''amour' stérile de la civilization urbaine moderne*" (the sterile love of modern urban civilization).[80]

Russell wryly notes, however, that unless society's attitude toward marriage and population changes, this aspect of the depopulation problem will produce its own solution:

Women who have mental interests, who care about art or literature or politics, who desire a career or who value their liberty, will gradually grow rarer, and be more and more replaced by a placid maternal type which has no interest outside the home and no dislike of the burden of motherhood. This result, which ages of masculine domination have vainly striven to achieve, is likely to be the final outcome of women's emancipation.[81]

In developing this emancipated, upwardly-mobile, depopulating typist for *The Waste Land*, Eliot depicts by means of her "indifference" to the clerk's "assault," and the only "half-formed thought" that follows it, the very "placid" inheritance that Russell anticipates as her dysgenically enslaving legacy.

Through such images and ideas, Eliot manages to present himself as a potential eugenical hero: he is a member of the middle class in question, but he recognizes the "vitality and interest" of the lower class. He observes that "[i]n the music-hall comedians [the lower classes] find the artistic expression and dignity of their own lives."[82] Having been introduced to the music hall by Vivien in 1915, Eliot is proud to have been a member of the "audiences in England, and especially Cockney London, who had crowded to hear" Marie Lloyd.[83] He had also seen Nellie Wallace, Little Tich, and George Robey. The Tom-figure in *The Waste Land*, however, has not been to the music hall. He is stranded in his class by more than the typographical gap that separates him from the Cockney culture represented in the concluding section of Part II, for he attends only the middle-class revue – where he has heard the "Shakespeherian Rag" from Ziegfield's follies. Whereas the music hall represents the "artistic expression and dignity" of lower-class lives, "this is not found for any life in the most elaborate and expensive revue."[84]

Thus, even before the death of Marie Lloyd late in 1922, Eliot presents the music hall as something missing: it pervades the poem as an absence. As Southam points out, "[t]he original *Waste Land* opened with the monologue of a music hall rake." The speaker mentions Boston music-halls and early twentieth-century music-hall songs by name. Similarly, Southam suggests that "the cockney dialogue of the pub scene . . . may also come from the music-hall background."[85] Certainly the last line of this section does, for Eliot conflates Ophelia's "Good night, ladies" speech with the ubiquitous music-hall song "Good Night Ladies." Furthermore, John Hayward – drawing attention to Eliot's extensive repertoire of music-hall songs – suggests that the reference to Brighton's Metropole hotel derives from a George Robey song.[86] Such songs are all instances of the lower-class "music" in "The Fire Sermon" – especially "The pleasant whining of a mandoline" – that recalls the sense of community under threat in the modern "City" (*CPP* p. 69). Eliot works in the "City," but the apparently working-class mandoline accompanying the "clatter and chatter" in the world of "fishmen" is the instrument that Vivien gave him for his birthday in 1921, confirming Eliot's identification with the music of the lower classes (*CPP* p. 69).

Furthermore, the greatest threat to the music hall – the cinema – appears in the early drafts of the poem in the very terms of Eliot's critique of class, culture, and eugenics. Just as Aeneas recognizes his mother's divinity "by her smooth celestial pace," "So the close rabble in the cinema / Identify a goddess or a star." Like the middle class, the "sweating" "millions" of the lower class are passive before "the screen" and "In silent rapture worship from afar." Eliot's conclusion – "Thus art ennobles even wealth and birth, / And breeding raises prostrate art from earth" – is heavy with irony

(*WLF* p. 29). While the art of Virgil and the breeding of Venus may raise and ennoble, their modern analogues – cinema as "art" and the sweaty "breeding" millions – merely debase.

The music hall was threatened by more than the cinema and gramophone, however, for it had also become a prime site for prostitution. In an issue of *Shield* that Eliot read, John Cowen suggested that "[i]n London the principal prostitution markets are either in the music hall or in the street. . . It is difficult in a few words to convey a sense of the suitability of the music hall as a prostitution mart." The man who attends the music hall is tempted on all sides: "Sexual vice meets him on the stairs, sits beside him in the stalls, walks in front of him in the promenade; it is suggested by those around him, hinted at not obscurely on the stage; it surrounds him, pervades the air he breathes, stares him in the face."[87]

This dimension of the music-hall experience is also acknowledged in the poem. In each case, the music hall – whether American or English – is associated with prostitution. "Get me a woman" says the guy fresh from "the show" (*WLF* p. 5). Ophelia's song is the result of Hamlet's accusing her of being a whore and dismissing her to a "nunnery" or brothel, and Lil must compete with the "many" "Other girls" who will give Albert the "good time" he wants. Furthermore, "a weekend at the Metropole" derives from the phrase "a weekend at Brighton" – as Southam points out, a phrase "understood colloquially as an invitation carrying sexual implications."[88]

In 1922, the future of the music hall – and the future of lower-class culture – is under threat. The death of Marie Lloyd brings this threat home to Eliot: "You will see that the death of Marie Lloyd has had a depressing effect, and that I am quite incapable of taking any interest in any literary events in England in the last two months, if any have taken place."[89] Eliot identifies himself with the working man and the Melanesian: "incapable of taking any interest in any literary events," he is the working-man who has "lost some of his interest in life" and the Melanesian "deprived . . . of all interest in life." He is possessed of the "same listless apathy with which the middle and upper classes regard any entertainment of the nature of art." This middle-class apathy affects not only the poem's Tom-figure – bored by his recollection of "The Shakespeherian Rag" – but also the poem's author, for in dismissing as uninteresting the literary events in England of the last two months, Eliot also dismisses the just-published *Waste Land*.

Race suicide, it seems, will be both cultural and biological: "rapid-breeding cinema" culture will lead "rapidly" to the biological consequence of depopulation. Thus Eliot's observations two years later on reviewing F. W. Gamble's essay "Construction and Control in Animal Life": he notes that Gamble "begins with the arresting observation that 'zoological problems have become problems of control, and control, from implying mere restraint, has come to mean "quickening"'" and then applies "his conclusions to human civilization." Eliot's interest is piqued by the resemblance between Gamble's views and his own:

Bearing in mind his first statement, we read that "life under dominance (i.e. highly developed control) tends to exhaustion, whereas isolation leads to the renewal of activity at a lower level of complexity," and "in so far as isolation leads to greater 'individuation,' we may look to the isolated as the source of fresh individuality and power to wield dominance, to be paid for in time, however, with the inevitable price of diminished progress."

Eliot's conclusion – "We do not know what other zoologists say to this, but it looks as if one distinguished authority thought that a uniform civilization, in which the same films would be produced in every cinema of the world, was hardly a prospect to be desired" – has the effect of an "I told you so" and confirms that for Eliot the spectre of depopulation is no mere metaphor.[90]

The early drafts of *The Waste Land* anticipate his "Marie Lloyd" essay's image of human beings as regressing toward the state of "amorphous protoplasm" and this "Commentary" fear that the modern world is on the verge of biological "exhaustion." The typist in particular and Londoners in general represent primitive forms of life. Watching the typist and the young man, Tiresias foreknows "the manner of these crawling bugs" (*WLF* p. 33). London swarms with such bugs – or perhaps an even less evolved form of life:

> London, the swarming life you kill and breed,
> Huddled between the concrete and the sky;
> Responsive to the momentary need,
> Vibrates unconscious to its formal destiny.   (*WLF* p. 31)

Such images of regression from the biological status of human being figure the phenomenon of depopulation or race suicide that Eliot fears may be "the only solution" to the problem of regression from the cultural level that human being has achieved.

The imagery of biological regression in *The Waste Land* also functions in coordination with the assumption that human biological development recapitulates the history of the race – a lesson taught by MacBride, who emphasizes this aspect of animal development as a way of demonstrating his Lamarckian thesis about "the nature and mechanism of heredity." His interest is in the larval stage of development, intermediate between embryo and adult. Even "the small boy can be justly characterised as a human larva, for in body, but still more in mind, he is different from the adult." MacBride's attention is drawn by certain larvae that "are unquestionably reproductions of a former state of the race to which the parents belong." Like other fish, young flat-fish have eyes on both sides of their bodies; adult flat-fish, however, have eyes on the top side only. Like other bivalve molluscs, young American oysters possess a foot for locomotion; the adult does not. The marine animal known as the feather-star, MacBride points out, "has no stalk when adult and possesses the power of swimming from place to place, but when it is young it is rooted to the bottom by a stalk exactly like its fossil relatives." MacBride concludes that "[i]n the case of these larvae we may say that the life history 'recapitulates' the history of the race," a phenomenon that he explains as follows: "when an animal changed its mode of life . . . this usually happened at adolescence, and the new structures which were at first acquired as a reaction to the environment became, in course of time, so fixed in the animal's constitution that they appeared at progressively earlier periods in the life history and eventually independently of the environment at all." The phenomenon of "recapitulation" therefore "elucidate[s] the laws of heredity."[91]

That Eliot accepted MacBride's Lamarckian hypothesis in general is clear from his *IJE* essay. That he recalled this particular argument in support of the hypothesis is clear from the early drafts of *The Waste Land*. MacBride writes that a critic

might maintain that we have no proof that the ancestors of the flat-fish ever were like ordinary fish, or that the ancestors of the oyster ever burrowed, or, finally, that those of the feather-star were ever permanently fixed. The only conclusive proof would be furnished if some angelic recorder had watched the transformation slowly proceeding, and had left a duly attested account of the whole thing.[92]

Eliot borrows both the image of the observing eye and the idea that the "formal destiny" of evolutionary change is not evident to the life that participates in the "transformation": "swarming life . . . /

Vibrates unconscious to its formal destiny . . . / But lives in the transformations of the observant eye" (*WLF* p. 31). Like MacBride, Eliot implies that only the angelic eye can recognise the biological destiny implicit in changes of form and that only such an eye can see in distinct forms evidence of a continuous living process. MacBride's "angelic recorder" and Eliot's "observant eye" are themselves transformed into the Darwinian anthropologist in "The Beating of a Drum," where Eliot recalls MacBride's interest in the "recapitulatory element in development" when suggesting that Darwinism teaches that "the *nature* of the finished product . . . is essentially present in the crude forerunner."

In imagery suggesting biological regression, Eliot is making a point about the moral regression of modern human beings. Human development has become stunted at the larval stage – different from the adult stage "in body, but still more in mind." The inhabitant of the modern world is like Fresca – "Not quite an adult, and still less a child" (*WLF* p. 27). Or like Phlebas, who – undone in "the whirlpool" of physical disintegration – also regresses via the whirlpool of "recapitulation," for he has "passed the stages of his age and youth" (*CPP* p. 71). The images of crawling bugs, swarming life, and larval immaturity suggest a double problem: on the one hand, modern human beings have been arrested prematurely in their individual development; on the other hand, human culture as a whole is regressing.

The implications of this arrest in the larval stage of development are explained in contemporaneous essays. To E. B. Osborn's claim that "[y]outh knows more about the young than old age or middle age," Eliot replies that "[i]f this were so, civilization would be impossible, experience worthless."[93] His sense of the regressiveness involved in the worship of youth and adolescence is evident in his comparison of George Herbert and Henry Vaughan: "the emotion of Herbert is clear, definite, mature, and sustained; whereas the emotion of Vaughan is vague, adolescent, fitful, and retrogressive."[94] He hopes that "an exasperated generation may find . . . maturity as interesting as adolescence."[95] Our very status as human beings hangs in the balance: "what distinguishes the relations of man and woman from the copulation of beasts is the knowledge of Good and Evil . . . [T]he sexual act as evil is more dignified, less boring, than as the natural, 'life-giving,' cheery automatism of the modern world. . . So far as we are human, what we do must be either evil or good."[96] So much for the "bored," "automatic" typist. Such immature crawling, swarming inhabitants of the modern world represent a biological and moral "Peter-Pantheism" that Eliot abhors.[97] And yet the human regression – perhaps extinction – that they instance may be "the only solution."

Eliot's depiction of the hermaphroditic Tiresias is also involved in *The Waste Land*'s rumination on MacBride's Lamarckian conception of the mechanism of heredity. Recall that MacBride offers the example of hormones as a way of explaining chemically how acquired characteristics can become hereditary. He dwells in particular on "the inheritance of sex," pointing out that recent research has

assumed that the sexual cells . . . acquired their specific character through their power of absorbing sexual substances from the blood. These substances are termed *hormones*, and we may make the further supposition that a considerable amount of such hormones must be absorbed before they are able to affect . . . development, and consequently an exposure of many generations may be necessary before their influence becomes . . . engrained in the constitution of the animal.[98]

In introducing readers to the power of hormones, MacBride offers "evidence in support of the contention that maleness and femaleness are potentially present in both sexes" – that "there is in the human race no such thing as a completely male or a completely female organism. Every man possesses some traces of female characteristics, and every woman some male features."[99] It is all a matter of hormones, sexual characteristics depending on the balance of male and female substances in the blood. The proportions of the mixture vary infinitely, and hermaphroditism is always a possibility should the usual balances in men and women become dramatically imbalanced.

MacBride's account of the dramatic role of hormones in the chemical mechanism by which he imagines acquired character in general and sex in particular to be inherited may have been brought back to mind by the Eliots' apparent interest at this time in the role of hormones in Vivien's illnesses. Six months after completing *The Waste Land*, Eliot met Pound in Italy and discussed with him the possibility that Vivien's problems were glandular. In subsequent correspondence with Pound, Eliot reveals that he has been reading *The Glands Regulating Personality: A Study of the Glands of Internal Secretion in Relation to the Types of Human Nature* (1921) by Louis Berman, America's leading expert on hormones.[100] Apparently a friend of Pound's, Berman interests Eliot greatly: "I shall be glad to have a conversation with Berman if he arrives in this country"; "Ask him does he know a man named [Lancelot Thomas] Hogben who is writing a book on hormones, in England."[101] Eliot's interest in glands and hormones in general – if not his interest in Berman and Hogben in particular – presumably dates from before this time, for Vivien (finally encountering a specialist in June of 1922 who "mentioned glands as being the probable cause" of some of her troubles) confesses to Pound: "I must say I have often thought of this as a possibility myself."[102] It is likely that the Eliots had discussed the possibility that Vivien's illnesses were hormonal long before Eliot and Pound discussed the matter in Italy, *and* that Eliot initiated the discussion of glands at this time – to be pleasantly surprised by Pound's familiarity with Berman's work.

Thus Tiresias is more than a literary device "uniting" all the characters, such that "Just as the one-eyed merchant . . . melts into the Phoenician sailor, and the latter is not wholly distinct from Ferdinand Prince of Naples, so all the women are one woman, and the two sexes meet in Tiresias." According to Eliot, "[t]he whole passage from Ovid" explaining the history of Tiresias's hermaphroditic experience "is of great anthropological interest" (*CPP* p. 78). Eliot finds in the myth a version of MacBride's biological fact: "maleness and femaleness are potentially present in both sexes." Eliot's interpretation of Tiresias as biological hermaphrodite – "Old man with wrinkled female breasts" – implies that he interprets the myth anthropologically not as an account of sex-change (according to which Tiresias is *either* male *or* female) but as an account of hermaphroditic experience (according to which Tiresias is *both* male *and* female). Tiresias "blind" seer is also Hermaphroditus "throbbing between two lives" (*CPP* p. 68).

Tiresias is oppressed by the sameness of a repetitive history: he "Perceived the scene, and foretold the rest." This is a "scene" that he "can see." For Tiresias, history has become cinema. The stories "told upon the walls" in "A Game of Chess" similarly transform history into a projection onto a cinema screen. And the cinema that is contemporary culture is showing the same old film: "still the world pursues" a destructive relationship between men and women. Thus "civilization" has become "uniform," with "the same films . . .

produced in every cinema in the world." Thus the apathy, the boredom, and the loss of interest in life that are evident in the bedroom couple, Lil, the typist, and Tiresias. According to Eliot, this is the mood that eventuates in depopulation.

Tiresias is a figure for the biological exhaustion that grips the world. He is impotent because old. Female "breasts" and "dugs" are wrinkled: the childbearing years are past. Similarly, insofar as Tiresias is all men, he is not all man: the wrinkled state of his male genitalia is suggested by the image of the dead men "who lost their bones" and by the phallic description of the culture's stories of man's pursuit of woman as "the withered stumps of time." Tiresias is also impotent as hermaphrodite – whether young or old – for Ovid presents Hermaphroditus as "but half a man . . . enfeebled . . . weak and effeminate." Hermaphroditism is debilitation, a curse perpetuated by the "infected" waters of the pool in which Hermaphroditus bathed.[103]

Yet Tiresias also figures biological potential. However blasted in body or bored in mind by the repetitive assaults of history, Tiresias is a sign that despite the regressive tendencies of the modern world the story of human biology is not over. On the one hand, long before Ovid's pathologizing of hermaphroditism, hermaphrodeism was popular in the cultures of the eastern Mediterranean: the union in one being of the two principles of generation was worshiped as a sign of great fertility. On the other hand, according to MacBride, the hormones that have made such a person the sexually ambiguous human being that he is also have the power to make something else of human being itself. That is, according to MacBride's version of Lamarckism, something new in the way of human character can always be acquired and can become hereditary by means of the action of hormones.

This is how depopulation can be a "solution." It represents the possibility of wiping the slate clean. The end of one process of development can become the beginning of another. The "inevitable price," in the terms that Eliot borrows from Gamble, is "diminished progress," but the benefit is "fresh individuality and power" – an individuality and power that will be grounded in biological "isolation," for evolution occurs most rapidly in biologically isolated populations. Eliot comes to see an example of this evolutionary progress in the "inexhaustible . . . verse form" of the eccentric Ezra Pound: "in form he foreran, excelled, and is still in advance of our own generation and even the literary generation after us" – all because of "his complete and isolated superiority."[104] The concluding lines of *The Waste Land* anticipate both the biological argument to be articulated by Gamble and the cultural example to be provided by Pound ("*il miglior fabbro*"): the speaker is isolated culturally in the literary fragments shored against his ruins and isolated biologically as ascetic – waiting for the time to be propitious for the renewal of human being (*CPP* p. 59). Inflected by a Christianity not necessarily present in the concluding lines of *The Waste Land*, the same argument concludes "Thoughts After Lambeth" (1931): "The World is trying the experiment of attempting to form a civilized but non-Christian mentality. The experiment will fail; but we must be very patient in awaiting its collapse; meanwhile redeeming the time: so that the Faith may be preserved alive through the dark ages before us; to renew and rebuild civilization, and save the World from suicide."[105] Patience in the midst of the fragments and ruins of collapse will allow those few who stand against the modern world to renew human being – both culturally and biologically. The depopulation brought about by a new dark age will not only stop short of race suicide but will actually function eugenically so long as there is a biological and cultural reserve of "isolated superiority."

CHAPTER 7

The late eugenics of W. B. Yeats

To judge by the story of Yeats and eugenics told by several scholars, chief among them Elizabeth Cullingford, Paul Scott Stanfield, and David Bradshaw, Yeats was the last of the three writers I discuss to engage with eugenical discourse in a serious way.[1] Although acknowledging Yeats's longstanding concerns about degeneration, they agree that he becomes a full-blown eugenist only in the 1930s. In acknowledgment of this consensus, I have postponed consideration of the eugenical Yeats until after having aired the question of the eugenical interests of Woolf and Eliot – interests dating from much earlier in the century. My suggestion, however, is that Yeats was not the last of these writers to become interested in eugenics, but the first.

There can be no doubt about Yeats's interest in eugenics in the late 1930s. In *On the Boiler* (1939), his most explicitly eugenical work, Yeats pulls no punches. What he calls the "mob" does not need to know how to read and write: "Forcing reading and writing on those who wanted neither was the worst part of the violence which for two centuries has been creating that hell wherein we suffer."[2] Educate instead the descendents of the Ministers of the Treaty Government, for they, "if they grow rich enough for the travel and leisure that make a finished man, will constitute our ruling class . . . They have already intermarried, able stocks have begun to appear, and recent statistics have shown that men of talent are everywhere much linked through marriage and descent." Yeats's "if" here is no concession to the "environmentalists": "As intelligence and freedom from bodily defect increase, wealth increases in exact measure." The "if" merely acknowledges occasional exceptions to the rule, for "in every country the statistics work out the same average" (*Ex* pp. 413, 422, 422).

The modern world is degenerating – "visible in the degeneration of literature, newspapers, amusements" – because humankind is degenerating: "Since about 1900 the better stocks have not been

replacing their numbers, while the stupider and less healthy have
been more than replacing theirs." As we have seen, Yeats anticipates
"a prolonged civil war" brought about by "the multiplication of the
uneducatable masses" and hopes for "the victory of the skilful, riding
their machines as did the feudal knights their armoured horses."
Indeed, "[t]he danger is that there will be no war, that the skilled will
attempt nothing, that the European civilization, like those older
civilizations that saw the triumph of their gangrel stocks, will accept
decay." And so, "sooner or later we must limit the families of the
unintelligent classes" (*Ex* pp. 423, 425, 425, 426).

Yet even in these classes resides an ability that Ireland must not
waste: "Among those our civilization must reject . . . exist precious
faculties. . . I have noticed that clairvoyance, prevision, and allied
gifts, rare among the educated classes, are common among peasants." Any Irishness worth saving will depend on a eugenics
attentive to these faculties: "we must hold to what we have that the
next civilization may be born . . . These gifts must return . . .
Eugenical and psychical research are the revolutionary movements
with that element of novelty and sensation which sooner or later stir
men to action. It may be, or it must be, that the best bred from the
best shall claim again their ancient omens." This psychical genius is a
racial genius dependent upon biological genius: "We should count
men and women who pick, as it were, the dam or sire of a Derby
winner from between the shafts of a cab, among persons of genius, for
this genius makes all other kinds possible" (*Ex* pp. 436–37, 437, 430).

In *Purgatory* (1938), Yeats condemns the opposite of this biological
genius by means of similar horse-breeding imagery. Here the "grand-
dam" equivalent of the Derby winner – the lady of an ancient
household – picks badly. In what her son calls "a capital offence" she
marries "a groom in a training stable." In terms of Yeats's farmyard
eugenical symbols, this groom is her "horse at the Curragh" whose
"hoof-beats" torment their son. Implicitly a Derby winner who has
picked a cab-horse, this woman makes a dysgenical choice that
causes the bloodline for which she is responsible to degenerate.[3] The
mother's sin against eugenics is visited on the generations that follow.

Among the first to give serious attention to Yeats's interest in
eugenics, Cullingford is the most forgiving. In *Yeats, Ireland and
Fascism*, she suggests that Yeats's eugenics is "a desperate reassertion
of the potency of quality" in the face of the triumph of quantity via

"the windmills of the modern world, mass man and mass media."
On the one hand, she argues that Yeats first raises real problems (for
instance, Catholic Ireland needed a birth-control policy – if not
necessarily a eugenic one) but then obscures such issues by an
"unfortunate tone" and "repellant" "stridency." On the other hand,
"*On the Boiler* represents only one side of the aged Yeats" – a side that
even he did not necessarily take seriously. Thus she finds that "the
frenetic tone of *On the Boiler* suggests a man trying to convince himself
as well as his audience." In the end, although "Yeats was playing
with theories which in other hands were to have terrible applica-
tions," his "version of eugenic theory owes little to ideas about
breeding Aryan supermen, much to the Irish passion for breeding
race-horses."[4]

She judges Yeats more harshly in *Gender and History in Yeats's Love
Poetry*, in part because his eugenics is misogynistic. Here she condemns Yeats's "Eugenic racehorse rhetoric" in "A Bronze Head"
(1939) – where Maud Gonne, once "at the starting-post, all sleek and
new," is now imagined looking "with a sterner eye . . . / On this foul
world in its decline and fall; / On gangling stocks grown great, great
stocks run dry." This rhetoric "reinforces the vulgar stereotype of the
woman as nervous thoroughbred filly." Furthermore, the poem is "a
poetic betrayal" because of Yeats's "poetic implication of Gonne in
his eugenic program" – belying the fact that "[s]he was interested in
Hitler's Germany, as were numerous Irish people, not for eugenic but
for nationalist reasons."[5] As I will argue in the following chapters,
however, whether in the case of Yeats's Irish passion for racehorses or
in the case of Gonne's passion for Irish nationalism, the assumption
that Irishness precludes a hard-line negative eugenics is doubtful.

Stanfield is even more thorough than Cullingford in his survey of
the writing that reflects Yeats's interest in eugenics at this time,
effectively highlighting the eugenical themes in the poetry and plays
of 1938 and 1939. In "The Old Stone Cross" (1938), we learn that
degeneration prevails "Because this age and the next age / Engender
in the ditch" (*Poems* p. 598); "The Statesman's Holiday" (1939)
makes the same point: "Riches drove out rank, / Base drove out the
better blood, / And mind and body shrank" (*Poems* 626). Yeats had
recently encountered the statistics proving his longstanding suspicion
that mind and body were degenerating in Raymond B. Cattell's *The
Fight for our National Intelligence*, to which he refers readers in his notes
to *On the Boiler*.[6] Stanfield aligns Yeats with his persona Mannion in

"Three Songs to the One Burden" (1939).[7] Mannion suggests that because "[t]he common breeds the common" and "[a] lout begets a lout," the solution is to "Throw likely couples into bed, / And knock the others down" – simple and brutal eugenical common sense (*Poems* pp. 605–06). Cullingford implies that Yeats here uses Mannion to expose "by exaggeration the anti-individualist, anti-democratic, class-biased, and racist nature of eugenics." Yeats is not Mannion: "By making him a degenerate descendent of the sea-god Manannan, . . . Yeats ironically undermines his authority."[8] Yet one might also argue the opposite: that Yeats actually designs to align himself with Mannion, for Mannion's blood is about as distant from Manannan's as Yeats's is from that of the Middletons – the eugenic relatives that Yeats celebrates in both "Three Songs to the One Burden" and "Are You Content" (1938). The figure undercut is thus not Mannion, but Yeats, for, as Stanfield points out, "Mannion's purposeful brutality has the advantage" over the "acquiescence" of Yeats's relative Henry Middleton "since the latter has arrived at the point of sterility while the former at least holds the possibility of regeneration."[9] Even so, as Stanfield also notes, Yeats figures his own regenerative antidote to this sterility in the aesthetic solution to degeneration outlined in "Under Ben Bulben" (1939): "Poet and sculptor, do the work . . . / Bring the soul of man to God, / Make him fill the cradles right" (*Poems* p. 638).[10]

In his account of Yeats's eugenics in the late poems and plays, Stanfield argues that in the 1930s "Yeats was not converted to eugenics, but rather found in it a scientific diagnosis of modernity that complemented his own intuitive diagnosis." He notes that as early as the turn of the century, Yeats had *intuited* that modern human beings were degenerating, that better breeding would reverse this trend, and that the family would have to be the mechanism for maintaining or developing a breed superior to the degenerate masses – all points that he would make in *On the Boiler* and the eugenical poems of the late 1930s. His interest in eugenics was therefore a marriage of convenience, and the convenience was to be entirely his: "Yeats was willing to go along with the reasonings and statistics of the eugenists when they proved that modern man was degenerate, but not when they seemed to prove that there remained anywhere a larger residuum of the old heroic stuff than there remained in the Irish aristocrat and the Irish countryman."[11]

Bradshaw's documenting of Yeats's involvement in eugenics is the most thorough. Criticizing Stanfield's suggestion that Yeats was just one of many caught up in the wide appeal of eugenics at this time, noting instead that "by the mid-1930s the eugenics movement had become more polarised and less sure of itself than it was in its Edwardian heyday," he implies that Yeats's late enthusiasm for eugenics is due less to the force of the eugenics movement than to the force of his own eugenical convictions. Not only did "the alarmist, hereditarian eugenics promoted in *On the Boiler*" strikingly deviate "from the attitudes and approach which were concurrently being espoused by [C. P.] Blacker and other influential figures in the Eugenics Society," but "the stridency of the initial formulation of his views outdid even Cattell's lurid prognostications in places."[12]

Bradshaw's work reveals Yeats's interactions with Cattell, Blacker, and other members of the Eugenics Society. We now know when Yeats joined the Eugenics Society, when he read *The Fight for our National Intelligence*, what back issues of *The Eugenics Review* interested him and why, what debates interested him so much as to lead to correspondence with Blacker, and so on. Especially interesting is Bradshaw's revelation that Yeats asked Blacker to send him copies of C. J. Bond's 1928 Galton Lecture ("Causes of Racial Decay") and R. A. Fisher's 1926 essay "Problem of the Decay of Civilization." Citing Bond's recommendation that the unfit be segregated and sterilized, for instance, Bradshaw writes that "[i]t is tempting to suggest that Bond's goal of biological apartheid was at the forefront of Yeats's mind when he commenced writing *Purgatory* shortly afterwards."[13] In Bradshaw's exemplary essay, the emergence of *On the Boiler* from the eugenics movement of the 1930s could not have been better demonstrated.

In fact, all three scholars – whether apologizing for Yeats or condemning him – effectively highlight eugenical dimensions of his work during the late 1930s. Yeats's notorious celebration of embodied experience in his late poems is clearly not an indiscriminate approval of the body. One must remember the warning of "the man in the golden breastplate" in "The Old Stone Cross" (1938):

> Because this age and the next age
> Engender in the ditch,
> No man can know a happy man
> From any passing wretch;
> If Folly link with Elegance
> No man knows which is which. (*Poems* p. 598)

In the concluding stanza, although apparently condemning actors like Laurence Olivier as "lacking music" because they mute the poetry in Shakespeare's lines (believing "it is more human / To shuffle, grunt and groan"), Yeats does not really leave the theme of dysgenical engendering. The "actors" in question who excite Yeats's "spleen" are the degenerate men and women of stanza two who treat reproduction disrespectfully. Whether in the ditch or in a bed, these sexual actors deny the more than human dimension of sexual intercourse. They "shuffle, grunt and groan, / Not knowing what unearthly stuff / Rounds a mighty scene" (*Poems* pp. 598–99). In other words, these sexual actors are not directed by a eugenical ideal. And so, however much, like Eliot, Yeats valued the sacred purpose of life and art, he also, again like Eliot, nonetheless acknowledged that our "unearthly stuff" entails upon poets and their readers alike a special responsibility with regard to the earthly stuff: the embodied human being must strive for the "Profane perfection of mankind" (*Poems* p. 639).

Although the assumption common to these studies is that Yeats's formal discovery of eugenics came late, both Bradshaw and Stanfield draw attention to the eugenics latent in Yeats's "pre-eugenical" writing. Bradshaw, for instance, notes Yeats's complaint in *Estrangement* about "the new ill-breeding of Ireland, which may in a few years destroy all that has given Ireland a distinguished name in the world."[14] Yet he suggests that words like these are merely "the metaphors which he had deployed in his vilification of Edwardian Ireland" – metaphors that "anticipate the scientific 'evidence' he would encounter in the writings of Cattell," and so metaphors important in "accounting for the pull which eugenics exerted on Yeats's mind." Similarly, the dysgenic theme of *Purgatory* "is anticipated by the 'crazy salad' of dysgenic misalliance in 'A Prayer for my Daughter.'"[15] The real eugenics appears in the 1930s; anything before this is anticipation.

Similarly, Stanfield identifies deceptively eugenical postures in *On Baile's Strand*, *The King's Threshold*, and "If I Were Four-and-Twenty." In *On Baile's Strand* (1903), Cuchulain expresses the fear that a divinely descended heroic race is being "marred . . . in the copying," no longer mating with those "fitted to give birth to kings" (*Plays* pp. 485, 487). Stanfield suggests that "*On Baile's Strand* shows how readily Yeats figured class differences as differences in race or kind, and how readily he imagined modern barrenness as a consequence of degeneration, the triumph of the weak stocks over the great by weight of numbers."[16] Similarly, *The King's Threshold* (1903), by means of Seanchan's teaching that poets "made the golden cradle" that allowed children to "be born to majesty" (*Plays* p. 266), implies "that the imaginings of poets created the human race as it now exists, and that the imaginings of poets will eventually create an even greater race."[17] The eugenics here is deceptive because, according to Stanfield, Yeats has not yet discovered eugenics. Even the concern expressed in "If I Were Four-and-Twenty" (1919) that a bad choice in marriage could deprive a family of its "biological force" is deceptively pre-eugenical.[18] The eugenical themes of *On Baile's Strand*, *The King's Threshold*, and "If I were Four-and-Twenty" – respectively, "the degeneration of man," "regeneration through the right kind of art," and "regard for the best family stocks" – are merely "three ideas that contributed to Yeats's later interest in eugenics." The same ideas "lie near the center of Yeats's final blast at the public, *On the Boiler*" – a work in which his turn-of-the-century pre-eugenical intuitions are now "supported by new evidence from the new science of eugenics."[19]

Yet although Cullingford, Stanfield, and Bradshaw agree that Yeats's first meaningful engagement with eugenics dates from the 1930s, Stanfield's suggestion that in the 1930s the science of eugenics was either new as a science or new to Yeats is misleading. It is also misleading to suggest that its statistical evidence of degeneration was new – either to the science or to Yeats. Nor is it accurate, I will argue, to say that the early poetry, drama, and prose merely anticipate the serious eugenics of the 1930s. Yeats's interest in eugenics involves a much longer story, and dates from a much earlier time.

Bradshaw himself acknowledges that "it would be wrong to assume that [Yeats] was entirely unfamiliar with eugenicist ideas before joining the Eugenics Society in 1936."[20] He points both to people Yeats knew and to books that he owned as possible sources of knowledge about eugenics long before he joined the Eugenics Society or read Cattell's book. Among the eugenical books in his library were Francis Galton's *Hereditary Genius* (1869) and William McDougall's *National Welfare and National Decay* (1921). The copy of *Hereditary Genius* in his library is the 1914 edition, and since it has George Yeats's name on it the book presumably entered the library when they married in 1917, or sometime thereafter. It contains statistical analysis of the frequency of the appearance of genius in the upper classes – the very statistics that Yeats had hoped in the late 1930s to find updated in Cattell's book or in other work by members of the Eugenics Society.[21] McDougall's book is not nearly as laden with statistics as either Galton's or Cattell's, but, as we shall see, it explains the problem of the differential birthrate in terms similar to Cattell's. Furthermore, it is clear that Yeats lived at a time when, whether he knew it or not, he lived amongst friends and acquaintances who were eugenists. As Bradshaw notes, among the eugenists that Yeats knew personally were his doctor Norman Haire and his one-time lover Florence Farr. As we shall see, there were many others.

Following up such hints and guesses by Bradshaw about the eugenical books and the eugenists themselves that Yeats knew is instructive in this attempt to answer the question, "What did Yeats know about eugenics and when did he know it?" In each case, one finds reason to believe that Yeats was a eugenist long before his card-carrying days of the late 1930s.

The case of Haire is particularly interesting. The Harley Street gynecologist who performed the Steinach operation on Yeats in 1934, Haire was a member of the Eugenics Society from 1921 to 1934.[22] Phyllis Grosskurth points out that he was famous for performing the Steinach operation as a rejuvenation cure, for the "radical practice of performing vasectomies . . . as a means of birth control," and for "his preoccupation with selective breeding."[23] He had published widely on questions of sex, birth control, and the Steinach operation, including such books as *The Encyclopedia of Sexual Knowledge* (1934), of which he was general editor, *How I Run My Birth Control Clinic* (1929), *The Comparative Value of Current Contraceptive Methods* (1928), *Hymen; or the Future of Marriage* (1927), *Rejuvenation: the Work of Steinach, Voronoff and Others* (1924), and *Recent Developments of Steinach's Work* (1923).[24]

In the promotion of birth control, Haire was almost as active – if not nearly as famous – as Marie Stopes and Margaret Sanger. Indeed, Yeats's reference in *On the Boiler* to the need for the Irish government to send "doctor and clinic" to "limit the families of the unintelligent classes" is probably an allusion not to Stopes or Sanger but to his doctor Haire – the birth control campaigner he knew personally (*Ex* p. 426). Haire was also an advocate of sterilization for unfit breeders, earning Havelock Ellis's support in his sterilizing of mentally defective patients.[25] In fact, he was Ellis's mouthpiece for advice to the Eugenics Society about controversial sterilization legislation that the Society proposed in 1931.[26] Ellis and Haire argued that voluntary sterilization was a medical matter – a procedure not requiring an enabling law, and a cause not likely to be advanced by inviting the interference of ignorant legislators. As Bradshaw notes, Haire resigned from the Eugenics Society in 1934 because he disagreed with "what he took to be its position with regard to voluntary sterilization" when, despite his advice just three years before, another sterilization bill was proposed.[27] It was at precisely this time – the spring of 1934 – that Yeats consulted Haire about the Steinach operation and shortly thereafter underwent the procedure.

As Steinach's associate Paul Kammerer points out, the operation involved "a ligation (vasoligature), followed by a severing (vasectomy) of the spermatic duct, . . . applied only to one of the two spermatic ducts, in the event that (aside from sexual ability) the propagative ability is to be conserved, restored, and prolonged." The rejuvenating effect of the operation, according to the knowledge and the terms of the time, was explained as follows:

The sexual glands consist . . . of two main tissues . . . The generative tissue, or the generative gland proper, takes care of the exterior excretion (*excretion*). The interstitial tissue, however, called the "puberty gland" by Steinach, takes care of the inner secretion (*incretion*). The fluids prepared in this tissue mix uninterruptedly with blood circulation, gaining a strong chemical influence . . . in the preservation of general vitality.

Interference with the spermatic duct results in compensatory processes in the neighboring sex gland. . . [T]he result consists of a retrodevelopment of the generative gland proper . . . At the expense of this deterioration or retrodevelopment, the interstitial gland proliferates; . . .the excretion, for the time being, is surpassed, thus gradually stimulating the incretion of those substances (*"hormones"*) which are responsible for a heightening and preserving of vitality and joy of life.[28]

Thus the Steinach operation promised to turn the outwardly directed fountain of germ plasm into an inwardly directed fountain of youth.

According to Hone, depressed by ill health and a general lack of vigor, Yeats first learned of "the rejuvenating cure" from a friend who "described the contents of Steinach's book with great impressiveness and the appropriate gesticulations."[29] Apparently, Yeats "hurried away to read the volume in Trinity College Library."[30] Hone's suggestion that Yeats read an account of the operation by

Steinach himself is extremely unlikely, as Steinach published no account of his work in English before Yeats died and Yeats did not read German, the language in which Steinach otherwise published. Yeats's surviving library indicates that he owned a copy of a book that includes a description of the Steinach operation, Peter Schmidt's *The Conquest of Old Age: Methods to Effect Rejuvenation and to Increase Functional Activity* (1931), which Yeats presumably acquired in advance of his operation. Schmidt was a respected surgeon and great promoter of the operation, in many ways the German equivalent of Haire in this respect. To Steinach's claim that "within modest limits, the process of aging can be influenced" he added his own observation (based on case notes on "several thousand males"): "Considering the range and intensity of the results which were produced, one may be permitted to safely say that, by means of vasoligation on man, decidedly more than a restoration 'within modest limits' has been achieved."[31] Schmidt reported a success rate of 50 percent, the effect appearing within four to six months and lasting two to three years. Perhaps explanation enough of Yeats's decision in favor of the operation, Schmidt's book is not likely to have been the one that Yeats sought out in Trinity College Library, for there were many other books available, all of them focusing more directly on Steinach's work.

Yeats may have read George F. Corners' *Rejuvenation: How Steinach Makes People Young* (1923), which assured readers that the operation creates an "organic condition analogous to that of youth."[32] He may have read Paul Kammerer's *Rejuvenation and the Prolongation of Human Efficiency: Experiences with the Steinach-operation on Man and Animals*, to which Harry Benjamin (the American equivalent of Haire) contributed an introduction arguing that "[t]he progress of senility can be retarded; sometimes even more than only 'within modest limits' as Steinach so conservatively expressed it."[33] He may even have read Haire himself, who warned in *Rejuvenation: the Work of Steinach, Voronoff, and Others* that doctors had to be careful not to cut tiny nerves and blood vessels in the area of the incision if the operation were to be a success – advice perhaps as likely to instill fear of the operation as confidence in Haire himself.[34]

Whichever of the many books and pamphlets describing Steinach's work that Yeats read, the information offered by them was much the same. Arnold Lorand's account of Steinach's experiments is typical in its readiness to suggest the transferability of the results of

Steinach's operation on rats to human beings. Steinach operated on "old marasmic rats of the age of twenty-eight to thirty months – an age corresponding in rat life to the eighties or more in human subjects." Noting that the operation increased the life-span of the rats by 25 percent, Lorand suggests that "it would seem possible in this way, if one were permitted to apply these findings to the human race, to add about twenty years to the life of a man already about eighty years old." The operation promised to increase not only the length of life, but also the quality of life. Initially moribund, emaciated, and sexually lethargic, the rats were transformed by the operation:

New hair grew all over their bodies . . . At the same time, they were as agile and erect as young rats in the prime of life . . . Their behavior in the sexual sphere after the operation was equally remarkable . . . Before the operation . . . [a] young female rat placed in their cage evoked no interest whatever. . . After the operation, however, these previously impotent old rats turned into sexually active young males.

Lorand is summarizing Steinach's *Verjungung* – the monograph that inspired the books about his operation, and the one in which Steinach described the cases of three men upon whom the operation was performed. Lorand highlights what would have caught Yeats's attention:

These persons felt much younger than their age; their fatigued state disappeared. Their symptoms of arteriosclerosis, dizziness, shortness of breath, tremor, etc. also disappeared or were improved. . . The sexual desire reappeared and was very pronounced. Potency was returned to the normal of their younger years in at least two of the three cases, and in the third, a man of seventy-two years with pronounced arteriosclerosis, sexual desire reappeared after a long interval, and natural satisfaction of it was possible.[35]

That reports of Steinach's work like these should interest a sixty-nine year old Yeats "dejected" by old age in general and frustrated in particular by an "impotence . . . caused by arteriosclerosis" is not surprising.[36]

The Steinach operation greatly interested eugenists – being regarded as one of many important "measures to encourage fertility of the gifted" – and was frequently discussed in terms of its eugenical potential.[37] Rejuvenation was the necessary prelude to eugenical procreation by older people, for the prevailing prejudice was that procreation by the old and senile would produce enfeebled offspring

– a prejudice evident not just among eugenists, but in society as a whole (thus Stephen Dedalus dismisses his friend Cranly as "the child of exhausted loins").[38] Such reservations "regarding the inferior quality of progeny begotten at an advanced age" were understood by Kammerer to be "eugenical objections."[39] Such objections were obviated, of course, for those who had a successful Steinach operation.

More interestingly, the Steinach operation also served the argument of eugenists who believed in the inheritance of acquired characteristics, for the Lamarckian assumption that the germ plasm of the old had acquired not just age but heritable wisdom allowed one to argue that one should not "neglect / Monuments of unageing intellect," but rather embrace them – *if* they had indeed become rejuvenated (*Poems* p. 407). Kammerer makes this argument in *The Inheritance of Acquired Characteristics*, where "[m]entioning the Steinach Method gives [him] occasion to dwell on . . . combining rejuvenation with inheritance of acquired characteristics." For Kammerer, "[p]ropagation at a mature age, after a life crowded with valuable experiences – verily, this would be an ideal realization, if, in spite of the number of years lived through, youthful strength still makes this possible. To realize this ideal, within certain limits, seems to be possible now by taking recourse to modern methods of rejuvenation." Given that Steinach's rats appeared to pass on to their progeny the intensified sex gland activity that the operation had induced, Kammerer suspected that rejuvenation was a heritable acquired characteristic and that therefore even in human beings "it may be possible to bring rejuvenation effects to bear upon succeeding generations."[40]

Steinach was known to eugenists because of his association with Kammerer. Their experiments in biology were cited to support a Lamarckian conception of heredity. In *Biogenetic Marvels: the Romance of Biology, Disclosing Man's Infinite Potentialities* (1925), G. B. Starkweather eagerly and with satisfaction cited their work as contradiction of the "almost unanimously agreed" judgment of "orthodox 'science'" that Lamarck "was wrong." Steinach and Kammerer had proven Lamarck's claim that "the transmission of acquired characters was a natural biological law":

I have wearied of reiterating my Lamarckian attitude, and now dwell upon it again, because . . . Dr. Steinach, with his associate, Dr. Kammerer, has bred generations of salamanders, a lizard-like creature with the chameleon's power of adapting itself to a background. . . Those kept in orange, turned increasingly orange, while those kept in darkness turned increasingly black. The orange parents had young with strong orange tints and the offspring of the artificially blackened salamanders were abnormally black.[41]

MacBride, of course, had impressed Eliot with the same Lamarckian argument in 1916–17, citing the same experiments: "These experiments of Kammerer constitute the most complete proof that the functional response excited in one generation by the environment has its effect in the next generation . . . in a word, *that acquired qualities are to some extent inherited*." Responding to the objection that these experiments had not revealed a mechanism by which to explain a theory of the inheritance of acquired characteristics, MacBride suggested first that "the important thing is not our conception of *how* the thing happens, but the proof that it *does* happen," and, second, that chemicals like hormones might be responsible for environmentally induced alterations in an individual's germ plasm – precisely the direction in which Steinach took his experiments.[42] The work of Steinach and Kammerer, in short, was a lifeline to Lamarckian eugenists otherwise at odds with the prevailing orthodoxy in the science of heredity.

And so, by the time of the operation – he decided for it himself "after consultation with a doctor who would give no opinion either way" – Yeats would have learned a good deal about eugenics both through his discussions in advance of the procedure with Haire (the greatest British expert on the procedure) and through any research about Steinach's work that he undertook on his own.[43] The Steinach operation, long seen as a metaphor for Yeats's determination to put on the mask of "the wild old wicked man" and thereby dwell triumphantly in "the foul rag and bone shop of the heart," is thus also a part of the story of his involvement with eugenics – a story predating his membership in the Eugenics Society and his reading of Cattell by at least several years (*Poems* pp. 587, 630).

Although Virginia and Raymond Pruitt argue that any positive results of the operation on Yeats are attributable to psychological rather than physiological factors, it is clear that Yeats himself believed that the operation had been a success. He "astonished" the friend who had jestingly recommended the operation "when, a month or two later, he strode into his office looking like another man, and said, 'I had it done.'"[44] Yeats clearly meant to credit the new stride and the new mood to the operation. Impotent once again in his sixties – he spoke of the return (from the days of his early affair with Olivia Shakespear) of his "inhibition" – Yeats understood, as Cullingford points out, that although the impotence was "[o]nce a nervous problem, the 'inhibition' was now organic."[45] Thus one reason for the Steinach operation.

From this point of view, it is interesting to note that, unable to reach climax several months after the operation, Yeats thought to himself "perhaps after all . . . this nervous inhibition has not left me" – implying that he still believed that the operation had been physiologically successful and that his impotence was to be explained, as of old, by nervousness.[46] Haire apparently concluded in consulting with Yeats after the procedure "that the operation had no effect upon his sexual competence. He could not have erections."[47] The sexual bravado evident in the late poetry may be "a pathetic over-compensation for impotence," but if so, Yeats himself would seem to have understood the problem to have been psychological, and not directly physiological.[48] A. Norman Jeffares concludes that the operation gave Yeats "a new self-confidence" and that "his interest in sex was stimulated."[49] Virginia Pruitt suggests that "Yeats believed that his own 'lust' and 'rage' were physiologically assured after the operation, and his herculean and unabated creative energy apparently derived from that belief."[50]

This remarkable confidence in the physical changes caused by the operation is evident in the poem most often associated with Yeats's post-Steinachian sexual stridency – "The Wild Old Wicked Man" (1938). Read biographically, this poem confirms Yeats's confidence in his physical sexual abilities and implies that Yeats was indeed aware of the eugenical implications of the Steinach operation. Arising out of his attempt to persuade Lady Elizabeth Pelham to become sexually intimate with him, the poem advertises the wild old wicked man's virtues as a lover. Among these are decidedly eugenical virtues.

Cullingford, however, reads the poem as a defense against impotence: the old man replaces his penis with words "that can pierce the heart," whereas the "young man" can "but touch": "A man unable to have an erection has a vested interest in the idea that words go deeper than penises" (*Poems* p. 588).[51] Women should know, the old man suggests, that he "Can touch by mother wit / Things hid in their marrow bones" (*Poems* p. 589). Cullingford sees this "mother wit" as lesbian knowledge: "Women know what women like; men feminized by age and impotence understand, as lesbians do, those female pleasures not dependent upon an erect penis."[52] Perhaps so, but the phrase "mother wit" was given a eugenical context for Yeats – it is the "natural capacity" of a population – in the Galton lecture by Bond that Blacker sent Yeats at the beginning of 1938 (during the period when "The Wild Old Wicked Man" was being written).[53] The wild old wicked man is not suggesting that he cannot produce an erection; rather, he suggests both that he has the same "touch" as the young men (after all, he is "A young man in the dark"), and also that he has *more* in his touch than the young men have in theirs. The logic is not the "either-or" of "take their touch or my words," but rather the "both-and" of "take from me the special offer of both touch and words." And so although Cullingford finds that "the refrain 'Daybreak and a candle-end' undercuts his sexual bravado with its suggestion of drooping, melting wax,"[54] one might just as well argue that the candle that has burned till dawn confirms what the speaker implies: that the old man who is a "young man in the dark" can stay up all night.

Like Parnell, knowing "as few can know" that "All men live in suffering," the old man implies that "bitter wisdom . . . enriched his blood" (*Poems* pp. 589, 543). This claim is quite literal: rejuvenated, a wild old wicked man can pass on the wisdom acquired with age – precisely the eugenical result anticipated from the Steinach operation. In the old man's enriched blood is the "mother wit" of Ireland that descends first through his ancestors and second through a wit acquired in the living of his life. Such is the germ plasm that the old man offers to the women of the modern world. If the woman preoccupied with the "old man in the skies" will not have him, perhaps the more welcoming "Girls down on the seashore" who "turn down their beds" will. Or in Yeats's case, if the English Lady will not avail herself of the opportunity he offers, he may well have to pick a Derby Winner from between the shafts of a cab. Whether as the post-Steinach Yeats or as the old man inexplicably still wild and wicked, such a man, the poem's eugenical logic implies, can put wit in a womb if he be allowed to lie "Upon a woman's breast" (*Poems* p. 590). Impotence may be a problem for the aged Yeats – whether caused by artireosclerosis or a longstanding "nervousness" with women – but his wild old wicked man is no lesbian wannabe. The argument that Yeats makes through him is that eugenical good fortune awaits the woman who can tease from him a germ plasm reinvigorated by the Steinach operation and full of a mother wit augmented by a lifetime's experience.

I conclude that Yeats had researched the Steinach operation thoroughly, was confident that his own operation had rejuvenated him physiologically, and was vitally aware of the operation's eugenical implications for his own status as a late breeder.

As we have seen, Bradshaw also points out that Yeats's library contains books on eugenics, including two important works owned by his wife George Yeats: "a copy of the 1914 edition of Francis Galton's *Hereditary Genius* (1869) and William McDougall's *National Welfare and National Decay* (1921) . . . the first of which is the seminal text and the second a prominent book in the annals of eugenics."[55] Galton's book began the accumulation and analysis of statistics that became a staple of eugenical research and would culminate in Cattell's work, while McDougall argued the main eugenical line "that the upper social strata, as compared with the lower, contain a larger proportion of persons of superior natural endowments" – not putting the argument "from the purely biological standpoint," but offering instead "a presentation of the case for eugenics from a more psychological standpoint and on a broad historical background."[56]

McDougall, for instance, is the likely source of one of Yeats's favorite lines signifying the dysgenic state of modern Ireland. Yeats's famous fascist marching songs "Three Songs to the Same Tune" (1934) make the eugenic argument that "Great Nations flower above," but that occasionally the time comes for those like the Blueshirts to march "When nations are empty up there at the top" (*Poems* pp. 547, 548). Similarly, in "Blood and Moon" (1928), Yeats contrasts the time past when an "arrogant power / Rose out of the race" with the time present of the "modern nation . . . / Half dead at the top" (*Poems* pp. 480, 482). Bradshaw notes that "Yeats brooded on the impermanence of civilizations throughout his life, but in his last years his interest in . . . writings . . . on the rise and fall of cultures markedly intensified," and so he suggests that "Fisher, Bond and Cattell, who explained the demise of civilizations in terms of a withering and adulteration of the best, could hardly have failed to arouse Yeats."[57] True enough, yet McDougall was available to Yeats long before he read Fisher, Bond, and Cattell. In *National Welfare and National Decay* (1921), McDougall addresses the same subject and uses the very words that Yeats does: "Civilizations decay because they die off at the top" (p. 8). Again, McDougall's book and Yeats's apparent recourse to its arguments and phrasing appear well before the 1930s.

McDougall's thesis is that "the great condition of the decline of any civilization is the inadequacy of the qualities of the people who are the bearers of it," and so he observes with regard to the question of a nation's social and political organization that "[t]he truth is that forms of organization matter little; the all important thing is the quality of the matter to be organized, the quality of the human beings that are the stuff of our nations and societies" (pp. 36, 7). Yeats reproduces this argument in *On the Boiler*: "If ever Ireland again seems molten wax, reverse the process of revolution. Do not try to pour Ireland into any political system. Think first how many able men with public minds the country has, how many it can hope to have in the near future, and mould your system upon those men" (*Ex* p. 414).

Other of McDougall's points about eugenics appear in Yeats's writings. McDougall suggests that "modern feminism is withdrawing more and more of the best of the women from marriage and motherhood," quoting S. H. Halford's essay "Dysgenic Tendencies" to the effect that "there seems no other prospect, if the full feminist ideal be realized, than the entire extinction of British and American intelligence within the next two or three generations."[58] Yeats refers to this danger in his advice to Lady Dorothy Wellesley in response to her suggestion that women of genius could not be expected to have children: "raising his hand and speaking like the prophets of old, [Yeats] replied: 'No, we urgently need the children of women of genius!'"[59] Although Cattell had warned of the dangers of the differential birthrate, this warning had long been a staple of eugenical texts and so of course it appears in McDougall's: "the superior half of the population is ceasing to produce children in sufficient numbers to replace their parents, while the lower half continues to multiply itself freely and is the source of all increase of population" (*National Welfare*, pp. 159–60). As early as a 1925 Senate speech against a law to prevent women from being appointed to certain positions in the civil service because they might leave employment should they marry, Yeats implies the same concern expressed later to Wellesley: "there is the danger of making it difficult for women to marry and discouraging marriage if there is any undue discrimination against women on the ground that they will withdraw from the Service on marriage."[60] In the Ireland of 1925, the assumption is clear: to discourage women from marriage is to discourage women from having children. Such talented women as the civil service might attract should not be kept from marriage, for this is to rob Ireland of their children. As this is the argument of eugenists in general, and as this is the argument of McDougall in particular, there is no reason to deny that Yeats here expresses full-blown eugenical beliefs.

Similarly, Yeats's definition of the Anglo-Irish people in his speech to the Irish Senate on divorce (1925) reflects McDougall's interest in a culture's eugenically originary moment. McDougall notes that

Professor Flinders Petrie . . . advances a theory which claims to explain both the rise and fall of . . . [civilization]. He supposes that every cycle is initiated by a biological blending of two races; that this gives to the blended stock a new energy which carries it up the scale of civilization; that, after about one thousand eight hundred years, this effect is exhausted and that, in consequence of loss of vigor, decline inevitably sets in. (*National Welfare*, p. 34)

It may well have been in response to this passage that Yeats acquired his own copy of Petrie's *The Revolution of Civilization* (1922). The main tenets of McDougall and Petrie are evident in a speech to the Irish Senate warning Catholic Ireland that outlawing divorce will deny to the protestant Irish what they consider a right:

We against whom you have done this thing are no petty people. We are one of the great stocks of Europe. We are the people of Burke; we are the people of Grattan; we are the people of Swift, the people of Emmet, the people of Parnell. We have created the most of the modern literature of this country. We have created the best of its political intelligence. Yet I do not altogether regret what has happened. I shall be able to find out, if not I, my children will be able to find out whether we have lost our stamina or not. . . If we have not lost our stamina then your victory will be brief, and your defeat final, and when it comes this nation may be transformed.[61]

Of Yeats's attempts in general to define the Anglo-Irish, Seamus Deane notes that his language is "partly genetic, partly environmental."[62] His language here is certainly biological, and talk of a stock and its stamina, as shown through subsequent generations and as measured against the success of other strains in the battle for existence, is vaguely eugenical. Against the background of the ideas of McDougall and Petrie, however, the eugenics is clearer: the combination of Anglo blood and Irish blood has created a new political intelligence and a modern literature in Ireland. It is clear that Yeats expects this stock to triumph and thereby transform the nation. The correspondence of this biological account of Ireland's present culture with McDougall's and Petrie's association between advancing civilization and biological blending is confirmed by Yeats's explanation of Irishness in "Bishop Berkeley" (1931):

Born into such a community [with a "sense for what is permanent, as distinct from what is useful"], Berkeley with his belief in perception, that abstract ideas are mere words, Swift with his love of perfect nature, of the Houyhnhnms, his disbelief in Newton's system and every sort of machine, Goldsmith and his delight in the particulars of common life that shocked his contemporaries, Burke with his conviction that all states not grown slowly like a forest tree are tyrannies, found in England the opposite that stung their own thought into expression and made it lucid.[63]

English and Irish cultures were distinct. The great stock responsible for the literature and the political intelligence of modern Ireland resulted from a crossbreeding of the English and Irish stock of the eighteenth century. That this modern Irish culture comes of being born not just in the right place but also of the right people is confirmed by Yeats's claim that Berkeley offers "the only philosophical arguments since Plotinus that are works of art, being so well-bred, so sensible."[64] The sensible thought is bred in the bone: it is as much a matter of significant blood as a matter of significant soil.

Asserting that "Yeats had learned the notion of an essential racial 'signature' both from his Anglo-Irish mentors and from the English Romantics," Deane warns that his attempt to define the Irish race "is not . . . to be confused with the cruder racial theories so pervasive in the Europe and Ireland of the thirties."[65] In fact, Yeats's thinking about race is inextricably confused with such eugenical thought. Deane finds that Yeats has defined Irishness as pre-seventeenth-century Englishness – an Englishness lost to the industrial revolution but preserved in Ireland: "The colony, Ireland, has now become the motherland of historical memory. The actual motherland, England, has become degraded past recognition."[66] A well-argued and accurate enough account of a perverse colonialism in Yeats, Deane's own language acknowledges its eugenical dimensions. What Deane sees as insidious cultural colonialism is from the eugenical perspective of McDougall and Petrie a matter of colonizing germ plasm. And so, in light of the close thematic and verbal parallels between *National Welfare and National Decay* and the poetry and prose of the 1920s and 1930s, there is no need to defer Yeats's acquaintance with and serious interest in eugenical texts until the late 1930s: this interest is earlier than and continuous with his later reading.

Bradshaw actually hints that for Yeats a very personal interest in eugenics might have emerged as early as 1910. He points out that Florence Farr advertised eugenical beliefs about breeding: "I do not think that we shall ever get mankind to carry out the eugenic ideal of careful breeding, but I do think we might come to a time when the natural instinct of a woman for the fit father of her child will be a very important factor in the arrangements made for the existence and benefit of future generations."[67] Bradshaw suggests that "it is more than likely that she and Yeats would have discussed careful breeding" – presumably because they were engaged in an affair occasionally between 1903 and 1907.[68] In the year Farr published *Modern Woman: Her Intentions* (1910), Yeats was certainly familiar with her views on marriage – which he summarized as "only . . . meet now & again like sensible people: that is the only endurable kind of marriage" – and had not surprisingly reached the correct conclusion that she was "not of a domestic temperament."[69] So Bradshaw may well be correct in suggesting that they talked about these things.

Farr's belief in "the natural instinct of a woman for the fit father of her child" seems to be the point of view that Yeats rebuts in his claim in "If I Were Four-and-Twenty" that the origin of the family (and thereby the origin of civilization) is not a matter of "mere instinct": "A single wrong choice may destroy a family, dissipating its tradition or its biological force, and the great sculptors, painters, and poets are there that instinct may find its lamp."[70] On the other hand, Farr's talk of a woman's instinct in these matters certainly predates Yeats's later references to eugenically adept man-pickers – both *On the Boiler*'s "daughter of a bar-maid man-picker who had doubled her own mettle with that of a man whose name she had forgotten or never known" and "Man-picker Niamh" of "News for the Delphic Oracle" (1939) (*Ex* p. 433, *Poems* p. 611). Her influence in this matter may extend as far as Yeats's argument that "[w]e should count men and women who *pick*, as it were, the dam or sire of a Derby winner from between the shafts of a cab, among persons of genius, for this genius makes all other kinds possible" (*Ex* p. 430, emphasis mine). Cullingford suggests that "Yeats's use of the word 'pick' implicates 'Hound Voice,' in which the speaker and his lovers 'picked each other from afar,' in the eugenic program" (*Poems* p. 622).[71] If so, one might make the same claim of man-pickers who appear in Yeats's poems even before the 1930s, including the "barbarous crowd" of those who "pick and choose" unwisely in "His Phoenix" (1916), and the ambitious mermaid of "A Man Young and Old" (1927) who – having "found a swimming lad, / Picked him for her own, / Pressed her body to his body" – unintentionally drowns him (*Poems* pp. 354, 452–53).

Of course Bradshaw explores a very interesting question indeed in "The Eugenics Movement in the 1930s and the Emergence of *On the Boiler*," yet an equally interesting question concerns the emergence of Yeats's 1930s' membership in the Eugenics Society and his earlier acquaintance with eugenics. Eugenics was both in the Edwardian air Yeats breathed and in the Georgian library he kept. Yet there was much more in the air and much more in the library than readers of Yeats have yet realized. Follow Bradshaw into Yeats's library, crack the backs of the books there, and one finds eugenics everywhere. So just how early can one date Yeats's acquaintance with eugenics, and what was the impact of such an introduction to eugenics?

CHAPTER 8

Yeats and stirpiculture

Yeats's earliest acquaintance with eugenics dates from the turn of the century when he was sent for review a copy of Allan Estlake's *The Oneida Community* (1900), subtitled "A record of an attempt to carry out the principles of Christian unselfishness and scientific race-improvement."[1] Known neither as a Christian nor as a eugenist in 1900, Yeats was presumably offered the book because of his well-known interest in spiritualism, for chapter eight is titled "A Definition of Spiritualism" and chapter nine, "Investigation of Spiritualism in the Oneida Community." Yeats wrote no review of the book, however, and, as Edward O'Shea notes, many pages of the copy of the book that is preserved in Yeats's library are uncut, so one might suspect that he did not even read it.[2] Yet it is certain that Yeats read Estlake's book, and it is likely that its influence is responsible for much of the eugenics in Yeats's early work.

The Oneida Community was established in 1848 by John Humphrey Noyes. As J. M. Whitworth notes, "[c]onvinced that the second coming was past, Noyes concluded that he was living in the age of the fulfilment of Christ's prophecies, and hence that perfect holiness and sinlessness were not only attainable in this life, but that only persons who could lay claim to such perfection were truly Christian."[3] Determined to demonstrate such holiness and sinlessness in a functioning Christian community, Noyes summoned followers to central New York state where the eighty-seven people who heeded his call would practice the radical selflessness that he believed was required of Christians regenerated into sinlessness by the second coming. The selflessness preached in the name of "Bible Communism" was most notoriously practiced in sexual relations, for, according to Noyes,

When the will of God is done on earth as it is in heaven, there will be no marriage. The marriage-supper of the Lamb, is a feast at which every dish is free to every guest. Exclusiveness, jealousy, quarrelling, have no place there . . . In a holy community there is no more reason why sexual intercourse should be restrained by law, than why eating and drinking should be.[4]

This communism of affections was formalized as complex marriage, the practice of sharing oneself sexually within the community – a practice that prevailed until its unpopularity outside the community led Noyes to recommend its abandonment in 1879.

Supplementing Noyes's interest in regenerating the spirit through sinlessness was his interest in regenerating the body through selective breeding. He had signalled such hopes as early as *Bible Communism* (1853):

The physiologists say that the race cannot be raised from ruin till propagation is made a matter of science . . . [P]ropagation is controlled and reduced to a science in the case of valuable domestic brutes; but marriage and fashion forbid any such system among human beings. We believe the time will come when involuntary and random propagation will cease, and when scientific combination will be applied to human generation as freely and successfully as it is to that of other animals.[5]

By the late 1860s, Noyes had introduced this breeding discipline to the community – calling the practice stirpiculture, acknowledging in the Latin root *stirpem* (stock) the farmyard model of this "scientific propagation":

It is one thing to seek in any existing race the best animals we can find to breed from . . . and it is another thing to start a distinct family and keep its blood pure by separation from the mass of its own race. . . The terms "thorough-bred," "blood-stock," "pure blood," etc., have no meaning except as they refer to this method of segregation. This indeed is the principal work of modern science . . . It deserves a distinct name, and we will take the liberty to call it *Stirpiculture*.

Monogamy abandoned, complex marriage would allow one male to impregnate many females, as in the farmyard. But successful stirpiculture also requires abandonment of the incest prohibition: it "is an attempt to create a new race by selecting a new Adam and Eve . . . First there must be, in the early stages, mating between very near relatives, as there was in Adam's family; and secondly, there must be, in all stages, mating between members of the same general *stock* who are all related more or less closely."[6] Only in this way could the regenerated spiritual integrity of the human race come to reside in a body regenerated to the level of its original physical integrity.

Complex marriage abandoned in 1879 in the face of external hostility to the community, lack of discipline proliferating amongst younger members of the community, the health of Noyes himself failing, rivalry amongst potential successors increasing, and the appointment of Noyes's son as President causing great dissension, the grand experiment in Christian Communism collapsed in the early 1880s. The Oneida Community's assets were converted into a joint-stock company, which continues to this day. Its ideals and practices became the subject of books and essays, ranging from academic studies such as A. N. McGee's "An Experiment in Human Stirpicul-ture" in *The American Anthropologist* (1891) to Estlake's unabashedly hagiographical account of Noyes's work in *The Oneida Community*.[7]

Estlake was one of the three hundred members of the Oneida Community at the time of its dissolution in the early 1880s. Writing *The Oneida Community* after Noyes's death, Estlake remained a true believer – convinced that Noyes was "the most important and central" of Christ's "messengers" (p. 5). According to Estlake, "[i]t was no fault of [Noyes's] that he lived before the people were ready for him, any more than Christ was to blame for trying to teach a people what they were unable to receive" (pp. 1–2). Estlake's logic was simple: "Either John H. Noyes was a heroically good man or he was a diabolically bad one, and the Oneida Community was either a heaven of purity and bliss or it was a hell of wickedness and hypocrisy" (p. 51). And so, as Whitworth explains, "[w]ith a facility which his mentor would have admired, Estlake exculpated Noyes from blame for the collapse of the Community, and transferred the burden of guilt to the corrupt and unappreciative inhabitants of the external society." Estlake thus assumed the role of "Noyes's apologist" and "posthumous eulogist."[8]

Estlake's enthusiasm for the teachings of Noyes in general and his explanation of particular aspects of Community life so interested Yeats that he stole an Oneida Community member described by Estlake to serve as a character in *The Speckled Bird* – his unfinished novel from the late 1890s and early 1900s.[9] This fact is evident from a comparison of several passages in the two works. Estlake, attempting to counter skepticism about the possibility of so great an unselfishness as that required for the success of complex marriage, recounts at length testimony by a member of the Oneida Community (implicitly identified as "A") about a situation that would presumably have constituted a painful love triangle anywhere else but in the Community:

Charles C— . . . was deeply in love with Miss B— . . . This love was reciprocal. . . The Community, always solicitous to discourage selfishness in conjugal intercourse as in all other departments of life, . . . deemed it prudent that she should become a mother by some husband of her choice, and that Charles C— should choose some other sweetheart to woo for the purpose of maternity. . . This may have been a trial for Charles C— , but *he never harboured a jealous thought of the man who was united to the same woman; on the contrary, their common love was a bond of union, and after the child was born he loved it as tenderly and cared for it as devotedly as if it were his own*. . . One evening, when I was in Miss B— 's room, her child was so fretful that our efforts failed to soothe it. The door opened and Charles C— , taking the child from its crib so quietly that we were scarcely aware of his presence, carried it into his own room. . . His solicitude lest our courtship be interrupted . . . made an impression on my heart that can never be effaced. (*Oneida Community*, pp. 74–77)

It also made quite an impression on Yeats. In *The Speckled Bird*, the protagonist Michael Hearne listens to a member of the Oneida Community defending complex marriage as a "natural" practice, the opposite of and antidote for the "sex fever" induced by the practices of others (such as the celibacy imposed upon the member of the rival Fountain Grove Community with whom the member of the Oneida Community here argues): "'A fever,' said the disciple of Noyes, 'of an exclusive and selfish love. With us jealousy is unknown. I have myself helped to rock the cradle of a child that was born of one whom I had loved and of my successor in her affections'" (p. 73). The character in Yeats's novel is clearly Estlake's "Charles C—."

And so, in a sense, is Yeats himself. Autobiographical from beginning to end – Michael is clearly based on Yeats himself – *The Speckled Bird* is particularly autobiographical at this point. Yeats found himself in the same position as C – limited to a "spiritual marriage" with the woman he loved (Maud Gonne), a woman who was conceiving children by another (Lucien Millevoye) – and he was clearly intent on imposing the same situation upon his protagonist in *The Speckled Bird*. By mid-novel, Michael is determined to marry Margaret Henderson, whom Yeats soon marries off to another man by whom she will become a mother. Yeats apparently intended to develop the scene in the novel involving the man from the Oneida Community to highlight these issues even more. In revising what editor William H. O'Donnell identifies as the "final" version of the novel, Yeats made a note to himself that Michael's "interest in the conversation of the man of the Oneida Community and of the Fountain Grove man must be made rather keen. One must be made to see that his own love affair makes him vitally interested in all such things" (p. 222).

Yeats's note is ambiguous. On the one hand, Michael's keener interest in the conversation could be developed to indicate his interest in the nature of true love and ideal marriage – given that he has already proposed marriage to Margaret and been rejected – and to foreshadow more clearly the extent to which Michael would soon find himself in C's position. On the other hand, Michael and his friend Samuel Maclagan anticipate a great spiritual and secular "change" in the world – "from [their] meeting will come the overthrow of whole nations, but not for a long time. Nobody can tell how long, how many generations" (p. 59) – and it is clear that Maclagan expects eugenical breeding to be part of this change:

he went into the Greek Room [of the British Museum] and, standing in front of a statue of an athlete, he held out his arms and got Michael to feel their muscle and compare them with the muscles of the athlete. . . Then he spoke of the contrast between the form of Greek statues and the men and women who were looking at them. He said, "Men were once like that and now they are getting more and more miserable looking. But for them the world would get much worse, for everybody is trying, though half-heartedly enough, to become a little like them, but their endeavour gets fainter and fainter." (pp. 59–60)

In this passage written in 1902, one finds the same eugenical arguments offered in "The Statues" (1939): on the one hand, Greek statues made Europe great "when Phidias / Gave women dreams and dreams their looking glass"; on the other hand, Europe today is degenerate, "thrown upon this filthy modern tide / And by its formless spawning fury wrecked" (*Poems* pp. 610–11).

The Greek hope to incarnate beauty in human form via some form of association with beautiful statues was no doubt well known to Yeats. In "The Decay of Lying," Oscar Wilde's character Vivian notes that "[t]he Greeks . . . set in the bride's chamber the statue of Hermes or of Apollo, that she might bear children as lovely as the works of art that she looked at in her rapture or her pain. They knew that Life . . . can form herself on the very lines and colors of art, and can reproduce the dignity of Pheidias as well as the grace of Praxiteles."[10] Walter Pater quotes Winckelmann to similar effect: "By no people . . . has beauty been so highly esteemed as by the Greeks. . . The general esteem for beauty went so far, that the Spartan women set up in their bedchambers a Nireus, a Narcissus, or a Hyacinth, that they might bear beautiful children."[11] Whereas the Greek practices to which Wilde, Pater, and Wincklemann refer are clearly based on a belief in what Frazer described in *The Golden Bough* as sympathetic magic, Maclagan's punning acknowlegdment that the miserable degeneration that confronts the modern world will be overcome only after "many generations" – marking both the passing of time and acts of procreation – shows that Yeats has forced a biological synthesis here of previously distinct realms: ancient fertility rituals and modern eugenics.[12] Yeats conceives the beauty of Greek art as capable of making people seek sexual partners in whom such beauty is at least partially incarnated, thereby breeding back into the race the beauty that has been bred out.[13]

Given the conversation between Michael and Maclagan about the need for self-conscious eugenical goals in breeding, it is possible that Yeats meant to develop the passage in question to show Michael "vitally interested" in the stirpicultural dimensions of Oneida Community love. There is the beginning of such a turn in the declaration by the member of the Oneida Community that in sexual matters, Community members "are as natural as the Greeks" (*Speckled Bird*, p. 73) – not the Greeks that were homosexual, but the Greeks that Maclagan admires, the Greeks whose eugenical potential Estlake salutes: "It would be surprising if such a palpable possibility as cultivation of the human race had entirely escaped observation by the Grecian intelligence. . . If goodness, rather than physique, had been the Spartan ideal, . . . superior goodness conserving physical powers would have saved Greece from the emasculating debaucheries which led to her ruin" (pp. 96–97).

Certainly the Oneida Community's intervention in the relationship between Charles C— and Miss B—, which Estlake details carefully and which Yeats recalls fairly accurately, involved stirpicultural considerations. As A explains,

Not only temperament, but tendencies that were in any way objectionable, were recognised as being undesirable qualities to intensify by the uniting of two parents having the trait in common. Both Charles C— and Miss B— having been under criticism for a tendency to drift into exclusive relations in such manner as to jeopardise communistic love, it was found wrong to place them in conditions of stronger temptation. (*Oneida Community*, p. 75)

And there is much more on stirpiculture in *The Oneida Community* than this passing reference by "A." Indeed, Estlake not only devotes a whole chapter to the topic (chapter seven, "Parentage"), but also discusses throughout the book the stirpicultural implications of everything from complex marriage to male continence and "the question of 'woman's rights'" – always championing stirpiculture with the same enthusiasm that he devotes to all of Noyes's ideas (p. 88).

In fact, all of the main assumptions of eugenists were presented to Yeats in the pages of *The Oneida Community.* "Stirpiculture is such an important factor in the redemption of the world," Estlake suggests, "that the surest way of getting the right sort of people is to have them born right," and so "it is the prerogative and the duty of all concerned to propagate from the best to the exclusion of the worst" (pp. 85–86). Like all eugenists, he complains of modern degeneration "in this age of perversions": "men and women defy natural laws relating to wise selection of the fittest, and consort wholly regardless of the parentage of future generations. . . oblivious of their liability to produce either genius or idiocy, health or disease" (pp. 86, 94). Like all eugenists, he sees the danger that lies in the differential birthrate: "the families of the most refined and of those whose means provide the best conditions for rearing and educating children are, from various causes, limited; while the poor, the ignorant, and the vicious breed like rabbits" (p. 86). The result is that "man has over-populated the world with a relatively worthless progeny" (p. 99).

Estlake even argues that "[t]he subjection of woman during so many ages" has made this condition "a second nature . . . Reliance on man has become a heredity." If woman is to be free, "Her ambition must be aroused to become the mother of a future and a better race." Similarly, the "young man, the victim of a sexual nature, stimulated into such abnormal cravings as to constitute a disease in the heredity of the race," must be taught discipline in order to overcome this disease (pp. 88–89). Lamarckian eugenist that he is, Estlake recognizes that the successful efforts of potential mothers and fathers to acquire these characteristics will change the heredity of the race only after several generations: "Although the regenerated nature of parents would modify environments of off-spring so as to accustom the young to be more receptive to higher influences, . . . it could not be expected that their changed character-istics would become hereditary in one or a few generations" (pp. 84–85).

The Speckled Bird suggests that Yeats read most of *The Oneida Community*, if not all of it. Although the man from the Oneida Community to whom Michael is listening is "Charles C—" insofar as the unselfish cradle-rocking is concerned, it is more accurate to describe Yeats's "disciple of Noyes" as a composite figure – a figure including aspects of "Charles C—," aspects of a number of other anonymous Com-munity members whom Estlake quotes, and aspects of Estlake himself. When the member of the Oneida Community in *The Speckled Bird* says "With us jealousy is unknown," for instance, he sounds very much like the anonymous member called by Estlake to testify about the salutary effects of the "Community spirit" upon his sexual desires: "Jealousy I never knew" (p. 70). When "the disciple of the Oneida community" explains, "When you abolish private property you necessarily abolish exclusive marriage" (p. 73), he sounds like Estlake: "in a state of life in which ownership did not obtain, property rights of any kind could not be maintained. This disability implied that a man could no more own a wife than anything else" (p. 83).

Similarly, that Yeats makes the novel's Mrs. Samuels complain that the members of the Oneida Community "believe in free love" shows that he noted Estlake's defense of the Community against this very charge:

the free love movement . . . attained such an unenviable reputation for licentiousness that John H. Noyes "set his face as a flint" against them, and was most careful to repudiate not only all of their practices, but to avoid any affiliation whatever with them . . . Notwithstanding the most careful precautions, it proved to be impossible to evade the bad reputation that had been gained by free lovers, so that the term "free love" as applied to the Oneida Community. . . carried with it the unsavoury odour that licentious-ness had laden it with. (p. 81)

Mrs. Samuels goes on to observe that "[t]hey pretend that there should not be any kind of fixed marriage, justifying it by the phrase in the Bible that there will be no marriage nor giving in marriage in heaven" (p. 73). Mrs. Samuels knows Estlake as well as Yeats does, for Estlake indeed proceeds to justify communistic love by Christ's answer to the question about whose wife the seven-times married woman would be after the resurrection: "Christ's answer, that 'in the resurrection they neither marry nor are given in marriage, but are as angels,' . . . helped the faithful . . . whose thoughts turned to the angels as denizens of the higher world they were seeking to live in" (p. 83). The member of the Oneida Community echoes Estlake's point: "Our founder had the courage . . . to realize that a happy community upon earth must be an image of the [community] of the angels" (p. 73).

Yeats also took note of the Community's practice of "criticism." In *The Speckled Bird*, the member of the Oneida Community assures his critics that communistic love and complex marriage are possible because "[c]ontinual criticism made in a spirit of charity keeps us from the Old World errors of exclusiveness" (p. 73). The Community's practice of criticism is mentioned in passing in the account of the relationship between Charles C— and Miss B— (they had been "under criticism for a tendency to drift into exclusive relations"), but Yeats's knowledge of criticism would have come from wider reading in the book, for although criticism is the subject of no single chapter it is presented throughout the book as the *sine qua non* of the Community (p. 75).

Criticism, according to Estlake's mixed metaphor, "was to the Community what ballast is to a ship"; it "was the bulwark against the influx of selfishness" (pp. 58, 42). It originated in a spiritual exercise Noyes had practiced in a society of fellow students intending to become missionaries: "One of the weekly exercises of this society was a frank criticism of each other's character for the purpose of improvement. . . At each meeting, the member whose turn was . . . to submit to criticism, held his peace, while the other members one by one told him his faults in the plainest way possible."[14] On the one hand, "[c]riticism was . . . a barrier to the approach of unworthy people from without," for "[u]nless a man is very earnest in the desire for improvement of character, any investigation of his inner life . . . is so distasteful that the ordeal of receiving a faithful criticism so as to profit by it is a crucial test of sincerity" (pp. 64, 58). Estlake cites the example of "one applicant for membership, who had been accustomed to the etiquette of society and the nice compliments with which people of that class are wont to entertain each other": "Every trait of my character that I took any pride or comfort in seemed to be cruelly discounted; and after, as it were, being turned inside out and throughly inspected, I was, metaphorically, stood upon my head, and allowed to drain till all the self-righteousness had dripped out of me" (p. 67). Accepted into the Community, this member confirmed his sincerity and the wisdom of the practice of criticism, in Estlake's eyes, by the conclusion of his letter: "To-day I feel that I would gladly give many years of my life if I could have just one more criticism from John H. Noyes" (p. 68).

On the other hand, criticism "was equally a bar to the development of evil influences within" the Community (p. 64). As one can see by this member's example, criticism did not end after the initial criticism of probationary members of the Community, but continued throughout one's life in the Community. It was especially sought out as relief from the influence of the world outside. After a day of dealing with curious visitors to the Community (as many as a thousand might visit in one day), "those who had been most exposed to contact with them usually offered themselves for criticism, that their spirts might be freed from contamination by worldly influences" (pp. 60–61). Similarly, those who had to travel as salesmen for the Community "would seek sustaining power . . . by asking criticism before starting out" and would find on their return that "a bath relieved them of the dust of travel and a criticism relieved them of any possible spiritual contamination" (p. 61). The assertion by the member of the Oneida Community in *The Speckled Bird* that "continual criticism" is necessary to keep Community members from "Old World errors" echoes this aspect of *The Oneida Community*'s discussion of criticism.

Instrumental in the success of criticism as such a bar to the development of evil influences within the Community was the spirit in which it was offered. According to Yeats's Oneida man, criticism was made in "a spirit of charity" (*Speckled Bird*, p. 73). This fact is also emphasized by Estlake, who celebrates the Community's "ability to impart criticism in that spirit which provokes love and not wrath, healing the wound it makes" (*Oneida Community*, p. 58). Criticism was an essential part of "the caresses of the truest hearts that ever throbbed with love to their fellow beings"; it thus lived in the Community member's memory as "the loving words of many true friends" (p. 61).

Estlake also asserts that criticism was the foundation of successful complex marriage, essential "for the training of the young and uninitiated" (p. 42). Indeed, without criticism there is no complex marriage, and without complex marriage there is no communism:

"complex marriage and criticism were of such vital importance that
. . . it would be impossible to perpetuate real communism of heart
without" them (p. 42). Estlake therefore claims that the voluntary
suspension of complex marriage in 1879 in the face of public
opposition to the practice can be seen in retrospect to have doomed
the Oneida Community:

Criticism . . . would become unavailable with the introduction of worldly
marriage, for the wife would no longer feel free to criticise her husband
publicly, nor would she tolerate his being criticised by others. . . [S]uffice it
to say, that criticism must die when worldly marriage begins, and that it
ceased under the changed conditions of the Oneida Community. (p. 42)

The importance of criticism to the success of complex marriage is the
very point emphasized by the member of the Oneida Community in
Yeats's novel. His assertion that "[c]ontinual criticism made in a
spirit of charity keeps us from the Old World errors of exclusiveness"
attributes to criticism the Community's success in overcoming
"exclusive and selfish love," "jealousy," and "sex fever" (*Speckled Bird*,
p. 73).

Yeats having read so much of Estlake's book and having taken note of
so many facts about the Oneida Community, did the ideas about
stirpiculture even register – let alone resonate – in his mind? There is
considerable evidence that they did. As we have seen, Maclagan
yearns for the generation-by-generation improvement of the race
that will accompany the mysterious spiritual "transformation" of the
world that he anticipates. Furthermore, there is also interesting
evidence in plays contemporary with his final work on *The Speckled
Bird* in 1902 – plays such as *Where There Is Nothing* (1902), *On Baile's
Strand* (1903), and *The King's Threshold* (1903) – that Yeats did indeed
take heed of the eugenical ideas advanced in *The Oneida Community.*
     In *Where There Is Nothing*, the protagonist Paul Ruttledge condemns
his brother Thomas not just for aligning himself with the world of the
magistrates, but also for bad breeding: "You have begotten fools"
(*Plays* pp. 1119–20). Stanfield suggests that Yeats's "interest in
Nietzsche" accounts for this "interest in breeding," but, as Katherine
Worth points out, Yeats professed to have been introduced to
Nietzsche by John Quinn in September of 1902, and "by that time, of
course, a draft of *Where There Is Nothing* was already in existence."[15] It
would seem more likely, therefore, that through Paul Ruttledge Yeats
echoes here not Nietzsche's contempt for bad breeding, but Estlake's.

These lines led to an exchange of opinions between Yeats and the *Times Literary Supplement* critic A. B. Walkley about these very children. Walkley complained about the loose structure of the play in general, citing in particular the line "You have begotten fools": "This, if you please, is the sole reference in the play to the fact that his brother has any children at all, and we know nothing of them."[16] This criticism ignores or misunderstands both stage directions in Act 1 that bring Thomas's children and a perambulator on stage to be admired by the adults and dialog throughout the play referring to these children. Assuming that Walkley had mistaken the children in Act 1 for Paul's children, Yeats wrote to Walkley to put him straight: "Those children were not Paul's but his brother's, in fact the fools that he begot."[17]

Since Walkley is correct to point out that we know nothing of these children, the confidence that Yeats shows – both through his own voice in his letter and through his character Paul's voice in the play – that one can declare children of whom we know nothing "fools" would seem to be based on hereditarian assumptions. After all, in the nineteenth-century world of the play, it is unlikely that the child in the perambulator would have been wheeled out to the admiring gaze of all had it already shown tendencies toward foolishness, imbecility, or idiocy. The confident reference by Yeats and Paul to these children as "fools" casts aspersions not so much upon the children as upon their parents: they have begotten unadvisedly. In the words of *Purgatory*, they have "Begot, and passed pollution on" (*Plays* p. 1049).

These misbegotten are the result of a bad marriage, or so both Paul and Yeats would have it, for to criticize Thomas for having "begotten fools" is to criticize his wife Georgina as much as Thomas himself. In fact, Yeats makes it clear that Thomas is merely Georgina's surrogate, marriage having made him her agent in defense of household and home (*Plays* pp. 1077, 1110). Georgina and Thomas represent the status quo, the mundane, and the radically practical – the things that drive Paul away. Georgina in particular is antithetical to Paul: she declares his hedge sculptures "nonsense"; she confesses that she "can't imagine why" he "won't come in and be sociable" and complains that he is "always doing uncomfortable things"; in the face of his tinker's dress and his allusive metaphorical language, she can only conclude that "he is going mad!" (*Plays* pp. 1066–67, 1084). As it amounts to much the same thing, she is as eager to give Paul a lesson in sociability as she is to give their friends "a lesson in croquet": in each case, she has "learned all the new rules" (*Plays* p. 1078).

According to Paul's interpretation of his subsequent mystical visions, these rules are a sign of the Fall: "Laws were the first sin. They were the first mouthful of the apple, the moment man had made them he began to die" (*Plays* p. 1137). Before this, men and women "wept and laughed and hated according to the impulse of their hearts," that is, "according to . . . mother wit and natural kindness" (*Plays* p. 1136–37). Georgina is therefore a daughter of Eve, a betrayer of mother wit. Her symbolic role as Law explains why Yeats surrounds her with magistrates. Friends of the family, these magistrates celebrate Georgina as the upholder of the "laws" that should prevail in the business of managing a household, having children, and preserving a family name. Mr. Algie says, "What a pleasure it must be to Paul to have you and the little ones living here. . . Man was not born to live alone" (*Plays* p. 1077–78). Mr. Joyce says, "you and Thomas will keep up the family name better than he would have done" (*Plays* p. 1085). Georgina's role as Law also explains why Paul proposes to marry Sabina Silver, for she represents the vagabond community of tinkers who live outside Georgina's law – as Paul says, "they are quite lawless. That is what attracts me to them" (*Plays* p. 1081).

This impulsive marriage seems to put Paul on the way to the ruin delineated in *Purgatory* where the bad marriage choice of the owner of a house like Paul's produces within two generations "A bastard that a pedlar got / Upon a tinker's daughter in a ditch" (*Plays* p. 1044). But there is a eugenical logic in Paul's behavior – precisely what is missing in the behavior of his *Purgatory* counterpart. Determined "to go back to the dark ages," Paul sees the tinkers as representing the realm of "mother wit and natural kindness" that he seeks (*Plays* pp. 1084, 1137). His implicitly eugenical goal in proposing to marry Sabina is the one acknowledged in *On the Boiler*. Since "clairvoyance, prevision, and allied gifts, rare among the educated classes, are common among peasants," and since "[t]hese gifts must return," Yeats implies that in order "to hold to what we have that the next civilization may be born . . . of our own rich experience" it will be necessary for a Paul to marry a Sabina: then "the best bred from the best shall claim again their ancient omens."[18] Paul's marriage to Sabina is implicitly a response to Thomas's marriage to Georgina: Sabina is to be the new Eve, redeemer of mother wit.

Yeats depicts his concerns about degeneration by means of farmyard imagery. Paul is first seen clipping hedges into the shape of birds. The stage directions state: "The hedge is clipped into shapes of farmyard fowl" (*Plays* p. 1064). The one he is working on, he tells his brother, "is a Cochin China fowl, an image of some of our neighbours, like the others" – a likeness Thomas would appreciate if he "could see their minds instead of their bodies" (*Plays* p. 1065). These neighbors are all "poultry" who "chirp or quack"; "they think in flocks and roosts" (*Plays* pp. 1069–70). In short, they are "like farmyard creatures, they have forgotten their freedom" (*Plays* p. 1069). Unlike the products of the farmyard eugenics celebrated by Noyes, these domesticated creatures represent biological degeneration, a decline in human being: "their human bodies are a disguise, a pretence they keep up to deceive one another" (*Plays* p. 1069). Paul's argument that his neighbors have become a domesticated breed preoccupied with maintaining family names, and that this tendency has produced a degeneration in terms of their human being, is an application of Estlake's similar observations: "What is called 'pure blood' of any type is not progressive. It is too narrow. Its tendency is too much toward pride of genealogy. People relying upon admiration of past achievements and reputation of ancestors, deteriorate" (*Oneida Community* p. 107). It is this deterioration through admiration of the wrong things that Yeats stages at the end of Act 1 when the children appear and "[a]ll gather round them admiringly" (*Plays* p. 1085).

That Walkley should not have noticed these children or noted that they are Thomas's is curious. Certainly Thomas's children were from the beginning an important element in Yeats's conception of the play and he wanted them to be noticed – if not admired. The first stage direction describes "[a] table with toys on it" and a subsequently omitted 1902 stage direction foregrounds these toys: "Paul yawns, takes up the ball and cup from table, and sways it" (*Plays* pp. 1064, 1065). Similarly, in subsequently altered 1902 dialogue, Paul also draws attention to this toy by declaring that he has to catch the ball "twenty times without missing" before he can go inside with Georgina (*Plays* p. 1067). Furthermore, even without such lines and stage directions, Yeats explained in his letter to Walkley that when the time came to stage the play he would direct it so as to focus even more attention upon these children: "I see the perambulator on the middle of the stage, or rather I cannot see it, for everyone is standing round it, stooping over it with their backs to me."[19]

Yeats signals his thematic intentions with regard both to the general attention to Thomas's children in Act 1 and to Paul's later denigrating reference to them in Act 3 by means of two rhetorical questions prompted by the tableau that he describes: "Is [the perambulator] not the conqueror of all idealists? And are not all these magistrates but its courtiers and its servants?"[20] Yeats's point here in part parallels Shaw's in his almost exactly contemporaneous and even more directly eugenical play *Man and Superman* (1903): idealists like John Tanner are conquered by the Life Force. Notwithstanding a Tanner's ambition to devote himself exclusively to intellectual creativity, biological creativity tends to prevail. But Yeats's point is also different – not that the ideal has been subordinated to the prerogatives of life, but rather that the individual has been subordinated to the prerogatives of the group.

In *Where There Is Nothing*, those who gather about the perambulator betray the mindset of the flock. Their admiration for Thomas's children is admiration for those who – unlike Paul and the vagabonds – "have no nonsense in their heads" (*Plays* p. 1086). What remnants of prelapsarian mother wit such a child might possess will be extinguished by the Law of the flock, which does not tolerate nonsense. Yeats's intended staging implies that people who "think in flocks and roosts" bequeath the same tendency to their children – both by nature and by nurture. Yeats and Paul thus have all the evidence they need to conclude that Thomas has "begotten fools."

In his contemptuous dismissal of Thomas's children, Paul implies that a perambulator deserves attention only if there is someone special in it: "There's nothing interesting but human nature, and that's in the single soul" (*Plays* p. 1070). Estlake makes the same point when identifying "pride of genealogy" as a source of racial deterioration: "Pride supplants appreciation of personal merit" (*Oneida Community*, pp. 107–08). Paul claims this singularity and personal merit for himself. No farmyard fowl, Paul is aligned instead with the tinkers' fighting cocks: "how you took to the cocks!" says Paddy Cockfight, "I believe you were a better judge than myself" (*Plays* p. 1122). Perhaps it takes one to know one: Paul, suffering bruised ribs from his fight with the forces of law and order, "is doubled up . . . like that old cock of Andy Farrell's" (*Plays* p. 1122). Paddy Cockfight, however, also knows a singular bird when he sees it, as he explains in describing his acquisition of his "new speckled bird": "The day I first seen him I fastened my two eyes on him, he preyed on my mind, and next night, if I didn't go back every foot of nine miles to put him in my bag" (*Plays* p. 1106). Similarly, having had to leave Paul behind because of his injuries, the tinkers return by play's end to reclaim him. Like Michael Hearne, Paul is this speckled bird – the speckled bird of Jeremiah, beset by other birds because of its singularity (Jeremiah 12: 9). Similarly, playing with the child's toy until he has caught the ball twenty times, and confused that the tinker's children should not confide in him as one of them, Paul positions himself symbolically alongside Thomas's children – available for inspection. But this bird of a different feather is not admired by the flock. In fact, he is set upon by the mother hen Georgina and avoided by the tinker children. His singularity and personal merit go unappreciated.

One of the play's most interesting eugenical concerns is the misunderstanding of inheritance evident in the behavior of Paul's fellow magistrates. They admire the wrong thing. They breed for the wrong reasons. By the sin of the Law, they have turned from the natural authority of the heart and mother wit to the abstract authority of genealogy, social position, and financial considerations. That children who are "fools" in comparison to the childlike Paul's singularity and personal merit should be admired for the genealogy, social position, and financial standing that they inherit is too galling a dispossession for Paul to endure. Although the magistrates recognize that, according to the law of primogeniture, Paul was to the manor born, Paul seems to be the only one to recognize that his authority derives not from Law but from mother wit.

The attention to the question of authority and inheritance diminishes after Act 1. The play's main concern is to take Paul from a world where material comforts and social conventions are *something* to a world where these things are nothing (the world of the tinkers) and then to a world where there is a more profound nothing that grounds experience of the divine (the world of the mystic and visionary). Such concerns seem far removed from eugenics, but when Paul leaves his home and the material values of the world represented by Georgina and the magistrates with the words "I have begun the regeneration of my soul," he echoes Estlake's theory about how individuals and cultures develop spiritual awareness. Understanding consciousness to be a function of a mind–body dualism in which the thought of a mind expresses itself as vibration through the mechanism of a material brain, Estlake explains why "[s]piritual perception can only be acquired through regeneration":

When thought develops cerebral structures capable of responding to higher
vibrations, this responsive faculty demands thoughts still higher to which it
may respond . . . [T]hought begetting thought, there must come a time
when vibrations attuned to material things fail to satisfy the cravings of
consciousness; and this yearning of the soul for higher vibrations of thought
must lead directly into regeneration as the only portal to experience on a
higher plane. (*Oneida Community*, p. 144–45)

Yeats comes close to quoting Estlake directly in Paul's line, "I have
begun the regeneration of my soul." For Estlake and Yeats alike, this
regeneration of the soul also requires the regeneration of the race.

These questions about the nature of authority and its manner of
inheritance become the main theme of Yeats's next play, *On Baile's
Strand* (1903). Although Stanfield describes it as showing tendencies
that have "much to do with his later interest in eugenics," it is better
described as showing an early interest in eugenics that is in some
ways as coherent and comprehensive as the well-documented later
interest.[21] Like Paul Ruttledge, Cuchulain complains of bad breeding
and degeneration: "Conchubar, / I do not like your children – they
have no pith, / No marrow in their bones, and will lie soft / Where
you and I lie hard" (*Plays* p. 481). Cuchulain is so convinced that a
trend toward degeneration has set in that he acknowledges both that
his own father would have bested him, had they fought, and that if he
himself had had a son, the father would again inevitably have
prevailed in combat: "For the old fiery fountains are far off / And
every day there is less heat o'the blood" (*Plays* p. 511). Mistakenly
believing that he has no children of his own, Cuchulain consoles
himself with the thought that at least he will "leave / No pallid ghost
or mockery of a man"; he will not be "marred . . . in the copying"
(*Plays* pp. 483, 485).
   Noting such implicitly eugenical lines and reviewing the publishing
history of the play, Stanfield suggests that none of the "passages
referring to degeneration appeared in the first published version of
the play, that of 1903. The play was heavily revised, and the idea of
degeneration introduced, sometime prior to the publication of the
play in *Poems, 1899–1905*, in 1906."[22] Yet in lines dating from the
earliest version of the play in 1903, Conchubar's expectation that
Cuchulain will obey his children simply because they have inherited
his kingly authority prompts the latter to draw attention to the
problem of inheritance: "Let your children / Re-mortar their

inheritance, as we have, / And put more muscle on" (*Plays* p. 507). Like Maclagan, Cuchulain can measure the degree of degeneration that each generation suffers by comparing present muscles with past muscles, and again like Maclagan he believes that muscles can be improved both within an individual lifetime and over generations – insofar as re-mortared muscle is inheritable as an acquired character-istic. Cuchulain's advice to Conchubar's children is quite eugenical, quite Lamarckian, and quite literal: acquire some muscle worth inheriting – thence comes hereditary authority.

In other lines from the 1903 version of the play – lines subsequently eliminated from the version of the play appearing in 1906 and afterwards – Yeats attributes to Conchubar a eugenical understand-ing of war. Criticized by the drunken Daire for having "hated peace" and thereby caused the death of many a great figure, Conchubar claims that the wars he waged were necessary – undertaken either "to strengthen Emain" or, more interestingly, to prevent dysgenic procreation: "When wars are out they marry and beget / And have their generations like mankind / And there's no help for it" (*Plays* p. 494). Having just asserted that he and his fellow kings, "Being the foremost of men," should "be much stared at and wondered at, and speak / Out of more laughing overflowing hearts / Than common men," Conchubar implies that the responsibility to remain aloof from "mankind" or "common men" in general bearing also applies to procreation (*Plays* p. 490). At times, therefore, he wages war to prevent the degeneration that threatens when his kings and queens begin to "marry and beget / And have their generations like mankind." Better that some should not beget than that they should beget unthinkingly and perhaps pass pollution on, for then "there's no help for it."

Apparently anticipating here the much later debate at the First Eugenics Conference and in *The Eugenics Review* about whether the effect of war was eugenic or dysgenic, Yeats actually imputes to Conchubar a perspective that he had encountered in *The Oneida Community*. According to Estlake, war is part of "nature's plan of evolution" (p. 102). On the one hand, nature promotes the "intensi-fication of tribal traits through long periods of clannish exclusive-ness"; on the other hand, it promotes "the merging of varying tribes and nations with their characteristic traits by means of conquest and captivity" (p. 102). So we learn that the clannish and exclusive Aoife boasts "that she's never but the one lover, and he the only man that had overcome her in battle," and so we see that the child of this union is a merging of the best aspects of the two parents (*Plays* p. 521). Estlake also observes that "[i]n the absence of more enlightened means of progression . . . History is replete with evidences of nature's plan of promoting higher civilization through suffering from the sword followed by pestilence, famine, and all the cruelties that man can be capable of inflicting" (*Oneida Community* p. 102). Yeats obliquely acknowledges the dysgenical correlative of Estlake's point when rereading *On Baile's Strand* in his own copy of his *Collected Works* of 1908, for in a never-published revision he changes Conchubar's explanation of Cuchulain's disdain for his children with "no pith / No marrow in their bones" from "You rail at them / Because you have no children of your own" to "You rail at them / Because the war and changes of land and sea / Have left you with no children of your own."[23]

Now that there is peace, however, Conchubar's great project is "to build up Emain that was burned / At the outsetting of these wars" (*Plays* p. 490). Emain will be strengthened only by ensuring that both the foremost buildings and the foremost people are made of the right stuff:

> It is the art of kings
> To make what's noble nobler in men's eyes
> By wide uplifted roofs, where beaten gold,
> That's ruddy with desire, marries pale silver
> Among the shadowy beams.   (*Plays* p. 490)

Like Sidney's artist, Yeats's artful king will make the brazen world golden, but the sexual metaphor directing gold to marry silver acknowledges that in Conchubar's project – unlike Sidney's – art and biology are intertwined. Cuchulain anticipates Conchubar's imagery but not his biological subtext: "while [Conchubar] talks of hammered bronze and asks / What wood is best for building, we can talk / Of a fierce woman" (*Plays* p. 478). Cuchulain underestimates Conchubar – both Conchubar's choice of metal, and his choice of people. The peace by which Conchubar plans to build both his city and his race (so long as gold marries silver, and both refrain from bronze) proves to be a much more sophisticated understanding of Cuchulain's narrower view of deep passion as "a difficult peace" ("a kiss / In the mid battle") between "the hot-footed sun, and the cold sliding slippery-footed moon" – a battle that has lasted "for three times the age / Of this long 'stablished ground" (*Plays* p. 478).

The revised version of the play reverses these roles, making Cuchulain the one who warns society about the threat of degeneration and leaving Conchubar the one who does not comprehend the eugenical issues at stake in the biological future of Emain. Nonetheless, the muscular advice of 1903 remains in the 1906 version of the play as evidence of the first version of its eugenical theme. It would seem, then, not that the much revised later version *introduces* the theme of heredity and degeneration to a play without such a theme, but rather that it greatly expands a theme present from the beginning – a theme about heredity and degeneration that is itself inherited and regenerated from *Where There Is Nothing*, *The Speckled Bird*, and *The Oneida Community*.

Whereas in *On Baile's Strand* Yeats develops more explicitly and more fully Paul Ruttledge's concerns in *Where There Is Nothing* about unrecognized hereditary authority, in *The King's Threshold* (1903) he both continues this meditation on the role of hereditary authority in the state and develops more explicitly and more fully Conchubar's suggestion in *On Baile's Strand* that art and biology work hand-in-hand in building a culture and a race.

The magistrate Paul Ruttledge has abandoned the law and his fellow magistrates in favor of mother wit and the impulses of the heart, but Seanchan finds himself expelled from the poet's traditional place in the national council because of the King's belief that "it is the men of law, / Leaders of the King's armies, and the like, / That should sit there" (*Plays* p. 289). Paul and Seanchan represent an authority different from and opposed to Law – an authority no longer recognized by their societies. *The King's Threshold* makes explicit what remains implicit in *Where There Is Nothing* and *On Baile's Strand*: the reason that dysgenic "fools" are begotten by this neglect of a wisdom older than Law. Thus Seanchan invites his oldest pupil to rehearse the weightiest argument that he has learned about why poetry ought to be honored:

> the poets hung
> Images of the life that was in Eden
> About the child-bed of the world, that it,
> Looking upon those images, might bear
> Triumphant children.   (*Plays* p. 264)

Yeats has more than Winckelmann, Pater, and Wilde in mind. Of "cripples" who beg food from him, Seanchan asks, "What bad poet did your mothers listen to / That you were born so crooked?" (*Plays* p. 299). Observing the eyes, ears, mouths, and feet of the court women, Seanchan concludes: "The mothers that have borne you mated rightly" (*Plays* p. 294). He recommends that they "Go to the young men": "Are not the ruddy flesh and the thin flanks / And the broad shoulders worthy of desire?" (*Plays* p. 294). Seanchan's love songs thus supplement Maclagan's statues and Conchubar's "art of kings" as inducements to eugenical mating. Whether a Greek statue in the British Museum, a king making "what's noble nobler in men's eyes," or a poet celebrating strength and beauty, art can serve as a way of determining the direction and of measuring the distance that the contemporary human being must travel biologically to return to the human ideal.

Without the arts, Seanchan suggests, the world "would be like a woman / That, looking on the cloven lips of a hare, / Brings forth a hare-lipped child" (*Plays* p. 265). Indeed, he terrifies the King's daughters by suggesting that "A little while before [their] birth," their kind mother was blessed by a leper and so may have bequeathed to her daughters "hands / That are contaminated" (*Plays* p. 296). He then wildly declares to the court as a whole, "There's no sound hand among you . . . / You are all lepers!" – symbolizing by his apparent delusion the biological contamination that will come from their neglect of the poet's eugenical authority. He is convinced that were he to have given in to the King, "The kiss of multitudes in times to come / Had been the poorer" (*Plays* pp. 305–06). In the end, both the original comic ending, which sees the King acknowledge Seanchan's authority, and the later tragic ending, which sees the King refuse to yield to Seanchan, agree that degeneration has set in such that "nor song nor trumpet-blast / Can call up races from the worsening world / To mend the wrong" done to Seanchan (*Plays* p. 312). Consistent with this assertion that the world is "worsening" is Yeats's eventual elimination from the play of the King's claim that despite momentary sympathy for Seanchan he is

> now all king again,
> Remembering that the seed I come of, although
> A hundred kings have sown it and resown it,
> Has neither trembled nor shrunk backward yet. (*Plays* p. 307)

Such lines are inappropriate given the eugenical premise of the play that the germ plasm of the nation – including the king's – has indeed trembled and shrunk backward through neglect of the poet's eugenical authority.

Not surprisingly, Seanchan's celebration of poetry's function as eugenical preserver and protector of humanity's biological future appears in Yeats's poetry of 1902 and 1903. Particularly prominent in the poems of these years, collected in *In the Seven Woods* (1904), is Yeats's interest to define woman's role in the eugenical enterprise. As stirpicultural poet, Seanchan coaches the women of the court to choose "ruddy flesh," "thin flanks," and "broad shoulders," but the poet's instructions to the men of the court with regard to what they are to seek in women is not so clear. In many of the poems of 1902 and 1903, however, Yeats hints that he sees women and poets as having parallel eugenical roles: their shared task is to educate and discipline man to direct his "ruddy desire" toward beauty.

In "Adam's Curse" (1902) woman's beauty parallels the poet's word – the poet declaring that "to articulate sweet sounds together / Is to work harder" than most others in the world, the "beautiful mild woman" declaring that she too "must labour to be beautiful," and implying that she must do so with "sweet sounds" similar to the poet's, for her "voice is sweet and low." The word *labour* here is loaded with double meaning, for the labor of the "beautiful mild woman" that the poem contemplates is as much a matter of the womb as a matter of the dressing table or proper schooling. That is, insofar as her beauty is concerned, Yeats marks the beautiful woman as a thing of the body, a being whose knowledge and function come of being born a woman: "To be born woman is to know. . . / That we must labour to be beautiful." Pace Simone de Beauvoir, Yeats's "beautiful mild woman" would have it that one is not only born female, but also "born woman." And born woman, one has knowledge, "Although they do not talk of it at school." This knowledge is different from the intellectual knowledge of men who "quote with learned looks / Precedents out of beautiful old books" (*Poems* pp. 204–05). Grounded in woman's body, it is implicitly instinctive or intuitive knowledge.

The beauty in question is the result of collaboration between the artist and the woman, a point Yeats makes in "Discoveries" (1906): "A wise theatre might make a training in strong and beautiful life the fashion, teaching before all else the heroic discipline of the looking glass, for is not beauty, even as lasting love, one of the most difficult of the arts?"[24] The playwright and the woman are teachers; their knowledge is a discipline; they instruct their audience with regard to human ideals of strength and beauty. Like Conchubar's "art of kings" that makes "what's noble nobler in men's eyes" and Seanchan's "heady craft" that commends the "wasteful virtues" of the nobility, the "art of beauty" trains people to make "strong and beautiful life the fashion" and thereby to acknowledge the beautiful people to be the aristocrats whose standards of strength and beauty are to be admired and emulated.

Like the art of kings and the craft of poetry, therefore, the art of beauty is also oriented toward eugenics. The discipline of the looking glass creates the beautiful woman who in turn serves as looking glass for the people. As Yeats put it in "The Statues" more than three decades later, the art of Phidias "Gave women dreams and dreams their looking glass" (*Poems* p. 610). The beautiful woman as looking glass parallels the artist as looking glass: each presents the beautiful ideal. Each thereby instructs men and women alike as to standards of beauty to be sought – through personal grooming and comportment in emulation of such beauty, through marriage to a person demonstrating such beauty, and through procreation that will combine the partners' individual beauties into a more beautiful descendent.

Seanchan makes it clear that strength is beauty's reward, for the eyes, ears, mouth, and feet of certain court women earn them the right to expect ruddy flesh, thin flanks and broad shoulders in a man. Yeats makes it clear in "Peace" (1910) that beauty is strength's reward, for Maud Gonne's beauty is a form such as "painters paint" – "a form / That could show what Homer's age / Bred to be a hero's wage" (*Poems* p. 258). In the poems of 1902 and 1903, Yeats presents himself as Homer and Pygmalion both, shaping Gonne's virtues to be his own reward and asking only that she learn this through an "Old Memory" (1904):

> Your strength, that is so lofty and fierce and kind,
> It might call up a new age, calling to mind
> The queens that were imagined long ago,
> Is but half yours: he kneaded in the dough
> Through the long years of youth.   (*Poems* p. 201)

Her beauty and strength are the looking glass that might make a new age if, like Maclagan's statues, such beauty and strength should inspire emulative behavior – emulation extending all the way to procreation. It is because of the procreative potential of her beauty, and despite his fear of the same commonness that Conchubar fears, that Yeats claims in "In the Seven Woods" that he has "forgot awhile Tara uprooted, and new commonness / Upon the throne" (*Poems* p. 198). Maud Gonne's beauty is the promise of a "new age," redemption from the nation's seed squandered – whether by King Guaire in *The King's Threshold* or Edward VII in England.

Insofar as she is attracting a strong man for herself by laboring to be beautiful, the beautiful woman's role as hero's reward is the same role Yeats defines for her in his later poetry: man-picker. Unfortunately, however, just as there are what Seanchan calls "bad poets" who can badly sing the wrong couples into bed, so there are beautiful women who can pick the wrong men – precisely as Gonne did in marrying John MacBride as a reward for his heroism against the British in the Boer War:

> My love is angry that of late
> I cry all base blood down
> As though she had not taught me hate
> By kisses to a clown.[25]

Practicing the discipline of the looking glass badly, neglecting to make "strong and beautiful life the fashion," the beautiful woman can at least teach a negative eugenical lesson by her bad art.

And so Yeats sees the beautiful woman as serving humankind in the eugenical way Estlake explains:

evolution was preparing a fitting instrument for the expression of consciousness, by selecting through animal instinct the fittest to procreate; as consciousness developed, intuition took the place of instinct, and the female element being by nature more intuitional than the male, provided better conditions for co-operation with nature in the progression of the race. (*Oneida Community* p. 100)

Intuition, however, is not infallible and therefore must be supplemented

by an intelligent system of love relations, so that when through education or other means a desired brain development has been achieved, it may not be lost by injudicious mingling with undesirable strains, but be intensified and made permanent by an infallible intuition which will surely follow any intelligent attempt to improve humanity by looking for the best conditions and traits most desirable for transmission. (p. 101)

Estlake agrees with Shaw that until the "raw force" of Life builds human beings up "into higher and higher individuals, the ideal individual being omnipotent, omniscient, infallible, and withal completely, unilludedly self-conscious," the woman will have to do by intuition the job that self-consciousness will eventually inherit: the labor of the Life Force.[26] In Yeats's version of this story, the intuitive faculty of woman as man-picking hero's reward is educated and directed by poetry – an intellectual supplement serving the biological function of the higher stirpicultural intelligence that Estlake anticipates.

Looking back at Gonne's beauty from the perspective of *The Trembling of the Veil*, Yeats glosses his 1902 and 1903 poems about her beauty in the very terms that he would revisit in "The Statues": "her face, like the face of some Greek statue, showed little thought, her whole body seemed a master-work of long laboring thought, as though a Scopas had measured and calculated, consorted with Egyptian sages, and mathematicians out of Babylon, that he might out-face even Artemisia's sepulchral image with a living norm."[27] Here are "[t]he lineaments of a plummet-measured face" in the direction of which Yeats sees both the ancient Greeks and the modern Irish procreating in his 1939 poem. Stimulus of an intuitive force, Maud Gonne need show no more self-consciousness than a Greek statue or "boys and girls, pale from the imagined love / Of solitary beds" (*Poems* p. 610). As the result of generations of breeding both by evolution and by poetry, however, her body will inevitably give the appearance of forethought. It is not coincidental that in "Old Memory" Yeats finds her beauty "calling to mind / The queens that were imagined long ago," for her beauty is the result of the collaboration between the poet's imagining of those queens and the people's breeding of such queens as the heroic king's reward. Thus in *The Trembling of the Veil* Yeats recalls that "there was an element in her beauty that moved minds full of old Gaelic stories and poems."[28] She is reminiscent of these others because she is both literally and figuratively descended from them. Intuitive man-pickers laboring to be beautiful and intellectual poets belaboring the strong and beautiful life have thus conspired eugenically to produce the "living norm."[29]

The eugenical issues evolving in the novel, the plays, and the poetry of 1902 and 1903 are brought to a focus in Yeats's 1903 Preface to Lady Gregory's *God's and Fighting Men* (1904). Written in late 1903, it gathers together in a single paragraph a surprisingly large number of images, words, and phrases from the plays and poems composed during 1902 and 1903 – in each case, an image, word, or phrase associated in these works with his development of aspects of the stirpicultural eugenics of *The Oneida Community* that interested him. In doing so, Yeats made this Preface the site for the transfer of eugenical ideas from the realm of myth and legend to the realm of contemporary Irish society and politics.

Celebrating the Gaelic legends that Lady Gregory had translated in both *Cuchulain of Muirthemne* (1902) and *God's and Fighting Men* (1904), Yeats observes: "We cannot say how much that literature [of "Gaelic-speaking Ireland"] has done for the vigour of the race, for who can count the hands its praise of kings and high-hearted queens made hot upon the sword-hilt, or the amorous eyes it made lustful for strength and beauty?"[30] This is the goal for "wise theatre" that Yeats announces in "Discoveries" – the goal of making "a training in strong and beautiful life the fashion." Hoping that a popular modern theater might duplicate its success, Yeats suggests that the old popular literature has made so substantial a contribution to the vigor of the race that it is difficult to quantify. On the one hand, it has strengthened the state the way the "art of kings" strengthened Emain – that is, by making kings and queens "much stared at and wondered at" by those who would be called to serve them with sword. Seanchan's claim is similar:

> not a man alive
> Would ride among the arrows with high heart,
> Or scatter with an open hand, had not
> Our heady craft commended wasteful virtues. (*Plays* p. 290)

On the other hand, popular literature has strengthened the state biologically in the same way that Seanchan, Conchubar, and even Maclagan would – by gently knocking likely couples into bed through art's directing of them toward ideals of strength and beauty.

With the heat of the blood diminishing in the one, and the King's seed worsening in the other, both *On Baile's Strand* and *The King's Threshold* contemplate communities threatened with the loss of their old aristocracy, and so echoes of these plays not surprisingly emerge from images, words, and phrases in an essay contemplating modern Ireland's plight in the absence of just such an aristocracy – an early and regular theme in Yeats's work, well-documented in Yeats scholarship. Yet Yeats also brings these plays to mind because modern Ireland and the old Ireland of Conchubar and Seanchan are all "worsening" because of dysgenic habits. As in *The King's Threshold* and *On Baile's Strand*, one of Ireland's most pressing problems is the problem of poetry and eugenics.

In old Ireland, Yeats implies, the poets were, like Seanchan, part of the national council – if not formally, at least informally. Even when they were not actually members of government, by means of the "old stories" they left, the Gaelic poets counseled – and to a certain extent governed – through their poetry. They "helped to sing the Old Irish and the old Norman-Irish aristocracy to their end. They heard their hereditary poets and story-tellers, and they took to horse and died fighting against Elizabeth or against Cromwell" (Preface p. 133). Similarly, even "when an English-speaking aristocracy had their place, it listened to no poetry indeed, but it felt about it in the popular mind an exacting and ancient tribunal, and began a play that had for spectators men and women that loved the high wasteful virtues" (p. 133). This old Ireland is dead and gone – not just because the old aristocrats are dead and gone, but also because the old poets are dead and gone. In their poetry was to be found the nation's "habit of mind" – still sufficiently vigorous in the eighteenth-century to have influenced the English-speaking successors to the old Irish and old Norman-Irish aristocracy, but no longer so (p. 132).

The loss of the aristocracy, the loss of poetry, and the loss of the nation's habit of mind are the same thing. The old aristocracy "heard their hereditary poets"; their English-speaking successors "listened to no poetry" but felt "the popular mind" about them; but there is no more aristocracy "in an age that has lost the understanding of the word" (p. 133). The word "aristocracy" was understood in past ages because "the art of kings" commended "laughing overflowing hearts" (*Plays* p. 490) and the poet's "craft" commended "wasteful virtues" (*Plays* p. 290). The aristocracy was the product of the habit of mind produced by values commended in art. In "The Trembling of the Veil," Yeats recurs to this point in explaining the appeal of Maud Gonne's beauty to the people of Ireland: "she looked as though she lived in an ancient civilization where all superiorities whether of mind or body were part of public ceremonial, were in some way the crowd's creation."[31] In hearing the poets or feeling the popular mind, aristocrats performed the roles written for them by the poets, the roles expected of them by the spectators – the ones who stared at and admired Conchubar's kings and queens, the "women by the churn / And children by the hearth" in Seanchan's time who, hearing "a song about enchanted kings," "caught up the song / And murmured it" (*Plays* p. 290). Yeats recalls Conchubar's and Seanchan's understanding of the mechanism that produces aristocracy in the Preface: "When one reads of the Fianna, or of Cuchulain, or of any of their like, one remembers that the fine life is always a part played before fine spectators" (p. 133). In the end, "when the fine spectators have ended, surely the fine players grow weary, and aristocratic life is ended" (p. 133). The English-speaking aristocracy lasted only so long as they "had for spectators men and women that loved the high wasteful virtues," and such spectators exist only so long as "something of the habit of mind" of Gaelic-speaking Ireland "remains in ways of speech and thought and 'come-all-ye's' and poetical sayings . . . when Gaelic has gone and the poetry with it" (pp. 132–33).

Despite the suppression of Gaelic-speaking Ireland since the time of Elizabeth and the time of Cromwell, Yeats identifies a point when an Irish habit of mind, an Irish poetry, and an Irish aristocracy might have been renewed: when the English-speaking aristocracy took the place of the old Irish and old Norman-Irish aristocracy. Listening to no poetry but feeling the impress of the remnants of the popular mind that the old poetry had produced, English-speaking aristocrats performed versions of the *sprezzatura* and generosity that Ireland's remaining fine spectators expected. Yeats celebrates the "gentlemen of the eighteenth century" who went out "to fight duels over pocket-handkerchiefs, and set out to play ball against the gates of Jerusalem for a wager, and scatter money before the public eye" (p. 133). They produced "an epoch of such eloquence the world has hardly seen its like" (p. 133). Performing the role of aristocrats, maintaining an eloquent literature, and perpetuating as best they were able the habit of mind impressed upon them, they simply did not survive long enough to establish themselves. They lost "their public spirit and their high heart" and grew "querulous and selfish" (p. 133). In Yeats's judgment, "[h]ad they known the people and the game a little better, they might have created an aristocracy in an age that has lost the understanding of the word" (p. 133).

To know the people and the game a little better is to know the poetry better – for therein resides the habit of mind that produces the game or play, the people as spectators, and the aristocrat as player.

An English-speaking aristocracy performing a play written by Gaelic-speaking poets "played out life not heartily but with noise and tumult" (p. 133). The aristocrat's "high heart" was not in it because it was not an entirely Gaelic heart; Conchubar's "laughing overflowing heart" was beating in a foreign language. The aristocrat's "public spirit" lapsed into selfishness because it was not entirely one with the Gaelic public whose spectral remnants inspirited them as best it could; Seanchan's "wasteful virtues" were commended in a foreign language. The community of poet, spectator, and performer was fractured in what Yeats called "that splendid misunderstanding of the eighteenth century" (p. 134). The "gentlemen of the eighteenth century" were insufficiently like their descendent Maud Gonne – more thoroughly than they "the crowd's creation," the creation of "minds full of old Gaelic stories and poems."[32]

Yeats characterizes this fracture and this misunderstanding as at least in part a matter of blood. As explanation of the English aristocracy's pursuit of "the high wasteful virtues," Yeats writes, "I do not think that their own mixed blood or the habit of their time need take all, or nearly all, credit or discredit" (p. 133). Credit is due for the *sprezzatura* and generosity; discredit is due for the loss of "high heart" and "public spirit." Whatever the proportion of credit and discredit it deserves, a blood mixed of Gaelic and English strains is partially responsible for the cultural mix-up: the English-speaking aristocracy's inability to listen to the Gaelic poetry that it "felt about it" (p. 133).

Yet whatever discredit it deserves for the "misunderstanding of the eighteenth century," this mixed blood is marked with a "splendid" potential never realized – to Yeats's great regret and, according to Yeats, to modern Ireland's even greater regret. The English-speaking aristocracy "might have created an aristocracy in an age that has lost the understanding of the word" (p. 133). That is, it might have bequeathed an aristocracy to the modern Ireland in which Yeats writes, for his tense here indicates that Yeats's age is the one that "has lost the understanding" of aristocracy.

The *sprezzatura* and generosity of this English-speaking aristocracy is embodied in the one true aristocrat in *Where There Is Nothing*, Paul Ruttledge. Yeats suggests in his essay that when one reads of the Fianna, Cuchulain, and the like, "[t]here one also notices the hot cup and the cold cup of intoxication" (p. 103) – an echo of Paul's determination "to drink contentedly out of the cup of life, out of the drunken cup of life" (*Plays* p. 1104). This splendid drunkenness is "in honour of [his] wedding" to Sabina: "I'll have all the public-houses thrown open, and free drinks going for a week!" (*Plays* p. 1104). The retrospective gaze of Yeats's essay confirms that Paul's intoxicating marriage to Sabina represents a potential mixing of the blood of old Ireland and its English-speaking aristocracy – one way to create "an aristocracy in an age that has lost the understanding of the word" (as Paul's has). According to Yeats, the mixed blood of the English-speaking aristocracy helped to produce a people of "impulse" – "the impulse that made those gentlemen of the eighteenth century fight duels over pocket-handkerchiefs . . . and scatter money before the public eye" (Preface p. 133) – the same "impulse of their hearts" by which, according to Paul Ruttledge, the men and women in Eden lived (*Plays* p. 1136).

Seanchan sees the same potential from a mixing of blood in his vision of the stars in a frenzy, "about to marry / Clods out upon the ploughlands, to beget / A mightier race than any that has been" (*Plays* p. 301). Seanchan hears the stars singing praise of the same *sprezzatura* and generosity that Yeats celebrates in the English-speaking aristocracy:

> It was praise of that great race
> That would be haughty, mirthful, and whitebodied,
> With a high head, and open hand, and how,
> Laughing, it would take the mastery of the world. (*Plays* p. 301)

This is the same race "of more laughing overflowing hearts / Than common men" that Conchubar wars to preserve (*Plays* p. 490). The gentlemen of the eighteenth century who begin with a "high heart," follow its "impulse" fitfully, but in the end live life "not heartily," are the half-hearted descendents of Conchubar, Seanchan, and Paul Ruttledge.

Blood's the thing. Conchubar would preserve it, Seanchan would forestall its worsening, and Paul Ruttledge and the Maud Gonne of Yeats's poems would regenerate it. The problem of modern Ireland, as Yeats sees it in 1903, is that the evolution of Irish blood has been thwarted by recent history. Had the English not intervened in Ireland, the old Irish and old Norman-Irish aristocracy might have endured – the Gaelic poetry and the Gaelic habit of mind uninterrupted, spectators and players enjoying the same play. Had individuals acted differently, or had conditions been otherwise, the

English-speaking aristocracy might have created a new aristocracy out of their mixed blood – *provided they had had time*. The art in which the nation's "habit of mind" resides is "made, not by the artist choosing his material from wherever he has a mind to, but by adding a little to something which it has taken generations to invent" (Preface p. 132). The several generations between the eighteenth century and Yeats's own would hardly have been enough to develop the new literature, the new habit of mind, and the new aristocracy that Yeats imagines.

The old Irish and the old Norman-Irish aristocracy gone, even its English-speaking successor gone "after an epoch of such eloquence the world has hardly seen its like," there is no recourse but to begin the process again:

If we would create a great community – and what other game is worth the labour – we must create the old foundations of life, not as they existed in the splendid misunderstanding of the eighteenth century, but as they always exist when the finest minds and Ned the beggar and Seaghan the fool think about the same thing, although they do not think the same thought about it. (pp. 133–34)

Mixed blood produced misunderstanding because there was not sufficient continuity between beggar and fool, on the one hand, and fine mind, on the other (p. 103). According to Yeats, aristocrat and fine mind appear at the apex of a pyramidal cultural structure; spectators, fine and otherwise, constitute increasingly broader levels – the lowest levels comprising beggars and fools. In eighteenth-century Ireland, Yeats finds a Gaelic base incompatible with an English apex: the structure crumbles.

There is more biology here than meets the eye, for Yeats's story of race, habit of mind, and aristocratic fine mind is essentially a transformation of Estlake's account of the evolution of advanced civilizations and advanced individuals:

The various civilisations that have existed in historic and prehistoric epochs have been expressions of just so much thought as in any particular civilisation, the consensus of intelligence possessed by the people was capable of attracting and expressing. Every civilisation has been the result of a long period of evolution or incubation, during which the masses had been to some extent educated sufficiently to develop a change, however slight, in brain tissue capable of responding to higher vibrations. The consensus of increased brain activities of the people contributed to the intelligence of a smaller proportion of the population who stood out in bold relief upon the pages of history, and whose erudition reacted to raise the standard of education among the masses. (133–34)

Yeats's description of a Gaelic-speaking Ireland that has been made a vigorous race through the process of developing a "habit of mind" or "thought" by "adding a little to something which it has taken generations to invent" is similar. This thought is continuous between bottom and top – between fool and fine mind: it is not "only among the poor that the old thought has been for strength or weakness" (p. 133). Like Estlake, Yeats characterizes this thought as the expression of racial consensus, as the outcome of generations of incubation and evolution, as the embodiment of a hermeneutic circle involving the masses and an elite group. Even the equanimity he evinces in the face of the disappearance of the old aristocracy and the old thought matches Estlake's: "The history of nations demonstrates the wisdom of processes of evolution in which nature develops intelligence by the mixing up of differing civilizations by sinking the old in the oblivion of preparation for the new" (p. 108). When Yeats declares that to "create a great community . . . we must recreate the old foundations of life," he is not recommending a return to the "old thought," but rather a return to a state of civilization in which the thought of the race is continuous between fool and fine mind. Thence will come a new poetry, a new habit of mind, and a new aristocracy.

These texts of 1902 and 1903 – *The Speckled Bird, Where There Is Nothing, On Baile's Strand, The King's Threshold, In the Seven Woods,* and the Preface to Lady Gregory's *God's and Fighting Men* – show the deep impact of Yeats's reading of *The Oneida Community.* Under the heading "Stirpiculture," Yeats was introduced by Estlake to a wide variety of turn-of-the-century eugenical perspectives that appear in these works: the belief that biological degeneration had set in, the conviction that self-consciousness about breeding could supplement evolution's now-thwarted law that only the fittest should survive, the assumption that aristocrats represented superior elements of the national germ plasm, the consequent fear of the differential birthrate, and the interest in promoting positive eugenics.

Furthermore, as Stanfield has shown, revisions to *On Baile's Strand* show that eugenical issues concerning degeneration and heredity continued to interest Yeats between 1904 and 1906. Similarly, lines added to *The King's Threshold* at this time continue to develop the play's concerns about the poet's eugenical role, for in such new lines

Seanchan explains that by his hunger strike against the king's banishing of the poet from the national council he is "labouring / For some that shall be born in the nick o' time": "how could they be born to majesty / If I had never made the golden cradle?" (*Plays* p. 266). As late as "Sailing to Byzantium" in 1926 and his Senate speech on Irish coinage in 1928, in fact, one finds Yeats recalling passages from Estlake's book.

In "Sailing to Byzantium," the first stanza's images of natural sexual activity culminate in the lines: "Fish, flesh, or fowl, commend all summer long / Whatever is begotten, born, and dies" (*Poems* p. 407). Estlake had used the same phrase to explain the decorum that prevails in nature when sexual activity is initiated by the female: "From the pollen that falls in response to the suggestion from the appropriate pistil that conditions are prepared to retain it, to the animal, whether fish, flesh, or fowl, the same principle obtains, the female inviting the male" (*Oneida Community* p. 88). As much as the "aged man" wants "out of nature," he seems simultaneously to resent that "all neglect" the tattered old man aligned with "eternity" and "unageing intellect" (*Poems* pp. 407–08). From the point of view of the eugenical arguments Yeats regularly makes both before and after this poem, the aged man's complaint about the frenzied sexual activity of the youth in the first stanza is not that the young procreate, but that they procreate in dysgenical neglect of the monuments of unearthly stuff that rounds their activity.

In his Senate speech, Yeats refers disparagingly to the "eugenics of the farmyard" as the reason the committee on coinage chose a more realistic depiction of a bull over the design that Yeats himself preferred.[33] Yeats's reference to farmyard eugenics is an ironic recollection of Noyes's stirpicultural model of eugenics – *ironic* because Yeats's complaint is that farmyard eugenics has robbed Ireland of the eugenical potential latent in the image of the bull produced by artistic license: Yeats's bull is not an ideal bull for the farmyard, but rather an altogether human ideal – a type of the strength and beauty toward which the human community ought to direct its breeding.

Unless there are clear verbal echoes like these, however, discriminating Estlake's discrete influence on Yeats becomes complicated after 1908, for a new influence arises both to renew Yeats's interest in eugenics and to redefine it, sending him in a variety of new and sometimes surprisingly personal eugenical directions.

CHAPTER 9

Yeats and The Sexual Question

In the late 1990s, many in Switzerland were distressed to learn that the person whose face had adorned the Swiss 1,000 franc bank note since 1978 was a eugenist responsible for the canton of Vaud's 1928 sterilization law – a law sanctioning the sterilization of, among others, the "feeble-minded, morally weak, idiotic and promiscuous," and a law admired by the most infamous eugenist of all, Adolf Hitler himself.[1] The face on the country's largest denomination bill was that of Auguste Forel – not only a eugenist, but also one of Europe's most prominent neurophysiologists at the end of the nineteenth century (parts of the brain are named after him) and, at the beginning of the twentieth century, one of its most prominent psychiatrists – author of the popular guide to sexual hygiene that Yeats owned.

First published as *Die sexuelle Frage* (1905), Forel's book *The Sexual Question* took its place alongside Havelock Ellis's *Studies in the Psychology of Sex* (1897–1928), Richard Krafft-Ebing's *Psycopathia Sexualis* (1902), and Sigmund Freud's works as a seminal influence in the twentieth century's so-called sexual revolution.[2] Understanding themselves to be destroying the conspiracy of silence about sex, understood by their societies to be violating taboos, understood by Foucault to be agents for the incorporation of the body within the production of truth by scientific discursivity ("It was a time when the most singular pleasures were called upon to pronounce a discourse of truth concerning themselves, a discourse which had to model itself after that which spoke . . . of bodies and life processes – the discourse of science"[3]), these figures were and remain notorious – whether prosecuted by Foucault or, in Ellis's case, by the British courts.

Despite the open hostility of the medical profession and the general public, Forel campaigned hard in this cause, however conceived. Resigning his professorship, he spent much of his thirty years in nominal retirement researching and writing about human sexuality. He became one of the first presidents of the World League for Sexual Reform, the principles of which (drafted in 1928) reflected many of the ideas that he had begun to promote twenty years before in *The Sexual Question* – ranging from support for such liberal and progressive causes as "Political, economic and sexual equality of rights of men and women," "The liberation of marriage (and especially divorce) from the present Church and State tyranny," and "Birth control, so that procreation may be undertaken only deliberately and with a due sense of responsibility," to support for the cause we find so unliberal and unprogressive: "Race betterment by the application of the knowledge of eugenics."[4]

Writing about the relationship between alcohol and heredity in the late 1890s, delivering papers like "Malthusianism or Eugenics" in the first decade of the twentieth century, and dispensing eugenical advice freely in *The Sexual Question*, Forel was among the first – if not necessarily among the foremost – of the first generation of eugenists.[5] As such, he extended Yeats's knowledge of turn-of-the-century eugenics far beyond what Estlake had taught him, for Forel was a scientist, deriving his eugenics not from John Humphrey Noyes and stirpiculture's subjective and arbitrary "eugenics of the farmyard," but from the apparently objective number-crunching of Francis Galton himself.[6]

One cannot read many pages of *The Sexual Question* without encountering explanations, interpretations, and evaluations of human sexual behavior from a eugenical perspective, and one cannot read at length in the book without encountering a broad range of the early eugenist's concerns. On the question of just what characteristics can be inherited, Forel has an opinion: "Everything may be transmitted by heredity, even to the finest shades of sentiment, intelligence and will, even to the most insignificant details of nails, the form of the bones, etc." (p. 30). On the question of whether acquired characteristics can be inherited, Forel has an opinion: despite "facts invoked by Weismann against the heredity of acquired characters," Forel is able "to conceive the possibility of an infinitely slow heredity of characters acquired by individuals, a heredity resulting from prolonged repetition" (p. 17). On the question of whether the distinguished people in society constitute a biologically elite class, Forel also has an opinion: he does not accept the "superficial assertion" that "the qualities of higher forms of man are exhausted in a few generations, while the mass of mediocrities continually produce new genius," for "[i]t is inconceivable that the laws of heredity should make an exception of the mental qualities of man" (p. 33).

Forel's fears about degeneration are the typical fears of eugenists at this time. People often select reproductive partners unwisely – "A common woman will lower the level of offspring of a distinguished husband, and inversely" – and people often live unwisely – creating a hereditary taint to be passed on by blastophthoria: "By blastophthoria, or deterioration of the germ, I mean . . . the results of all direct pathogenic or disturbing action, especially that of certain intoxications, on the germinal cells, whose hereditary determinants are thus changed" (pp. 33, 36). Alcohol represents the biggest blastophthoric threat:

No doubt the peculiarity of badly supporting alcohol is inherited by ordinary heredity as a hereditary disposition, but it is not this which produces the alcoholic degenerations of the race. . . The spermatozoa of alcoholics suffer like the other tissues from the toxic action of alcohol on the protoplasm. . . [T]he children resulting from their conjugation become idiots, epileptics, dwarfs or feeble minded. (p. 37)

Thus "[t]he combination of a bad selection with blastophthoric influences constitutes the great danger for humanity, and it is here that a rational sexual life should intervene" (p. 44).

Forel also draws attention to the "grave" dangers in the differential birthrate. One danger is that "for reasons of economy, the intelligent, educated and cultured marry less often and procreate fewer children" (p. 295). Similarly, because "the most incapable and immoral classes of the population are those who trouble least about their maximum number of children," the "blind and thoughtless propagation of degenerate, tainted, and enfeebled individuals is another atrocious danger to society" (p. 464, 423).

The emancipation of women, which Forel generally supports, contributes to this problem insofar as it supports "the modern tendency of women to become pleasure-seekers, and to take a dislike to maternity" (p. 137). Its most virulent form emerges as "Americanism" – the desire to remain "young and fresh as long as possible, fearing the dangers and troubles of childbirth and the bringing-up of children" (pp. 331–32). Should the pleasure seeking involve alcohol or narcotics, and should the emancipated woman reluctant to have children be intelligent, educated, and cultured, the results of emancipation are dysgenic.

In fact, Forel perceives here a "grave social evil, which rapidly changes the qualities and powers of expansion of a race, and which must be cured in time, or the race will be . . . supplanted by others" (p. 137). Like Pearson, Rentoul, the Whethams, and so many other early eugenists, Forel raises the spectre of race suicide: the misguided "form of emancipation of women is absolutely deleterious and . . . leads to degeneration, if not extinction of the race" (p. 332). What was once a battle for survival amongst individuals has now become a battle for survival amongst races: "we know that certain of the lower races, such as the pigmies, the Veddas and even the Negroes, are inaccessible to a higher civilization . . . We shall, therefore, have to choose finally between the gradual extinction of these races or that of our own" (p. 361).

As for most eugenists at this time, the rational sexual life that Forel favors involves both positive and negative eugenics. On the positive front: "The principal task of a political economy which has the true happiness of men at heart, should be to encourage the procreation of happy, useful, healthy and hard-working individuals" (p. 465). Always a harder sell, negative eugenics required longer and more careful justification:

To build an ever-increasing number of hospitals, asylums for lunatics, idiots and incurables, reformatories, etc.; to provide them with every comfort, and manage them scientifically, is no doubt a very fine thing, and speaks well of the progress and development of human sympathy. But . . . by concerning ourselves almost exclusively with human ruins, the results of our social abuses, we gradually weaken the forces of the healthy portion of the population. (p. 465)

A certain rhetorical flourish also helped the argument: "The law of heredity winds like a red thread through the family history of every criminal, of every epileptic, eccentric and insane person. And we should sit still and witness our civilization go into decay and fall to pieces without raising the warning and applying the remedy?" (p. 427). Negative eugenics is a necessary element in this remedy: "it is not sufficient to combat the excesses of criminal and dangerous individuals . . . by placing them under supervision and preventing them doing harm. It is also necessary to attack the cause of the evil by preventing their germs from being reproduced" (p. 390). Besides, negative eugenics is in the long run the kindest way of proceeding: "By attacking the roots of the evil and limiting the procreation of the unfit, we shall be performing a work which is much more humanitarian, if less striking in its effect" (p. 465).

Precisely when Yeats read Forel's book is not clear. In a sense, he knew the book – or at least the patchwork of science, stereotype, and superstition that went into it – even before he acquired a copy of *The Sexual Question*. When apprised by Maud Gonne in 1905 of the behavior by her husband John MacBride that had precipitated the breakdown of their marriage – drunkenness, violence, seduction of Gonne's half-sister, sexual molestation of her daughter – Yeats was even then sufficiently persuaded of the connection between alcohol and sexual irregularity to conclude (as Forel would have done) that MacBride suffered "erotomania from drink."[7] Furthermore, as Yeats's biographer R. F. Foster points out, well before Gonne's appeal for help in this matter Yeats had heard "rumors about the marriage – some true (MacBride's drunkenness), some not (their baby Sean's epilepsy)."[8] The rumor-mongers who brought to Yeats this false tale of the son's epilepsy implicitly anticipate Forel's text: the alcoholic father's blastophthoric germs produce "alcoholic degenerations of the race"; his "children . . . become idiots, epileptics, dwarfs or feeble minded." Yeats's friend William Fay was another of those who introduced this text to him. He told the same blastophthoric tale about the dysgenic consequences of alcohol abuse when explaining to Yeats that the working-class woman of Dublin was often trapped in marriage to a drunken husband "who hands his besottedness on in the blood."[9] In many ways, then, *The Sexual Question* translated into the terms of science a eugenical text that Yeats had already picked up as eugenically informed Dublin gossip and class prejudice.

Yeats owned a copy of the first English version of *The Sexual Question* (1908), based on the second German edition (1906), also the basis of translations into French (1906), Italian (1907), and Norwegian (1913).[10] He certainly acquired this 1908 copy before 1920, for it is recorded in that year's index of his library's holdings.[11] Given that the book was so popular as to be reprinted in 1911 and ten times thereafter, the fact that Yeats owned a 1908 copy increases the likelihood that he had acquired it before 1911. Furthermore, evidence of his having acquired the book and read at least parts of it before 1911 appears in a number of texts – especially those concerned with the controversies over *The Playboy of the Western World*.

In "On those that hated 'The Playboy of the Western World,'
1907," first appearing in a diary entry dated 5 April 1909, Yeats
writes:

> Once, when midnight smote the air,
> Eunuchs ran through Hell and met
> On every crowded street to stare
> Upon great Juan riding by:
> Even like these to rail and sweat
> Staring upon his sinewy thigh.   (*Poems* p. 294)

On 8 March 1909 he wrote to Lady Gregory that "discontents
enlarge my diary," one of them being discontent with "men like
Griffith": "I wrote a note a couple of days ago in which I compared
Griffith and his like to the Eunuchs in Ricketts' picture watching
Don Juan riding through Hell."[12] Although Yeats attributes the
inspiration for his Don Juan allusion to a painting by his friend
Charles Ricketts, George Bernard Shaw was the one who had
brought the Juan figure back into prominence with *Man and Superman*.
He called the play's third act "Don Juan in Hell," a long and difficult
act which, although published as part of the play in 1903, was not
performed when the play was first staged in 1905, and was then
staged on its own in 1907. Yeats, Shaw's somewhat jealous rival, and
Ricketts, a designer of theater costumes, sets, and backdrops, certainly followed Shaw's work at this time. In fact, Ricketts himself
brought Yeats the gossip to which the play in question gave rise
(presumably because Granville Barker, "playing John Tanner in *Man
and Superman*, made himself up to resemble Shaw"): "Ricketts says
that [Robert] Farquharson says that Granville Barker is Shaw's
son."[13] It is likely that both Ricketts's painting and Yeats's interpretation of it were inspired by Shaw's play.

Yeats certainly interprets Ricketts's "Don Juan in Hell" in terms
appropriate to Shaw's "Don Juan in Hell." The latter is Shaw's
symbol of creative power – creative evolution striving to realize itself
both biologically and intellectually. Shaw outlines these ideas in the
long and playful letter to Walkley with which he introduces the
published version of the play, claiming at last to have written the
"Don Juan play" about the nature "of sexual attraction" that he
understood Walkley to have asked for and then carefully situating his
Don Juan in relation to his forbears: there is the "prototypic Don
Juan, invented early in the XVI century by a Spanish monk," who is
interesting for "the heroism of daring to be the enemy of God";

"Molière's Don Juan casts back to the original in point of impenitence; but in piety he falls off greatly"; in Mozart's version, "you have freedom in love and morality mocking exquisitely at slavery to them"; Byron's Don Juan "does not count for much" because he is "only a vagabond libertine." Shaw's conclusion is that at the beginning of the twentieth century, the story "is a full century out of date": Don Juan is now an intellectual – "concerned for the future of the race instead of for the freedom of his own instincts."[14]

Yeats updates the Juan figure in the same way. Both in his diary and in "On those that hated 'The Playboy of the Western World,' 1907," his thesis is the same: the artist now possesses the "sinewy thigh" that the eunuchs lack. Whereas the source of sexual power and attractiveness was once literally such a sinewy thigh and the phallus it betokened, sexual power and attractiveness now derive from intellectual and moral development rather than physical development. According to Yeats, the lack that the eunuchs bemoan as they review Synge's work is his intellectual and moral power. The eunuchs of Young Ireland are sterile: "Even if what one defends be true, an attitude of defense, a continual apology, whatever the cause, makes the mind barren . . ." People like Synge "delight in what is unforeseen, and in the mere spectacle of the world, the mere drifting hither and thither that must come before all true thought and emotion." In this posture lie Synge's power and attractiveness: "Only that which does not teach, which does not cry out, which does not persuade, which does not condescend, which does not explain, is irresistible."[15] Synge is the return of what Young Ireland repressed: "Synge was the rushing up of the buried fire, an explosion of all that had been denied and refused."[16] In the poem, Yeats makes it clear that "great Juan" is not the new phallic artist but the old-fashioned Juan: "Once," eunuchs stared in envy at the sinewy thigh. Now, Yeats explains in his essay and diary, they stare in envy at the writer's mightier pen. Even setting the poem at "midnight" consigns this primitive Juan to a dark time, for the Juan who was "Once" a benighted soldier is now an enlightened artist – like Synge, and Yeats.

In "J. M. Synge and the Ireland of his Time" (1910), Yeats makes it clear that this is why Synge is regarded by the eunuchs as a threat to Irish womanhood: not because his play impugns the moral integrity of Irish women, but because the eunuchs know that Irish women will be attracted to a man with such a pen – just as the women of Mayo are attracted to the artist-figure Christy Mahon. Thus Yeats's analysis of *The Playboy* controversies is relentlessly psycho-sexual. The "forty young men" who had "stamped and shouted and blown trumpets" to "silence what they considered a slander upon Ireland's woman-hood" mounted "a defense of virtue by those who have but little": "As I stood there watching, . . . Synge came up and stood beside me, and said, 'A young doctor has just told me that he can hardly keep himself from jumping on to a seat, and pointing out in that howling mob those whom he is treating for venereal disease.'"[17]

Politics and bodies are diseased, Yeats implies, because frustrated sexual desire has become morbid. In his diary and in "On those that hated 'The Playboy of the Western World,' 1907," the allusion to the eunuchs' envy of Don Juan's sexual prowess is meant to represent the feelings of "envy, revenge, jealousy and so on" of journalists and politicians like Arthur Griffith who had attacked Synge's plays – in Griffith's case, out of the belief that literature should be subordinate to politics. Yeats traces the same envy of power in the venereally diseased young men: their "ideas and images" – expressed in language "carried beyond life perpetually," and therefore "worn and cold" – reflect "a dread of all that has salt and savour." The not surprising result is that natural sexual desire is made morbid: "After a while . . . abstract thoughts are raised between men's minds and Nature, . . . till minds . . . cry down natural impulse with the morbid persistence of minds unsettled by some fixed idea."[18] The unnatural continence that their fixed idea demands of them turns them into the frustrated eunuchs that "rail and sweat" in envy of the great Juan, "for a secret feeling that what is so unreal needs continual defense makes them bitter and restless." And it also "makes the mind barren."[19]

Yeats's sexual analysis ultimately focuses on "the morbid persis-tence of minds unsettled by some fixed idea." This form of morbid sexuality, according to Forel, characterizes the hysteric: "Hysterical men and women have a very peculiar sexuality. . . . A single idea is sufficient in a hysterical subject, to produce the realization of what it represents. The passionate imagination may lead to opinions and actions which are absolutely contradictory" (*The Sexual Question* p. 261). Forel also explains that "the disorders of sexual life . . . almost exclusively originate . . . in the hereditary disposition of the brain of the individual" (p. 208). Yeats defines hysterics and traces their hereditary influence in similar terms: "Ireland for three generations" has pursued such fixed ideas until "at last a generation is like an hysterical woman who will make unmeasured accusations and believe impossible things, because of some logical deduction from a solitary thought which has turned a portion of her mind to stone."[20] The hysteria of minds unsettled by a fixed idea is passed down – leading to a hereditary condition that Yeats calls "the *hysterica passio* of Ireland."[21] And so, like Shaw's updated Juan John Tanner, Yeats is also "concerned for the future of the race": he must save Ireland from the blasted germs of its hysterics.

Yet that we should attribute Yeats's distinction in these texts between the biological and intellectual dimensions of sexual attraction to Shaw's explicitly eugenical delineation of the same distinction in *Man and Superman* is by no means clear. In Forel, one finds not only the definition of sexual hysteria that Yeats follows, but also the same distinction between the primitive attraction to sinewy thighs that "Once" prevailed and the more civilized attraction toward mental accomplishments that now prevails – according to Yeats and Forel. Furthermore, Forel makes his distinction between physical and intellectual attractiveness by recourse to the same Don Juan figure.

Like Yeats's Juan, Forel's Juan is more attractive for his physique than his metaphysics and so represents a relatively primitive, instinctive stage of sexual attraction: "In primitive peoples, hardiness and boldness in men were qualities which made for success. This explains why, even at the present day, the boldest and most audacious Don Juans excite most strongly the sexual desires of women" (p. 94). Forel is quick to point out, however, that things are changing: "In our time women become more and more enthusiastic over the intellectual superiority of man, which excites their desire. Without being indifferent to it, simple bodily beauty in man excites the appetite of women to a less extent" (p. 94). In the society of "the fashionable young lady . . . saturated with unhealthy novels," of course, "young women are much more easily seduced by the art of Don Juan," but the truth remains that "in higher civilizations man is in general more sought after than woman" (p. 116). There are more than a dozen other similar references to Don Juans in *The Sexual Question*.[22] In each case, just as in Yeats's poem, the great Juans are late Juans – a blast from the still recent past when primitive physical and instinctual behavior was the key to sexual attraction.

Yeats, Forel, and Shaw all agree that the story of sexual attraction needs to be modernized eugenically: sinewy thought should excite

more desire than a sinewy thigh. Yeats and Forel are perhaps more
confident than Shaw that what *should* be the case actually *is*. Shaw
regularly undercuts Tanner's intellectual pretensions, concluding the
play with Ann Whitefield's casual dismissal of Tanner's ideas as mere
"talking" – all the while "caressing his arm" (the arm of one with a
"slimness of youth," a "high chested carriage of the shoulders," and
an "Olympian majesty" that combine to "suggest Jupiter" – and to
suggest perhaps that Ann finds the physique more attractive than the
meta-physique).[23] As guarantee of good germ plasm, the women that
Yeats and Forel admire look not to the thigh or the arm, but to the
mind. But the greatest difference between the modern Juans of
Shaw and Yeats is that the latter's is positioned in a homosocial
narrative. Although Yeats's Juan is inevitably a phallic symbol, like all
the other Juans, Yeats presents his Juan not as an explanation of or
even in connection with female desire but rather in connection with
and as an explanation of male feelings of sexual inadequacy and
unfulfillment.

The key to this function of the Don Juan figure in Yeats's analysis
of the political situation in Ireland is the figure of the eunuch. In a
later extract from the diary in question, Yeats makes his diagnosis
more sexually explicit: "the political class in Ireland . . . have
suffered through the cultivation of hatred as the one energy of their
movement, a deprivation which is the intellectual equivalent to the
removal of the genitals. Hence the shrillness of their voices. They
contemplate all creative power as the eunuchs contemplate Don Juan
as he passes through Hell on the white horse."[24] Forel explains the
physiological consequences of the removal of the genitals from
the male:

Castration is the term applied to the extirpation of the sexual glands. When
it takes place in infancy it causes considerable change in the whole
subsequent development of the body, especially in man . . . *Eunuchs* are men
castrated, usually in infancy. . . Male human eunuchs have a high-pitched
voice, a narrow chest; they remain beardless or nearly so . . . On the other
hand, if the sexual glands of an adult are removed, his body is not sensibly
modified. (*The Sexual Question* p. 25)

Of course Yeats would not have needed Forel to inform him of
what was presumably common knowledge: the effects of the removal
of the testicles upon the voice of the castrato. But he would probably
have needed Forel to inform him of the importance of the removal of
the genitals before puberty if the general effects of this procedure on

the development of the body and mind as a whole were to occur.[25] It is precisely this knowledge that Yeats reveals in "J. M. Synge and the Ireland of his Time" when he complains that nationalists of the Young Ireland persuasion have made themselves "barren" by "substituting arguments and hesitations for the excitement at the first reading of the great poets which should be a sort of violent imaginative puberty."[26] Young Ireland will never experience such a puberty because it has been castrated in infancy.

In adapting the diary entry above for publication as "Estrangement: Extracts from a Diary Kept in 1909" in *Autobiographies* (1914), Yeats changed the phrase "the intellectual equivalent to the removal of the genitals" to "the intellectual equivalent to a certain surgical operation."[27] Forel points out that the important thing is not the removal of the genitals, but the removal of the sex glands:

The characters of castrated individuals are due only to ablation of the sexual glands themselves – the testicles in man and the ovary in woman; mutilation of other sexual organs . . . such as the penis, womb, etc., produces no result of this kind. It would even appear to result from recent experiments that reimplantation of a sexual gland in any part of the body is sufficient to arrest the production of the special peculiarities of the eunuch. (*The Sexual Question* p. 26)

Yeats's revision is perhaps a concession to a squeamish public likely to be offended by such a direct reference to the sexual organs, but it also serves both to make the passage more scientifically accurate and to make it conform more closely to the information provided by Forel.

It is not just the physical character of the individual that is affected by this operation. Forel also describes the effect of castration upon the eunuch's personality and behavior: "Male human eunuchs . . . have an effeminate character, often intriguing. In both sexes there is a tendency to neurosis and degeneration" (p. 25). Yeats avails himself of this information in characterizing the situation of the young men and women brought up on the hatreds of nationalist politics: "Hatred must . . . create sterility. . . Hatred as a basis of imagination . . . helps to dry up the nature and make the sexual abstinence, so common among young men and women in Ireland, possible. The abstinence reacts in its turn upon the imagination, so that we get at last that strange eunuch-like tone and temper."[28] Forel's description of the eunuch's tendency toward degeneration is evident in Yeats's explanation of the "extreme politics" of the young nationalists as

being the result of despising "real life" and refusing "to accept
obtainable things": "a taste fed for long on milk diet thirsts for strong
flavours. In England the reaction would be vice, in Ireland it is
politics."[29] Ireland's politics, in short, is the expression of Ireland's
sexual degeneration, and this degeneration has become a blastophthoric inheritance: "Ireland has grown sterile, because power
has passed to men who lack the training which requires a certain
amount of wealth to ensure continuity from generation to generation,
and to free the mind in part from other tasks" – and to free the mind
especially from "hatred, envy, jealousy, revenge."[30] *Hysterica passsio*
can produce a fatal infertility.

The eunuch thus figures Yeats's understanding of the consequences of repressed sexuality – an understanding enabled by Forel.
Several years later in the same journal (18 May 1912), Yeats develops
the subject of the eunuch's deprivation further: "When any part of
human life has been left unexpressed, there is a hunger for its
expression in large numbers of men, and if this expression is
prevented artificially, the hunger becomes morbid . . . From this
cause have come . . . the obscene sentences written upon the walls of
jakes."[31] He had recorded the same observation in a more personal
form in his diary's account of his reaction to Gonne's refusal to
continue their sexual relationship (21 June 1909): "What end will it all
have – I fear for her & for myself – she has all myself. I was never
more deeply in love, but my desires, always strong, must go elsewhere
if I would escape their poison."[32] The morbidity of unexpressed
hunger leads to more than one kind of poison. In terms of his milk
metaphor, the morbidity of the hunger for something stronger than
milk can express itself either as alcoholism or extreme abstinence.
Like Forel, of course, Yeats is concerned not so much about the
hunger for milk and alcohol as about the hunger for sex – what Forel
calls "a natural appetite," which ought to be neither repressed nor
overstimulated: "in a natural appetite such as the sexual, the two
extremes of asceticism and excess lead to evil and unnatural aberra-
tions" (*The Sexual Question* p. 339). Forel's most morbid example of the
results of such repression as he and Yeats describe is the case "of a
monk who tore off his testicles in despair at being unable to conquer
his violent sexual appetite" (p. 422). Yeats and Forel clearly agree on
one result of the unnatural repression of the sexual appetite: the
eunuch.

Forel emphasizes many times and in many ways that the sexual

appetite is natural. His operating assumption is that "Man has as
much right to a certain agreeable satisfaction of his sexual appetite
. . . as he has to satisfy his hunger and thirst, as long as he does no
harm to anyone" (p. 290). Continence is possible, but not normal:
"Abstinence or sexual continence is by no means impracticable for a
normal young man . . . However, in the long run this state cannot be
considered as normal, especially when there is no hope of it coming
to an end in a reasonable time" (p. 81). Thwart the sexual appetite,
and it can become morbid. It can lead to "the bad habit of
masturbation . . . a habit which is both depressing and exhausting,"
with "its depressing action on sentiment and will" (p. 80). Similarly,
the combination of "sexual life with religious prescriptions" can
produce "a mixture of ridiculous prudery and continual eroticism"
(p. 346). Although Forel believes that "[i]n a general way, we may
accept the statement that many morbid conditions are known to
result from sexual excess, but few from continence," he acknowledges
that "[c]ontinence is not an easy matter for erotic individuals, and
requires a heroic internal struggle, especially in men" (p. 422). In
fact, "certain psychopaths and sexual hyperaesthetics often lapse into
a state of mental and nervous excitement from forced continence, so
that their neurosis becomes accentuated" (p. 422).

Perhaps most helpful to Yeats, after finally consummating his relationship with Gonne in 1908, only to be confronted immediately with
her refusal of further sexual intimacy with him (apparently because
of her religious scruples about the matter), was Forel's explanation
that the combination of "sexual life with religious prescriptions" can
produce "a mixture of ridiculous prudery and continual eroticism"
(p. 346).[33] In "King and No King," Yeats calmly and confidently
explains the defeat of their sexual hopes, implicitly blaming Gonne:
first there was the irrational declaration in the 1890s that she would
not marry ("that pledge you gave / In momentary anger long ago");
now there are the prescriptions of her Catholic faith ("And I that
have not your faith, how shall I know / That in the blinding light
beyond the grave / We'll find so good a thing as that we've lost?")
(*Poems* p. 258). Supported by Forel, Yeats implies that the one intent
on expressing sexual desire is healthy, the one intent on suppressing
it, morbid. Furthermore, Yeats's image of the love she has foregone is
perhaps his most mature: "The hourly kindness, the day's common
speech, / The habitual content of each with each / When neither

soul nor body has been crossed" (*Poems* p. 258). This surprisingly
domestic fantasy about a possible married future comes right out of
the section of *The Sexual Question* on "The Art of Loving Long": "For
the couple to find lasting and complete happiness in marriage, love,
however ideal it may be, should be accompanied by sexual enjoyment. In short, intellectual and sentimental harmony should be
combined with sensual harmony . . ." (p. 521). According to Forel,
such love "may be realized even when youth has passed," provided
that the tendency to succumb to the charms of others is forestalled by
"habit and imagination" (pp. 521–22). In more ways than one, Forel
has helped Yeats to imagine the "*Habitual* content of each with each"
(emphasis added).

Forel also enabled Yeats to explain to himself why Gonne had
agreed to marry John MacBride. In Forel's terms, she was simply one
of the fashionable ladies still susceptible to old-fashioned Don Juans.
Forel depicts such women as victims of "atavistic instinct":

The Don Juan experienced in the art of seduction approaches women with
audacity and *aplomb* . . . He has instinctively learnt one thing: viz., the
weakness of woman in the face of the male form, theatrical effects,
uniforms, an audacious act . . . [T]hese fireworks hypnotize her and silence
her reason . . . [S]he is then capable of enthusiasm for the most doubtful
cavalier and delivers herself to him bound hand and foot . . . (p. 120)

In Yeats's version of this story, her susceptibility to the major
MacBride arises not from her having read bad novels, however, but
from her having been born Helen – complete with the latter's ancient
Greek sensibility. Like Helen, she was "Bred to be a hero's wage,"
and like Helen, she rewarded heroism as she understood it: as the
primitive, physical, martial heroism of the soldier. Yeats understands
her to have offered herself as MacBride's wage for his service against
England in the Boer War. "No Second Troy" ambivalently describes
Gonne's sensibility in these matters as "not natural in an age like
this." From one point of view an elaborate compliment that exalts
her by condemning the modern world as inadequate to the second
Helen (the modern world contains "No Second Troy"), the poem
also implicitly identifies Yeats as no second Paris – a self-deprecating
gesture indeed *if* Yeats accepts Gonne's primitive version of heroism
("she would of late / Have taught to ignorant men most violent
ways"), but a rather self-congratulating gesture if (as it seems to me)
Yeats is criticizing Gonne's inability – "being what she is" – to
recognize the modern Juan's different form of heroism – the heroism

of the artist's intellectual endeavor (*Poems* p. 256–57). The old-fashioned Don Juan of "On those that hated 'The Playboy of the Western World,' 1907" is thus Major MacBride: the eunuchs who admire the great Juan are Griffiths and his like, precisely the admirers who took MacBride's side in his separation from Gonne.[34] The eunuchs are thus doubly dispossessed – not only lacking creative power, but also mistakenly envying the least adequate contemporary embodiment of such power.

Of course however much he needed Forel in 1908 and 1909 to explain the confusing events in his sex life at this time, it is also true that there was never a time after Yeats's own puberty when he did not need a book like *The Sexual Question* – something that he indirectly but unmistakably acknowledges in a memoir written in 1916 and 1917. He writes that he experienced sexual desire become morbid in the summer of 1897, which he called "the most miserable time" of his life.[35] His affair with Olivia Shakespear over, his sexual longing for Maud Gonne at a peak, he felt compelled to masturbate:

It was a time of great personal strain and sorrow. Since my mistress had left me, no other woman had come into my sexual life, and for nearly seven years none did. I was tortured by sexual desire and disappointed love. . . When desire became an unendurable torture, I would masturbate, and that, no matter how moderate I was, would make me ill. . . [M]y nervous system was worn out. The toil of dressing in the morning exhausted me, and Lady Gregory began to send me cups of soup when I was called.[36]

Writing in 1916 and 1917, Yeats imports Forel into this narrative of his sexual past – as much an interpretation of this sexual past as an account of it. Although guilt about masturbation in 1897 had made him ill, he now represents his masturbation to have been normal, not morbid – an instance of what Forel calls "compensatory masturbation": "This kind of masturbation may be called *compensatory*, because it does not depend on an anomaly of the sexual appetite, but serves to satisfy a natural want by compensation" (*The Sexual Question* pp. 228, 229). Forel's narrative of the effects of compensatory masturbation is similar to Yeats's:

Although depressing for those whose will power is overcome by an excitation which they cannot conquer, it is relatively the least dangerous form of onanism. At the most it leads to a certain amount of nervous and sexual exhaustion . . . The loss of substance from frequent seminal ejaculations is also more or less weakening . . . But what especially affects the nervous system, is the repeated loss of the will . . . (p. 229)

Looking back, Yeats knows why his mood was miserable, why his nervous system was worn out, why he was exhausted, and why he needed all those cups of soup. Moreover, apparently responding apologetically to Forel's advice that "[t]he man who, for some reason or another, cannot obtain normal coitus should content himself with nocturnal emissions" (p. 230), Yeats explains first that "[i]t never occurred to me to seek another love" and second that "A sexual dream was very rare" – although "[o]ne night" at this time he dreamed and awoke to find he "had emitted seed."[37] From his point of view in 1916 and 1917, Yeats interprets his sexual frustrations of 1897 according to a checklist of causes and effects provided by Forel.

The "Vision Papers" of 1919 also show Forel's influence. They suggest that Yeats was not the only one thumbing through Forel: George Yeats (or her daimon Ameritus) had also consulted *The Sexual Question*. The automatic writing session of 31 July was given over to the question of sexual health, the writer recommending that Yeats occasionally make love twice in an evening instead of just once: "Sexual health unaccustomed for some time to twice – therefore *gradually* try twice as always once will increase fatigue . . . Because you cease to be able to do more – it is like not taking enough exercise & a long walk exhausts you."[38] The writer is explaining Forel's "law of exercise":

the law of exercise is a general truth in the physiology of the nervous system. . . [E]very kind of nervous activity is increased by exercise. A man becomes a glutton by accustoming himself to eat too much, a good walker by exercising his legs. . . By neglecting certain activities or the provocation of certain sensations, these diminish in intensity . . . It is not surprising, therefore, to find this law in the phenomena of sexual appetite, which diminishes with abstinence and increases with repeated excitation and satisfaction. (Forel, *The Sexual Question*, p. 87)

Both as a bachelor and as a married man, Yeats faced many a sexual question – questions asked and answered against the background of the information and opinions provided by Forel in *The Sexual Question*.

Perhaps the most important of the sexual questions that Forel prompted Yeats to ask himself was whether he should get married and have children. In his "Conclusions," Forel makes it clear that someone like Yeats is one of what he calls the "Types to Perpetuate":

"men who are useful from the social point of view . . . should be induced to multiply. If they are endowed with clear intelligence and an active mind, or with an intellectual or artistic creative imagination, they constitute excellent subjects for reproduction" (*The Sexual Question* p. 512). Trusting woman's instinctive exclusivity in the matter of sexual selection, Forel believes that the fact that "[a]t the present day . . . cultured and intelligent women are . . . much less attracted by man's physical strength than by his intellectual superiority or genius . . . gives us a very important indication of the selection we desire" (p. 511). From the eugenical point of view, Yeats finds himself regarded as a well-endowed individual and begins to contemplate the responsibilities that such an endowment brings.

In "Pardon, Old Fathers" (dated 1912–14 by Yeats), he acknowledges that he is a member of a eugenically well-endowed family. He rehearses the deeds of past Yeatses, Butlers, Armstrongs, Middletons, and Pollexfens – daring merchants, generous scholars, courageous soldiers – as proof that he is a member of a family with hereditary values worth preserving. Yeats's ancestors have done their eugenical part by bequeathing to the poet a blood kept pure: "Merchant and scholar . . . have left me blood / That has not passed through any huckster's loin" (*Poems* p. 269). Given such blood, Yeats raises the question of his responsibility to have children of his own: the pardon he seeks from his old fathers is for having "no child" to "prove your blood and mine" (*Poems* p. 270).

This poem confirms that Yeats has come to regard blood and breeding as more than a figure of speech for the aristocratic kind of manners and attitudes of which he approves. In his diary of January 1909, the biological import of his references to the "ill-bred in manner," "the ill-breeding of the mind," "the new ill-breeding of Ireland," and the admirable "old blood" of the "well-born" is ambiguous: are the words "blood" and "breeding" used literally or figuratively? In "Pardon, Old Fathers," however, the specification of the "loins" as the mechanism of inheritance confirms that between 1909 and 1914 Yeats has come to understand heredity to be a function of the sexual reproduction of germ cells.[39]

Forel's role in this literalization of an ambiguous metaphor is suggested in a number of ways. Associating the "ill-bred," the "rude," and the "clown" with mechanism (whether as the machine, the newspaper, argument, or logic), and associating the "well-born" with "charm" ("Is not charm what it is, perhaps, because it is an escape from mechanism?"), Yeats suggests that charm is a matter of heredity: "Is not all charm inherited? – whether of the intellect, of the manners, or of character, or of literature?"[40] This confidence in the comprehensiveness of the hereditary mechanism echoes Forel's: "Everything may be transmitted by heredity, even to the finest shades of sentiment, intelligence and will" (*The Sexual Question* p. 30). Similarly, although both Yeats and Forel agree that "[i]t is inconceivable that the laws of heredity should make an exception of the mental qualities of man" – especially "the qualities of higher forms of man" (such as the quality Yeats calls "charm") – they also agree that there are exceptions that prove the rule (p. 33). Forel acknowledges that "our pathological degenerations and our crossbreedings are so infinitely complex that at any time atavism may produce . . . better children derived from bad parents" (p. 512). Similarly, Yeats acknowledges that "[w]hen we are moved to intolerance by some provincial folly or stupidity, one should look on the man or woman and think: 'From that blood may yet come some man of genius, perhaps the saviour of the race.'"[41]

Forel prompts a debate within Yeats about his broad eugenical responsibilities as poet versus his personal eugenical responsibilities as potential procreator. On the one hand, Yeats implies in his diary and in various poems of 1910 that his eugenical role is Seanchan's role: to give eugenical direction to breeding couples. In "A Woman Homer Sung," Yeats declares that as poet who "wrote and wrought," he has put Maud Gonne's beautiful body into words:

> I dream that I have brought
> To such a pitch my thought
> That coming time can say,
> "He shadowed in a glass
> What thing her body was." 　　　　　　(*Poems* p. 255)

In "Peace," he suggests that this body/poem displays "a form / That could show what Homer's age / Bred to be a hero's wage" (*Poems* p. 258). This form has the same potential as Maclagan's Greek statues:

> "Were not all her life but storm,
> Would not painters paint a form
> Of such noble lines" I said.
> "Such a delicate high head,
> So much sternness and such charm,
> Till they had changed us to like strength?"[42]

Homer's hero educated to desire a woman such as Helen is Yeats's Irishman educated to desire a woman such as Gonne. In each case the desire is directed toward eugenical improvement: Homer and Yeats alike strive to change their people in the direction of a heritable strength – in Yeats's case, "charm."

Maclagan's eugenical statues have certainly returned to Yeats's mind at this time. In his 1909 diary, he criticizes the unusual "broken" bodies in Augustus John's etchings:

A gymnast set to train the body would find in all these some defect to overcome, and when he had overcome them he would have brought them in every case nearer to that ancient canon which comes down to us from the gymnasium of Greece, and which when it is present marks, like any other literary element, a compact between the artist and society, a purpose held in common with his time to create emotions or forms which nature also desires.

The compact in question is eugenical, and John has abrogated it, for he is not interested "in the social need, in the perpetual thirst for ever more health and physical serviceableness, for bodies fitted for the labour of life." Quoting Blake, Yeats criticizes John's work as Noyes would have: "It is a powerful but prosaic art, celebrating the fall into division not the resurrection into unity." Like Maclagan, Yeats finds that the best chance of resurrecting the body into its original unity resides in the ancient canons of the Greek gymnasium: "The old art, if it [had] gone to its logical conclusion, would have led to the creation of one single type of man, and one single type of woman, in whom would have been concentrated, however, by a kind of deification, the capacity for all energy and all passion."[43]

Even when Yeats seems to confine the poet's improving task with regard to nation and race to that of providing cultural nourishment, the poet's eugenical mission is implicit. In the diary of 1910, he suggests that

A nation can only be created in the deepest thought of the deepest minds . . . who have first made themselves fundamental and profound and then realized themselves in art. In this way they rouse into national action the governing minds of their [time] – few at any one time – by an awakening of their desire towards a certain mood and thought which is unconscious to these governing minds themselves. They create national character.

Those who have realized themselves in art in the service of national character are creating the "charm" that Yeats sees as heritable: "To

oppose the new ill-breeding of Ireland . . . I can only set up a
secondary or interior personality . . ., and this personality . . . must
be always gracious and simple. It must have that slight separation
from immediate interests which makes charm possible." National
character is created by the cultural environment provided by the
poets: "The more unconscious the creation, the more powerful. A
great statesman . . . should have grown into and find about him
always . . . the nobleness of emotion created and associated with his
country by its great poets. If a man is not born into this, he cannot
acquire it . . . It is this culture that makes the birth of heroes possible
. . ." In writing thus of "inherited culture," Yeats does not necessarily
imagine it as heritable via the loins, but he implies here that
statesman and hero are not only to the manor born, but also to the
manner born. There is a sense, that is, in which charm cannot be
acquired. And so, of the interior personality that will display such
charm, Yeats confesses: it is, "alas, to me only possible in my
writings."[44]

The relationship between the artist's imagination and the aristocracy's blood is something that Yeats celebrates more and more.
He initially observes that "[a] great lady is as simple as a good poet.
Both possess nothing that is not ancient and their own . . . They
assume certainties, to the one fashions, to the other opinion, and re-
mould all slightly." He ultimately suggests that the source of this
"re-moulding" – whether in fashionable society or in society as a
whole – is the poet: "Every day I notice some new analogy between
[the] long-established life of the well-born and the artist's life. We
come from the permanent things and create them, and instead of
old blood we have old emotions and we carry in our head that
form of society which aristocracies create now and then . . ."[45]
The relationship is circular: the poet imagines the world and the
aristocrat makes the world thus imagined (as in *The King's
Threshold*).

In explaining the poet's role in this process of creating the
"nobleness of emotion" by which the statesman and hero make
the nation and race, Yeats not surprisingly recalls his character
who first made this claim on behalf of poets, Seanchan: "This is
the golden cradle which in my *King's Threshold* Seanchan would
prepare for his future children."[46] Seanchan had indeed used the
image of the golden cradle to explain his impact on future
children:

> I am labouring
> For some that shall be born in the nick o' time,
> And find sweet nurture, that they may have voices,
> Even in anger, like the strings of harps;
> And how could they be born to majesty
> If I had never made a golden cradle?   (*Plays* p. 266)

As in the diary entry, the poet is here the cultural nurturer. Yet Seanchan in this speech merely supplements the definition of the poet as eugenical director of national breeding that he had elicited from his pupils earlier in the play (just as Yeats supplements his own play, for this passage was added after the first appearance of the play in 1903 and before its 1906 revision). By means of the golden cradle, one is not just nurtured in sweetness, but also *born* to majesty. Seanchan claims responsibility for an elite bloodline. He is responsible for the creation of the aristocratic class in general (by having "commended wasteful virtues") – and responsible for the king's position at the head of this class ("the King's money would not buy, / Nor the high circle consecrate his head, / If poets had never christened gold . . . / Precious") (*Plays* p. 290). By making an elite culture for such a class and such a king to acquire, the poet has made both a culture and a blood to be transmitted thereafter by heredity. However much they disagree about how its strength should be expressed and whether it has "shrunk backward," both the King and Seanchan recognize that at the heart of their contest is the question of how best to preserve the king's "seed" (*Plays* p. 307).

Yeats indirectly recalls the passage from *The King's Threshold* about Seanchan's "golden cradle" even earlier in his diary when commenting on the bad temper of some of the younger members of the Abbey Theatre: "All these young people are the first generation in their families to do intellectual work, and though with strong, fresh and simple imagination and unspoiled taste, prolonged application is difficult to them. They have no acquired faculties. Most of them are naturally sweet-tempered, but they have no control over their tempers once they are aroused."[47] It is too early for the actors and directors in the Abbey Theatre to display sweet voices "even in anger" because the culture that they are acquiring has yet to become hereditary. Estlake, Forel, and Yeats agree that the process by which an individual and a race acquire heritable "charm" is a slow one.

Having embodied Maud Gonne in poetry, therefore, Yeats has fulfilled his eugenical mission as Seanchan did: he has given dreams their looking glass. Faithful to the old art, faithful to the ancient canons of the Greek gymnasium, and faithful to the form of woman Homer sung, Yeats would seem to have done all that he could to promote the birth of the Irish superman and superwoman. Yet his recollection of Seanchan's words is in fact a misrecollection – a misrecollection that suggests that Yeats recognizes a further responsibility in the name of eugenics – a personal responsibility that he has yet to address. In his diary, Yeats misremembers Seanchan's golden cradle as something he "would prepare for his future children." Yet Seanchan speaks of the nation's children, not his own. I read these "future children" not as Seanchan's, but as Yeats's.

The question whether Yeats himself should have children had begun to surface in the diary some time before this. As early as 25 February 1909, Yeats chafes at the suggestion that a cardinal virtue is the domestic one: "Evil comes to us men of imagination wearing as its mask all the virtues. I have known, certainly, more men destroyed by the desire to have wife and child and to keep them in comfort than I have seen destroyed by harlots and drink." The energy in this passage comes from his sense that he is contradicting received opinion that vice consists of "harlots and drink" and that virtue consists of "wife and child." But he also seems to be suggesting that he does indeed have wife and child: "I thought myself free, loving neither vice nor virtue; but virtue has come upon me and given me a nation instead of a home." Returning to these thoughts a few days later in his diary, Yeats declares that "the chief temptation of life" for him is to become active in public affairs and confesses that compared to this temptation "[i]t is easy to give up all thoughts of wealth and of domestic life *even*."[48] He thus implies that the temptation of domestic life is the second greatest temptation in his life at this time. These conflicting claims – that he does not want a wife and child, that perhaps he wants a wife and child (but not as much as he wants to be a public man), that in fact he already has a wife and child in the form of Ireland – put Yeats on the path to the reflections about childlessness in "Pardon, Old Fathers."

Whatever other pressures were brought to bear on Yeats at this time to turn his thoughts toward the subject of marriage and children (whether by family members, friends, lovers, or a sense of society's general expectations in this regard), Forel seems to have been responsible for Yeats's understanding of the eugenical dimensions of the question. Time and again in *The Sexual Question* Forel lays out the same opposition between wife and child, on the one hand, and harlots and alcohol, on the other, that one finds in Yeats's diary entry:

No doubt excesses [of the sexual appetite] disturb the ties of marriage and of family. . . It must, however, be admitted that their satellites, the venereal diseases, and their most common companion, alcoholism, are in reality the greatest destroyers of health, and make much more considerable ravages in society than the artificial increase and abnormal deviations of the sexual appetite itself. However, the latter by themselves often poison the mind and social morality . . . Immoderate sexual desire provoked in men by the artificial excitations of prostitution . . . renders difficult the accustomance to marriage, fidelity and ideal and life-long love for the same woman. (*The Sexual Question* p. 89–90)

Furthermore, Forel emphasizes that the desire for wife and child is the supreme virtue – claiming that he has provided in *The Sexual Question*

irrefutable proof that family life and the sentiments of sympathy between husband and wife, parents and children, constitute the phylogenetic basis of the sexual relations of humanity. Whatever may be the egoistic polygamous instincts of man, we can affirm that a natural and true monogamy constitutes the highest and best form of his sexual relations and of his love. (p. 380)

In fact, in the case of "excellent subjects for reproduction," like Yeats, childlessness is a social vice:

From the social point of view it is absolutely unjust that men who procreate children should alone bear the burden of the future generation. We know the egoistic proverb of the celibates, who say: "I have the right to take life easily, to enjoy myself and be idle, if I renounce the happiness of having children, either of my own accord or from necessity." This proverb, which may be transposed into "after me the deluge," cannot be recognized by any healthy social legislation. It is the duty of the State to relieve large families, to facilitate the procreation of healthy children, and to impose more work and taxes (for instance, artificial families) on sterile individuals. (pp. 382–83)

Forel is particularly harsh on "The Old Bachelor." Although he is capable "of finding . . . compensation in hard intellectual work or in some other employment," the old bachelor "needs compensation for the absence of love and family": "In a word, the object of life is partly wanting in the best of old bachelors, and this void not only affects his sentiments but his whole mental being. His general tendency to pessimism and egoism would be sufficient alone to provoke an energetic protest against the abandonment of social power to celibates" (p. 128). In his diary, Yeats actually accepts what Forel implies: that the life he is living at this time is a subject for pathology. Of his diary for the first part of 1909 Yeats writes: "I dare say that these notes, if some chance eye light on them, may seem morbid; but they help me to understand myself, and I remember hearing a man of science once argue that all progress is at the outset 'pathological.' I know that I have already made moral gains."[49]

Against this background, Yeats's argument that "the renunciation of the artist is those things which in others are virtues" is understandable.[50] Forel has made him defensive about his unmarried status. Claims that to marry a wife and have a child was the natural thing to do, that it was the normal thing to do, that it was the prudent thing to do – whatever claims like these that Yeats encountered in family, friends, lovers, or his own conscience – had no noticeable effect on Yeats. The claim that it was the eugenical thing to do, however, and the charge that not to do it was egoistic, combined to create for Yeats a sexual and psychological question that had to be addressed. His gesture of pointing to Ireland as his wife and child is a way of claiming that he already has the artificial family with which Forel would tax him.

Similar defensiveness is evident in other passages in his diary and in "J. M. Synge and the Ireland of his Time." In the latter, a lengthy quotation from *The Aran Islands* culminates in Synge's description of the shipping of shrieking pigs and the telling-off he received for being unmarried:

The women were over-excited, and when I tried to talk to them they crowded round me and began jeering and shrieking at me because I am not married. A dozen screamed at a time, and so rapidly that I could not understand all they were saying, yet I was able to make out that they were taking advantage of the absence of their husbands to give me the full volume of their contempt.

The folk wisdom of which Yeats is generally so enamored apparently complements Forel's point of view on the irresponsibility of the unmarried man, and so he defensively characterizes it here as "but the hysterical excitement of the women over the pigs." Explaining that Synge was a man whose "hidden passion" found "expression by its choice among the passions of others," Yeats reveals his own hidden passion about marriage by this choice among the hidden passions of Synge.[51]

In his diary, Yeats defends himself against hysterical women and
Forel alike by raising the possibility that he bears a hereditary taint:

I begin to wonder whether I have and always have had some nervous
weakness inherited from my mother. . . In Paris I felt that if the strain were
but a little more I would hit the woman who irritated me . . . The feeling is
always the same . . . It often alarms me; is it the root of madness? So violent
it is, and all the more because I seldom lose my temper in the ordinary
affairs of life.

Does this bad temper mean that Yeats is no better than the young
people of the Abbey Theatre – the first generation of their families to
do intellectual work? They "are naturally sweet-tempered, but they
have no control over their tempers once they are aroused." Either
Yeats bears a hereditary taint of madness or he can not yet list sweet
temper and charm amongst his "acquired faculties."[52] Lady Gregory
is the eugenical ideal – "Being honor bred," she is therefore "Bred to
a harder thing" than the need to triumph in controversy – but
outside his poems, Yeats himself is not (*Poems* p. 291).

The trajectory from eugenical poet of Seanchan's type to potential
procreator with a more personal conception of his eugenical responsibilities is described by Yeats's use of the word "barren" during these
years. As the Seanchan poet suffering an unreconcilable breach with
Maude Gonne because of her marriage to MacBride, the poet suffers
from "barren thoughts" (*Poems* p. 257). The poet's thoughts are
barren of her, barren of her form, and therefore eugenically barren.
He is no better than the eunuchs whose minds are "barren."[53] In
"Pardon, Old Fathers," however, the poet seeks forgiveness "for a
barren passion":

> Pardon that for a barren passion's sake,
> Although I have come close on forty-nine,
> I have no child, I have nothing but a book,
> Nothing but that to prove your blood and mine.   (*Poems* p. 270)

The book was enough for the Seanchan poet, but for the poet with a
sense of personal eugenical responsibilities, it is time to think of "his
future children."

One of the final entries in his diary indicates the wider context of
Yeats's eugenical reflections in "Pardon, Old Fathers." The novelist
George Moore had satirized Yeats's pretensions to noteworthy –
perhaps even aristocratic – descent in articles appearing in the
January and February 1914 issues of *The English Review.*[54] Lady

Gregory and Hugh Lane procured the retraction of offending passages about themselves by threatening legal action. Yeats chose a different strategy. As Foster points out, "'Pardon, Old Fathers' . . . provided immediate therapy, and concentrated his mind on matters which Moore could not defile: WBY's family gods . . ."[55] Yeats also unburdened himself in his diary by drawing Moore's dysgenic family tree in a prose inversion of his own poem: "I have been told that the crudity common to all the Moores came from the mother's family, Mayo squireens, probably half-peasants in education and occupation, for his father was a man of education and power and old descent." Moore is one of the eunuchs that several generations of degeneration has produced: "His mother's blood seems to have affected him and his brother as the peasant strain has affected Edward Martyn. There has been a union of incompatibles and consequent sterility."[56] Edward Martyn is doubly sterile. On the one hand, like Moore, he is the product of degeneration by mixture with base blood: "I used to think that two traditions met and destroyed each other in his blood, creating the sterility of the mule. His father's family was old and honored; his mother but one generation from the peasant."[57] On the other hand, Martyn is the product of the blastophthoric degeneration that Forel describes: according to Yeats, Martyn's father's excessive sexual appetite bequeathed to his son "an always resisted homosexuality."[58] And so , "in Martyn the sterility is complete."[59] Unlike Moore, however, Martyn has "self-possession and taste" – the word "charm" having been replaced by "self-possession" during Yeats's revising process, presumably because in the diary charm is an aristocratic quality appropriate neither to Martyn nor to Moore.[60] The example of Martyn and Moore also explains the dysgenic tendency at the heart of Irish Catholicism:

Both men are examples of the way Irish civilization is held back by the lack of education of Irish Catholic women. An Irish Catholic will not marry a Protestant, and hitherto the women have checked again and again the rise, into some world of refinement, of Catholic households. The whole system of Irish Catholicism pulls down the able and well-born if it pulls up the peasant, as I think it does.[61]

Yeats seems to understand Moore's satirical attack upon him, Gregory, and Lane as another instance of Catholic Ireland's check to refinement: in essay, speech, poem, and play, the Seanchan poet has repeatedly offered himself as the metaphorical husband of his nation, but Catholic Ireland has yet to acknowledge his charm.

Although evidence of Yeats's having read *The Sexual Question* is perhaps less explicit than evidence of his having read *The Oneida Community,* the conjunction both in his writing about *The Playboy of the Western World* and in his diaries between 1909 and 1912 of issues and images such as Don Juans, the intellectual nature of modern sexual attractiveness, eunuchs, removal of genitals and surgical extirpation of sex glands, shrill voices, sexual hysterics, the dangers of repressing sexuality, and hereditary degeneration by inheritance of morbid sexuality suggests that Yeats was dipping into *The Sexual Question,* if not thoroughly absorbed by it, long before George was – perhaps as early as 1909. Moreover, its influence seems to have endured for many years – and in many ways, affecting everything from his love for Maud Gonne and his sex life in marriage to his opposition to "the new ill-breeding in Ireland."[62] From the point of view of Yeats's writing subsequent to 1909, one of the most important effects of the book is to enable him to supplement his biological understanding of degeneration with a psychological one – the consequence of which is a tendency to psychologize about the dysgenic behavior of both races as a whole (including the Irish) and particular individuals (including himself).

And so, having brought the story of Yeats's early interest in eugenics to about the year 1914, I round back to Bradshaw, for his essay "The Eugenics Movement in the 1930s and the Emergence of *On the Boiler*" identifies a number of the eugenical texts that Yeats acquired after this point. These texts greatly complicate any attempt to discriminate the continuing influence of Forel and Estlake upon the eugenical aspects of Yeats's work after *Responsibilities.* Certainly Forel defends the idea that mental abilities are hereditary, yet he is not necessarily the eugenist that Yeats has in mind when elaborating upon this idea in later years, for Forel's source is Galton, and by 1917 George Yeats seems to have introduced a copy of Galton's *Hereditary Genius* into her husband's library. Both Estlake and Forel write of the dangers of the differential birthrate that would preoccupy Yeats in later years, but so does McDougall, whose *National Welfare and National Decay* – another book in Yeats's library – appeared in 1921. Estlake believes that the cross-fertilization of peoples produces stronger races, but so does Flinders Petrie, whose theories were advertised by McDougall and whose *The Revolutions of Civilization* (1922) Yeats also owned.[63]

Yet whatever the contribution of Forel and Estlake to the development of Yeats's thinking about eugenics in the late teens, the 1920s,
and the 1930s, the impact of *The Sexual Question* and *The Oneida
Community* on the earliest formulations of his eugenical ideas is clear.
It is no longer possible to read Yeats's language of blood and
breeding in these early years as a naive, non-biological celebration of
an aristocratic environment – an environment perhaps capable
(regardless of heredity) of nurturing the manners and attitudes of
which Yeats approved. In the history of twentieth-century literature,
we must acknowledge that the poet who called himself one of the last
romantics was also, like Woolf and Eliot, one of the first eugenists.

Notes

INTRODUCTION

1 See Henry W. Rumsey, "On a Progressive Physical Degeneracy of Race in The Town Populations of Great Britain," in *Transactions of the National Association for the Promotion of Social Sciences* (London, 1871), pp. 466–72.

2 William Greenslade, *Degeneration, Culture and the Novel: 1880–1940* (Cambridge University Press, 1994), pp. 15, 29, 46, 46.

3 Robert Reid Rentoul, *Race Culture; or, Race Suicide? A Plea for the Unborn* (1906; rpr. New York and London: Garland, 1984), pp. 7–8.

4 See Daniel J. Kevles, *In the Name of Eugenics: Genetics and the Uses of Human Heredity* (New York: Knopf, 1985), p. 21; Karl Pearson, "On the Scope and Importance to the State of the Science of National Eugenics," in *The Scope and Importance to the State of the Science of National Eugenics* (London: Dulau, 1909), in *Eugenics Laboratory Lecture Series: The Francis Galton Laboratory for National Eugenics* (New York and London: Garland, 1985), p. 39.

5 Greta Jones, *Social Hygiene in Twentieth Century Britain* (London: Croom Helm, 1986), p. 25.

6 Herbert Spencer, *Social Statics, Abridged and Revised* (1884), in *The Works of Herbert Spencer*, 21 vols. (Osnabrück: Otto Zeller, 1966), vol. I, p. 147.

7 Francis Galton, *Inquiries into Human Faculty* (London: Macmillan, 1883), pp. 24–25.

8 F. C. S. Schiller, *Social Decay and Eugenical Reform* (1932; rpr. New York and London: Garland, 1984), pp. 28–29.

9 Galton, "Eugenics, its Definition, Scope, and Aims," in *Essays in Eugenics* (1909; rpr. New York and London: Garland, 1985), p. 42.

10 William C. D. Whetham and Catherine D. Whetham, *The Family and the Nation* (1909; rpr. New York and London: Garland, 1984), pp. 6–7.

11 Rentoul, *Race Culture*, pp. 1–10.

12 Schiller, *Social Decay*, p. 30.

13 Albert E. Wiggam, *The New Decalogue of Science* (New York: Bobbs-Merrill, 1923), p. III, cited in Kevles, *In the Name of Eugenics*, p. 59.

14 Julian Huxley, "Eugenics and Society," *Eugenics Review*, 28.1 (1936), 30, 30, 11.

15 In *The Meme Machine* (Oxford University Press, 1999), Susan Blackmore refers to this enduring difficulty for Lamarckians as "Weismann's barrier" (p. 59). Blackmore notes that many today still assume that "[b]iological evolution is not Lamarckian and cultural evolution is," but her own "conclusion apropos Lamarck is that the question 'Is cultural evolution Lamarckian' is best not asked" (pp. 59, 60). Whereas Lamarckism attempts to transpose models of transmission quite valid in the realm of culture to the realm of biology, Blackmore does the opposite. Following upon the work of Richard Dawkins, on the one hand, and Daniel Dennett, on the other, in theorizing the meme as a cultural replicator analogous to the gene (like the gene, selfish, but unlike the gene, not necessarily interested in the host organism's biological advantage), Blackmore develops memetic theory in such a way as to explain everything from the origins of our large brains and our language ability to the development of religions and the Internet.

16 T. S. Eliot, "Recent British Periodical Literature in Ethics," *International Journal of Ethics* [*IJE*], 28.2 (Jan. 1918), 270, 274.

17 Karl Pearson, *The Grammar of Science* (London: Walter Scott, 1892), p. 33.

18 Ethel M. Elderton, *The Relative Strength of Nurture and Nature* (London: Dulau, 1909), in *Eugenics Laboratory Lecture Series*, p. 33.

19 Lyndsay Andrew Farrell, *The Origins and Growth of the English Eugenics Movement 1865–1925* (New York and London: Garland, 1985), p. 163.

20 *Ibid.*, p. 51.

21 Huxley, "Eugenics and Society," 30.

22 Eliot, "Recent British Periodical Literature," 274.

23 Jones, *Social Hygiene*, p. 32; on Labour opposition to the Act, see pp. 43, 58, 103.

24 C. P. Blacker, Letter to J. R. Baker (15 Feb. 1933), Eugenics Society Papers, C 10, cited in Jones, *Social Hygiene*, p. 103.

25 Huxley, "Eugenics and Society," p. 30.

26 William C. D. and Catherine D. Whetham, "Decadence and Civilization," *Hibbert Journal*, 10.37 (Oct. 1911), 188.

27 Edith Bethune-Baker, Letter to the editor, *The Hibbert Journal*, 10.38 (Jan. 1912), 474.

28 Whetham and Whetham, "Decadence and Civilization," 187–88; Bethune-Baker, Letter to the editor, 476.

29 Thomas J. Gerrard, *The Church and Eugenics* (London: P.S. King, 1912), pp. 37, 19–20.

30 Thomas J. Gerrard, "The Catholic Church and Race Culture," *Dublin Review*, 149 (July 1911), 55–67.

31 See *Casti Connubii*, in *The Papal Encyclicals 1903–1939*, ed. Claudia Carlen Ihm, 5 vols. (Raleigh, SC: McGrath, 1981).

32 See Jones, *Social Hygiene*, pp. 58–62.

33 George Bernard Shaw, "The Religion of the Future," lecture delivered to The Heretics Society, Cambridge, 29 May 1911, in *The Religious*

Speeches of Bernard Shaw, ed. Warren Sylvester Smith (University Park, PA: Pennsylvania State University Press, 1963), p. 35.

34 George Bernard Shaw, *Man and Superman: a Comedy and a Philosophy* (1903; rpr. Harmondsworth: Penguin, 1985), p. 218.

35 On Beatrice Webb, see Angus McLaren, *Birth Control in Nineteenth-Century England* (London: Croom Helm, 1978), p. 190; Sidney Webb, *The Decline in the Birth Rate* (London: The Fabian Society, 1907), pp. 16–17.

36 Austin Harrison, "The State and the Family," *English Review,* 16.2 (1912), 283.

37 Feisal Mohamed, "Lawrencian Eugenics and the Mating Habits of the Sons of God and the Men of Quetzalcoatl," Seventh International Conference of the D. H. Lawrence Society of North America and the Phoenix Rising Society, Taos, New Mexico, 17 July 1998, pp. 7–8.

38 Bethune-Baker, Letter to the editor, 474.

39 Kevles, *In the Name of Eugenics,* pp. 64–65.

40 Jones, *Social Hygiene,* p. 56.

41 Kevles, *In the Name of Eugenics,* pp. 64–65.

42 Jones, *Social Hygiene,* p. 58.

43 Herman J. Muller, *Out of the Night* (1935; rpr. London and New York: Garland, 1984), pp. 104–06.

44 G. B. Shaw, Preface to *On the Rocks,* in *The Complete Prefaces of Bernard Shaw* (London: Paul Hamlyn, 1965), pp. 353–54.

45 H. G. Wells, *Anticipations of the Reaction of Mechanical and Scientific Progress upon Human Life and Thought* (London: Chapman and Hall, 1901), pp. 287–90, 298–99.

46 Rebecca West, Letter to Violet Hunt (1914), in Victoria Glendinning, *Rebecca West: a Life* (London: Weidenfeld and Nicolson, 1987), p. 55.

47 D. H. Lawrence, Letter to Blanche Jennings (1908), in *The Letters of D. H. Lawrence,* ed. James T. Boulton, 3 vols. (Cambridge University Press, 1979), vol. I, p. 81.

48 D. H. Lawrence, *Phoenix II: Uncollected, Unpublished, and Other Prose Works by D. H. Lawrence,* eds. Warren Roberts and Harry T. Moore (New York: Viking, 1968), p. 265.

49 J. M. Synge, *The Playboy of the Western World* (London: Eyre Methuen, 1961), pp. 101–02.

50 Aldous Huxley, "Science and Civilization," in *Aldous Huxley between the Wars: Essays and Letters,* ed. David Bradshaw (Chicago, IL: Ivan R. Dee, 1994), p. 112.

51 Aldous Huxley, "What is Happening to Our Population?", in *Aldous Huxley between the Wars,* pp. 150–51.

52 Jones, *Social Hygiene,* p. 49.

53 G. K. Chesterton, Review of *National Life from the Standpoint of Science* by Karl Pearson, *Speaker* (2 Feb. 1901), 488.

54 Jones, *Social Hygiene,* p. 49.

55 G. K. Chesterton, "On Evil Euphemisms," in *Selected Essays* (London and Glasgow: Collins, 1936), pp. 226–27.

56 G. K. Chesterton, "On a Humiliating Heresy," in *Selected Essays*, pp. 229–30.

57 James Joyce, *A Portrait of the Artist as a Young Man* (1916; rpr. Harmondsworth: Penguin, 1964), pp. 208–09.

58 F. Scott Fitzgerald, "Love or Eugenics," Princeton Triangle Show (1914), in Kevles, *In the Name of Eugenics*, p. 58.

59 Farrell, *English Eugenics Movement*, pp. 31–32.

60 See C. P. Snow, review of *Out of the Night* by Herman Muller, *Spectator* (1936) and Olive Schreiner, *Woman and Labour* (New York: Frederick A. Stokes, 1911), p. 269. I refer to Marie Stopes's alliance with the eugenics movement in Chapter 3. Naomi Mitchison, whose brother J.B.S. Haldane was the sometime eugenist and later critic of main-line eugenics, was elected a Fellow of the Eugenics Society in 1925 (see David Bradshaw, "Huxley's Slump: Planning, Eugenics, and the 'Ultimate Need' of Stability," in *The Art of Literary Biography*, ed. John Batchelor [Oxford: Clarendon Press, 1995], p.164; on Haldane, see Kevles, *In the Name of Eugenics*, pp. 127–28). Mencken called eugenics the "great moral cause" in *Prejudices, Sixth Series* (New York: Alfred A. Knopf, 1927), p. 233. On London, see Juan Leon, "'Meeting Mr. Eugenides': T. S. Eliot and Eugenic Anxiety," *Yeats–Eliot Review*, 9.4 (Summer/Fall 1988), 174.

61 Leon notes that Dean William R. Inge, "one of eugenics's most vocal enthusiasts," was "blasted in BLAST (1914), and A. R. Orage decried eugenists' plans as the last word in totalitarianism" ("'Meeting Mr. Eugenides'" 174).

62 Michel Foucault, *The History of Sexuality, vol. 1: An Introduction*, trans. Robert Hurley (New York: Vintage, 1980), pp. 140, 138, 26, 26, 54, 118.

63 Bernhard Radloff, *Will and Representation: the Philosophical Foundations of Melville's "Theatrum Mundi"* (New York: Peter Lang, 1996), p. 2.

64 Gillian Beer, *Arguing with the Past: Essays in Narrative from Woolf to Sidney* (London: Routledge, 1989), pp. 4–5.

65 See Mark Haller, *Eugenics: Hereditarian Attitudes in American Thought* (New Brunswick, NJ: Rutgers University Press, 1963), pp. 137–40; and see Kevles, *In the Name of Eugenics*, p. 115.

66 Various newspapers and news services carried stories about eugenics in the late 1990s. See, for instance, Bob Fenton, "Sweden faces its not-so-secret history of forced sterilization," *The Daily Telegraph*, August 1997; "Finns sterilized 11,000, newspaper reports," Associated Press, in *The Ottawa Citizen*, August 1997; "Forcible sterilizing continues, Swiss told," Reuters News Agency, in *The Globe and Mail*, 29 August 1997.

67 Jonathan Freedland, "The Dirty Little Secret of the Old British Left," *Guardian Weekly*, 7 September 1997.

68 Virginia Woolf, *The Diary of Virginia Woolf*, eds. Anne Olivier Bell and Andrew McNeillie, 5 vols. (New York: Harcourt, Brace, Jovanovich, 1977–84), vol. 1, p. 13.

69 Hermione Lee, "Biomythographers: Rewriting the Lives of Virginia ... *iticism*, 26.2 (April 1986), 107; Hermione Lee, *Virginia* ...nopf, 1998), p. 184.

... *Boiler* (1939), in *Explorations* (London: Macmillan,

..., *Yeats and Politics in the 1930s* (London: Macmillan,

...ford, *Yeats, Ireland and Fascism* (London: Macmillan,

"A Modest Proposal," in *The Irish Tracts: 1728–1733*, ed. ...xford: Basil Blackwell, 1964), p. 116. In "In Memory of ...W.H. Auden writes that "mad Ireland hurt you into ...H. Auden, *The English Auden: Poems, Essays, and Dramatic* ...*1939*, ed. Edward Mendelson (London: Faber and Faber,

...nt Periodical Literature in Ethics," 274. ... *Christianity and Culture* (New York: Harcourt Brace, 1968),

..."Gerontion," in *The Complete Poems and Plays of T. S. Eliot* ...er and Faber, 1969), p. 37, hereafter cited parenthetically in the text as *CPP*; John Carey, *The Intellectual and the Masses: Pride and Prejudice among the Literary Intelligentsia, 1880–1939* (London: Faber and Faber, 1992), p. 13.

77 Leon, "'Meeting Mr. Eugenides,'" 174.

78 Robert Crawford, *The Savage and the City in the Work of T. S. Eliot* (Oxford: Clarendon Press, 1987), p. 69.

79 Michael Coren, *The Invisible Man: the Life and Liberties of H. G. Wells* (Toronto: Random House, 1993), p. 69. Michael Foot, *The History of H. G. Wells* (Washington, DC: Counterpoint, 1995), p. 61.

80 Bradshaw, "Huxley's Slump," p. 168.

81 Donald Watt, "The Manuscript Revisions of *Brave New World*," in *Critical Essays on Aldous Huxley*, ed. Jerome Meckier (New York: G. K. Hall, 1996), pp. 78–79.

82 Carey, *The Intellectual and the Masses*, p. 21.

83 Greenslade, *Degeneration, Culture and the Novel*, pp. 258, 10.

84 Jerome J. McGann, "The Text, the Poem, and the Problem of Historical Method," in *Literary Theories in Praxis*, ed. Shirley F. Staton (University Park, Pa.: University of Pennsylvania Press, 1987), p. 212.

85 Marouf Arif Hasian, Jr., *The Rhetoric of Eugenics in Anglo-American Thought* (Athens, GA and London: University of Georgia Press, 1996), p. 23.

86 Foucault, *History of Sexuality*, pp. 101, 101, 27, 101.

87 Thomas Hardy, "In Tenebris" II, in *The Complete Poetical Works of Thomas*

Hardy, ed. Samuel Hynes, 5 vols. (Oxford: Clarendon Press, 1982), vol. I, p. 208.

1 VIRGINIA WOOLF'S HEREDITARY TAINT

1 Lee, "Biomythographers," 107.
2 Virginia Woolf, *Orlando* (Oxford University Press, 1992), pp. 294–95.
3 Lee, "Biomythographers," 107.
4 T. S. Eliot, "Milton I," in *On Poetry and Poets* (London: Faber and Faber, 1957), p. 139; Lee, "Biomythographers," 108.
5 *Ibid.,* 111.
6 Woolf, *Diary,* vol. I, p. 13. This incident seems to resurface in *The Pargiters* and *The Years,* the danger represented by imbeciles transformed into the sexual threat represented by the implicitly imbecilic flasher with "the horrible face" who exposes himself to the young Rose. See Virginia Woolf, *The Pargiters: the Novel-Essay Portion of the Years,* ed. Mitchell A. Leaska (New York: New York Public Library and Readex Books, 1977), pp. 42–43.
7 Virginia Woolf, *Three Guineas* (London: Hogarth Press, 1938), pp. 199, 200, 201, 201–02, 198.
8 Elizabeth Butler Cullingford, *Gender and History in Yeats's Love Poetry* (Cambridge University Press, 1993), p. 279.
9 Jonathan Rose, *The Edwardian Temperament 1895–1919* (Athens, GA and London: Ohio University Press, 1986), p. 138.
10 Stephen Trombley, *"All that Summer She was Mad": Virginia Woolf and her Doctors* (London: Junction Books, 1981), p. 208.
11 Roger Poole, *The Unknown Virginia Woolf* (Cambridge University Press, 1978), pp. 122–23.
12 Farrell, *English Eugenics Movement,* p. 250.
13 See, for example, "The Eugenics Education Society," *Times* (10 March 1909), 12; "Eugenics Education Society," *Times* (4 Feb. 1910), 6; "Eugenics," *Times* (6 May 1910), 4; Havelock Ellis, "Eugenics and St. Valentine," *Nineteenth Century,* 59 (1906), 779; C.W. Saleeby, "Eugenics: The Essential Factor in Progress," *Monthly Review,* 23.1 (1906), 47; Lionel Taylor, "The Social Application of Eugenics," *Westminster Review,* 170 (1908), 416–24; W. C. D. and C. D. Whetham, "Decadence and Civilization," *Hibbert Journal,* 10.37 (Oct. 1911), 179–200.
14 See Farrell, *English Eugenics Movement,* pp. 264–71.
15 Henrietta O. Barnett, "Some Principles of the Poor Law," *Cornhill Magazine,* ns 24.142 (Apr. 1908), 501, 503. Greenslade explains the campaign for national efficiency as a response to "the cancer of unfitness" at the heart of the empire as revealed by the unfitness of soldiers recruited for the Boer War (*Degeneration, Culture and the Novel,* pp. 83–84).
16 Virginia Stephen, review of *The Memoirs of Lady Dorothy Nevill,* in *Cornhill Magazine,* ns 24.142 (Apr. 1908), 472.

17 W. Duncan McKim, *Heredity and Human Progress* (1900; rpr. New York and London: Garland, 1984), p. 188.

18 See Farrell, *English Eugenics Movement*, pp. 213–15.

19 Virginia Woolf, Letter to Emma Vaughan (23 Oct. 1900), *The Letters of Virginia Woolf*, eds. Nigel Nicolson and Joanne Trautmann, 6 vols. (New York and London: Harcourt Brace Jovanovich, 1975–80), vol. I, p. 40. See also Farrell, *English Eugenics Movement*, p. 224, and *Problems in Eugenics: First International Eugenics Congress*, 2 vols. (1912; rpr. New York and London: Garland, 1984), vol. I, p. xiv.

20 Woolf was referring to Josiah Wedgwood as "Jos." by January of 1915. See *Diary*, vol. I, p. 21.

21 Josiah Wedgwood, *House of Commons Debates*, 28 May 1913, vol. LV, 243–44, cited in Jones, *Social Hygiene*, p. 34; Jones, *Social Hygiene*, p. 34.

22 Dan H. Laurence, editor, *Bernard Shaw: Collected Letters*, 4 vols. (London: Reinhardt, 1985), vol. III, p. 439. Woolf could have attended Shaw's first lecture, "Life" (27 October 1916), for she was up from Rodmell on the day in question, dining out in London. (See Woolf, Letter to Vanessa Bell [24 Oct. 1916], *Letters*, vol. II, p. 124).

23 Virginia Woolf, "A Sketch of the Past," in *Moments of Being: Unpublished Autobiographical Writings*, ed. Jeanne Schulkind (London: University of Sussex Press, 1976), p. 72.

24 George Bernard Shaw, Letter to H. G. Wells (7 Dec. 1916), in *Bernard Shaw: Collected Letters*, vol. III, pp. 441–42. See also Samuel Butler, *Luck, or Cunning?* (1887), in *The Works of Samuel Butler*, 20 vols. (1924; rpr. New York: AMS Press, 1968), vol. VIII, ch. 6.

25 Poole, *Unknown Virginia Woolf*, p. 122.

26 T. B. Hyslop, "The Mental Deficiency Bill, 1912," *Journal of Mental Science*, 57 (Oct. 1912), 555.

27 Virginia Woolf, *Roger Fry* (1940; rpr. London: Hogarth Press, 1990), p. 156. Greenslade mentions Hyslop as one of those of the "still resilient degenerationist mentality" who were still peddling the simplistic strategies for pathologizing modernism that were promulgated by Max Nordau in *Degeneration* (1895; rpr. London: William Heinemann, 1898). See Greenslade, *Degeneration, Culture and the Novel*, p. 130.

28 Maurice Craig, *Psychological Medicine* (London: J. and A. Churchill, 1905), p. 32.

29 Maurice Craig, "Some Aspects of Education and Training in Relation to Mental Disorder," *Journal of Mental Science*, 67 (1922), 228.

30 Trombley, *Woolf and her Doctors*, p. 208.

31 Peter F. Alexander, *Leonard and Virginia Woolf: a Literary Partnership* (New York: St. Martin's Press, 1992), p. 86.

32 On Leonard Woolf's attitude toward children, see *ibid.*, p. 85.

33 On these matters, see *ibid.*, pp. 67–69, 79–84.

34 Virginia Woolf, *Mrs. Dalloway* (1925; rpr. New York and London: Harcourt Brace Jovanovich, 1953), p. 150.

35 See Poole, *Unknown Virginia Woolf*, p. 167, for a suggestive reading of the same passage about Bradshaw.

36 George Savage, "On Insanity and Marriage," *Journal of Mental Science*, 57 (1911), 98, 100.

37 See Alexander, *Leonard and Virginia Woolf*, p. 38. See also Jean Thomas, Letter to Violet Dickinson (14 Sept. 1913), cited in Quentin Bell, *Virginia Woolf: a Biography*, 2 vols. (London: Hogarth, 1972), vol. II, p. 16n, and vol. I, p. 199.

38 George Savage, cited in *Report of Proceedings of the First International Eugenics Congress*, in *Problems in Eugenics*, vol. II, p. 68. It is tempting to speculate that the family to which Savage refers here is the Stephen family, for Savage knew of the family history of madness, having attended upon J.K. Stephen, Virginia Woolf's first cousin.

39 F.W. Mott, "Heredity and Eugenics in Relation to Insanity," in *Problems in Eugenics*, vol. I, p. 421.

40 Woolf, Letters to Violet Dickinson (14 Jan. 1905, mid-Feb. 1905, July 1905), *Letters*, vol. I, pp. 175, 179, 198.

41 F. W. Mott, cited in *Report of Proceedings of the First International Eugenics Congress*, in *Problems in Eugenics*, vol. II, p. 69.

42 Woolf, Letter to Vanessa Bell (Wednesday, July 1911), *Letters*, vol. I, p. 469.

43 See Savage, Sir George Henry, *Who Was Who: 1916–1928* (London: Adam and Charles Black, 1928).

44 See "National Association for the Feeble-Minded," *British Medical Journal* (22 May 1909), 1243–44.

45 Virginia Woolf, *To the Lighthouse* (New York and London: Harcourt, Brace, Jovanovich, 1927), pp. 155–56.

46 Megumi Kato, "The Milk Problem in *To the Lighthouse*," *Virginia Woolf Miscellany*, 50 (Fall 1997), 5.

47 George Newman, "Discussion on the Control of the Milk Supply," *British Medical Journal* (27 August 1904), 421–29.

48 "Milk and National Degeneration," unsigned article, *British Medical Journal* (16 April 1904), 908–09.

49 Kato, "The Milk Problem," 5.

50 Woolf, Letter to Vanessa Bell (28 July 1910), *Letters*, vol. I, p. 430.

51 Woolf, Letter to Clive Bell (18 April 1911), *Letters*, vol. I, p. 461.

52 Virginia Woolf, holograph draft (June 1933), *The Years*, Berg Collection, New York Public Library, in Lee, *Virginia Woolf*, p. 330.

53 *Ibid.*

54 *Ibid.*, p. 331.

2 BOERS, WHORES, AND MONGOLS IN *MRS. DALLOWAY*

1 *Problems in Eugenics*, vol. I, p. xv.

2 See Farrell, *English Eugenics Movement*, p. 234; Rentoul, *Race Culture*, p. 101; Whetham and Whetham, "Decadence and Civilization," 193.

3 Virginia Woolf, *Night and Day* (New York: Harcourt Brace Jovanovich, 1920), p. 88.

4 See, for example, *Mrs. Dalloway* pp. 28, 130, 145.

5 Karl Pearson, *National Life: from the Standpoint of Science* (London: Cambridge University Press, 1901), pp. 11–12, 21, 27.

6 Charles B. Davenport, "The Feebly Inhibited: 1. Violent Temper and its Inheritance," *Journal of Nervous and Mental Diseases*, 42 (Sept. 1915), 608; see also Kevles, *In the Name of Eugenics*, p. 53.

7 Jones, *Social Hygiene*, p. 33.

8 See *Problems in Eugenics*, vol. II, p. 57.

9 Virginia Woolf, *The Voyage Out* (1915; repr. London: Hogarth Press, 1957), p. 91.

10 Maria Sharpe, "Autobiographical History of the Men and Women's Club," pp. 2–6, Karl Pearson Papers, Cabinet II, D3/k, Archives, University College London, cited in Kevles, *In the Name of Eugenics*, p. 25.

11 Virginia Woolf, *Jacob's Room* (1922; London: Hogarth Press, 1960), p. 66.

12 Kevles, *In the Name of Eugenics*, p. 107.

13 Mary Dendy, cited in Savage, "On Insanity and Marriage," 105.

14 On Woolf's critique of evolution, see Elizabeth Lambert, "Proportion is in the Mind of the Beholder: *Mrs. Dalloway*'s Critique of Science," in *Virginia Woolf: Emerging Perspectives*, eds. Mark Hussey and Vara Nemerow (New York: Pace University Press, 1984), pp. 278–82. On Woolf and science more generally, see Gillian Beer, *Wave, Action, Dinosaur: Woolf's Science* (Tokyo: English Literary Society of Japan, 2000).

15 Does Mr. Bentley connect Einstein and Mendel as authors of theories of relativity?

16 Kevles, *In the Name of Eugenics*, p. 105.

17 Woolf, *Night and Day*, pp. 365–66.

18 Kevles, *In the Name of Eugenics*, p. 44.

19 *Oxford English Dictionary*: "Mongoloid: Belonging to one of the five principal races of mankind (according to Huxley's division)."

20 William C. D. and Catherine D. Whetham, "The Influence of Race on History," in *Problems in Eugenics*, vol. I, p. 241.

21 *Ibid.*, p. 240.

22 *Ibid.*, p. 242.

23 *Ibid.*, p. 240.

24 Savage, in *Proceedings of the First International Eugenics Congress*, vol. II, p. 68.

25 See *mongol* in *A Supplement to the Oxford English Dictionary*.

26 Kevles, *In the Name of Eugenics*, p. 160. See also, F. G. Cruikshank, *The Mongol in our Midst: a Study of Man and his three Faces* (London: Kegan Paul, Trench, Trubner, 1924).

27 Nordeau, *Degeneration*, p. 15. Greenslade traces the tendency to judge criminal types by look to Cesare Lombroso. See chapter five, "Criminal degeneracy: adventures with Lombroso," of *Degeneration, Culture and the Novel*.

28 Woolf, *The Pargiters*, pp. 42–43.
29 Michel Foucault, "The Eye of Power," in *Power and Knowledge: Selected Interviews and Other Writings 1972–1977*, ed. Colin Gordon, trans. Colin Gordon, Leo Marshall, John Mepham, Kate Soper (New York: Pantheon Books, 1980), p. 147.
30 *Ibid.*, p. 155.
31 *Ibid.*, p. 154.
32 Woolf, *Diary*, vol. II, p. 222.
33 Foucault, "The Eye of Power," p. 154; *ibid*.
34 Lee, *Virginia Woolf*, p. 329.
35 *Ibid.*, p. 186.
36 Greenslade, *Degeneration, Culture, and the Novel*, p. 228.

3 BODY AND BIOLOGY IN *A ROOM OF ONE'S OWN*

1 Woolf, Letter to Janet Case (21 May 1922), *Letters*, vol. II, p. 529
2 Virginia Woolf, *A Room of One's Own* (1928; rpr. London: Penguin, 1975), p. 48.
3 See Henri Bergson, *Creative Evolution*, trans. Arthur Mitchell (New York: Henry Holt and Company, 1911).
4 Woolf, Letter to Janet Case (21 May 1922), *Letters*, vol. II, p. 529.
5 Samuel G. Smith, *Problems in Eugenics*, vol. II, p. 36, vol. I, p. 486.
6 C. W. Saleeby, cited in *Problems in Eugenics*, vol. II, p. 37.
7 F.A. Woods, cited in *Problems in Eugenics*, vol. II, p. 56.
8 Whetham and Whetham, *The Family and the Nation*, p. 77.
9 Woolf, *The Voyage Out*, pp. 93–94.
10 Whetham and Whetham, *The Family and the Nation*, p. 80.
11 Woolf blamed her susceptibility to mental illness on the Stephens, claiming to have inherited a nervous system "used by my father and his father to dictate dispatches and write books with . . . To think that my father's philosophy and the Dictionary of National Biography cost me this." See Woolf, Letter to Ethyl Smith (27 February 1930), *Letters*, vol. IV, p. 48.
12 See Woolf's "inherited . . . ancestral dread" of her body in "A Sketch of the Past," p. 68.
13 Samuel G. Smith, cited in *Problems in Eugenics*, vol. II, p. 36.
14 Elaine Showalter, *A Literature of their Own: British Women Novelists from Brontë to Lessing* (Princeton University Press, 1977), pp. 263–64.
15 Rentoul, *Race Culture*, p. 30.
16 See *Problems in Eugenics*, vol. II, pp. 63–64, and Kevles, *In the Name of Eugenics*, pp. 90, 323–24.
17 Kevles, *In the Name of Eugenics*, p. 349.
18 Virginia Woolf, Letter to Molly MacCarthy (19 Jan. 1923), *Letters*, vol. III, p. 6.
19 On Woolf and birth control, see Christina Hauck, "Virginia Woolf and

the Body," in *Virginia Woolf: Themes and Variations*, eds. Vara Neverow and Mark Hussey (New York: Pace University Press, 1994), pp. 115–20.

20 Rentoul, *Race Culture*, p. 131.

21 Mrs. Macoy Irwin, cited in *Problems in Eugenics*, vol. II, pp. 36–7.

22 R.L. Dugdale, *The Jukes* (5th edn.; New York: G.P. Putnam's Sons, 1895), p. 26.

23 Whetham and Whetham, *The Family and the Nation*, pp. 65–66.

24 Michael F. Guyer, *Being Well-Born: an Introduction to Eugenics* (New York: Bobbs-Merrill, 1916), p. 194.

25 Foucault, *The History of Sexuality*, p. 139.

4 ELIOT ON BIOLOGY AND BIRTHRATES

1 T. S. Eliot, *The Idea of a Christian Society* (New York: Harcourt, Brace, 1940), pp. 14, 16, 16, 13, 16.

2 Eliot confessed that his "only real conversion, by the deliberate influence of any individual, was a temporary conversion to Bergsonism." See T. S. Eliot, "A Sermon Preached at Magdalene College Chapel by T. S. Eliot, O.M." (Cambridge University Press, 1948), p. 5.

3 See *Josiah Royce's Seminar, 1913–1914: as recorded in the notebooks of Harry T. Costello*, ed. Grover Smith (New Brunswick, NJ: Rutgers University Press, 1963).

4 Crawford, *The Savage and the City*, p. 68.

5 T. S. Eliot, "Recent British Periodical Literature in Ethics," 270.

6 *Ibid.*, 273.

7 E. W. MacBride, "The Study of Heredity: Part III," *Eugenics Review*, 8.3 (Oct. 1916), 218.

8 T. S. Eliot, "Studies in Contemporary Criticism," *Egoist*, 5.9 (Oct. 1918), 113.

9 T. S. Eliot, "Contemporanea," *Egoist*, 5.6 (June–July 1918), 84.

10 Eliot, "Studies in Contemporary Criticism," 113.

11 E. W. MacBride, "The Study of Heredity: Part II," *Eugenics Review*, 8.2 (July 1916), 144–45.

12 "The Study of Heredity: Part IV," *Eugenics Review*, 8.4 (Jan. 1917), 353.

13 Eliot, "Recent British Periodical Literature in Ethics," 274.

14 *Ibid.*, 274. On p. 273, Eliot quotes MacBride from page 353 of "The Study of Heredity: Part IV." On Eliot's University of London lectures, see Ronald Schuchard, "T. S. Eliot as an Extension Lecturer," *Review of English Studies*, n.s. 25.98 and 99 (1974), 163–73, 292–304.

15 T. S. Eliot, "A Sceptical Patrician," review of *The Education of Henry Adams, An Autobiography*, *Athenaeum*, 4647 (23 May 1919), 361.

16 Henry Adams, *The Education of Henry Adams, An Autobiography* (1918; rpr. Boston, MA: Houghton Mifflin, 1961), p. 230; Eliot, "A Sceptical Patrician," 361.

17 T. S. Eliot, "The Beating of a Drum," *Nation and Athenaeum*, 34.1 (6 Oct. 1923), 11.

18 T. S. Eliot, "Commentary," *Criterion*, 4.4 (Oct. 1927), 347.

19 Eliot, "The Beating of a Drum," 11; MacBride, "The Study of Heredity: Part I," *Eugenics Review*, 8.1 (Apr. 1916), 26.

20 Eliot, "The Beating of a Drum," 11.

21 *Ibid.*

22 Eliot, "A Sceptical Patrician," 361–62, 362; Matthew Arnold, "Shelley," in *The Last Word*, ed. R.H. Super (Ann Arbor, Mich.: University of Michigan Press, 1977), p. 327.

23 Eliot, "A Sceptical Patrician," 361–62.

24 T. S. Eliot, review of *Mr. Shaw and "The Maid"* by J. M. Robertson, *Criterion*, 4.2 (Apr. 1926), 390.

25 Kevles, *In the Name of Eugenics*, p. 29. See also Karl Pearson, *The Grammar of Science* (London: Walter Scott, 1892).

26 Eliot, "A Sceptical Patrician," 362.

27 T. S. Eliot, "Commentary," *Criterion*, 4.4 (Oct. 1927), 346, 345–46, 346, 346, 347.

28 T. S. Eliot, "Literature and the Modern World," *American Prefaces*, 1.2 (Nov. 1935), 19.

29 T. S. Eliot, "A Prediction in Regard to Three English Authors," *Vanity Fair*, 21 (Feb. 1924), 29.

30 T. S. Eliot, "Imperfect Critics," in *The Sacred Wood*, rev. edn. (London: Methuen, 1928), p. 45; T. S. Eliot, "The Possibility of a Poetic Drama," in *The Sacred Wood*, pp. 66–67.

31 T. S. Eliot, "The Idea of a Literary Review," *Criterion*, 4.1 (Jan. 1926), 6.

32 Eliot, review of *Mr. Shaw and "The Maid,"* 390.

33 MacBride, "The Study of Heredity: Part II," 140, 139–40, 140.

34 T. S. Eliot, "London Letter," *Dial*, 71.4 (Oct. 1921), 454–55.

35 T. S. Eliot, review of *God: Being an Introduction to the Science of Metabiology*, by J. Middleton Murry, *Criterion*, 9.35 (Jan. 1930), 335–36.

36 Foucault, *The History of Sexuality*, p. 139.

37 Eliot, "London Letter," 454, 455.

38 *Ibid.*, 455.

39 T. S. Eliot, "Commentary," *Criterion*, 6.6 (Dec. 1927), 482.

40 T. S. Eliot, "Observations," *Egoist*, 5.5. (May 1918), 69.

41 E.B. Poulton's Galton Lecture "Eugenic Problems after the Great War" was among the essays that Eliot read in reviewing *The Eugenics Review* for his *IJE* essay. See vol. 8.1 (April 1916), 34–49.

42 Eliot, "Observations," 69.

43 Eliot, "Commentary," *Criterion*, 6.6 (Dec. 1927), 481–83.

44 T. S. Eliot, "Commentary," *Criterion*, 12.46 (Oct. 1932), 78–79.

45 T. S. Eliot, "Charleston, Hey! Hey!" *Nation and Athenaeum*, 40.17 (29 Jan. 1927), 595.

46 See MacBride, "The Study of Heredity: Part IV," 351.

47 T. S. Eliot, "London Letter," *Dial*, 73.6 (Dec. 1922), 662–63.

48 Kevles, *In the Name of Eugenics*, p. 160. See also, Cruikshank, *Mongol in our Midst*.

49 T. S. Eliot, "Commentary," *Criterion*, 3.9. (Oct. 1924), 4.

50 MacBride, "The Study of Heredity: Part IV," 330, 330, 331, 331, 331–32, 350, 350, 350–51.

51 Eliot, "Recent British Periodical Literature in Ethics," 274. See also MacBride, "The Study of Heredity: Part IV," 355, and E. W. MacBride, Letter to the Editor, *New Statesman* (17 March 1917).

52 T. S. Eliot, *Notes towards the Definition of Culture* (New York: Harcourt, Brace, 1948), p. 107.

53 E.P. Cathcart and A.M.T. Murray, "A Study in Nutrition: an Inquiry into the Diet of 154 Families in St Andrews," *MRC Spec. Rep. Ser.*, no. 151 (1931), p. 50, cited in Jones, *Social Hygiene*, p. 80.

54 Eliot sees more to the story of poverty and bad nutrition than heredity: "I hope . . . that the reader . . . has read, or will immediately read, *The Peckham Experiment*, as an illustration of what can be done, under modern conditions, to help the family to help itself." See *Notes towards the Definition of Culture*, p. 107.

55 Eliot, *Notes towards the Definition of Culture*, p. 126.

56 See Jones, *Social Hygiene*, pp. 25–41.

57 Eliot, *Notes towards the Definition of Culture*, pp. 76–77 (emphasis added).

58 T. S. Eliot, *After Strange Gods* (New York: Harcourt, Brace, 1934), p. 18.

59 Eliot, *Notes towards the Definition of Culture*, pp. 14, 13, 19, 77.

60 MacBride, "The Study of Heredity: Part IV," 331–32; Eliot, *Notes towards the Definition of Culture*, p. 23.

61 Eliot, *Notes towards the Definition of Culture*, p. 23.

62 Angus McLaren, *Birth Control in Nineteenth-Century England* (London: Croom Helm, 1978), p. 11.

63 Leonard Darwin, "Quality *Not* Quantity," *Eugenics Review*, 8.4 (Jan. 1917), 297.

64 A. K. Chalmers, "The Declining Birth-Rate: its Causes and Effects," *Eugenics Review*, 8.4 (Jan. 1917), 322.

65 John W. Taylor, *On the Diminishing Birth Rate* (London: Ballière, Tindall & Cox, 1904), pp. 11–13.

66 Eliot, "Recent British Periodical Literature in Ethics," 274–75.

67 Chalmers, "Declining Birth-Rate," 322, 323, 323, 327–28.

68 "Causes and Effects of the Declining Birth Rate," *Shield*, 3rd ser., 1 (Oct. 1916), 142.

69 Chalmers, "Declining Birth-Rate," 328.

70 Eliot, "Recent British Periodical Literature in Ethics," 275.

71 Darwin, "Quality *Not* Quantity," 307.

72 Eliot, "Recent British Periodical Literature in Ethics," 274.

73 Darwin, "Quality *Not* Quantity," 314

74 Eliot, "Commentary," *Criterion*, 6.6 (Dec. 1927), 483.

5 TO BREED OR NOT TO BREED: THE ELIOTS' QUESTION

1 Foucault, *The History of Sexuality*, pp. 124–25.
2 T. S. Eliot, Letter to Eleanor Hinkley (24 April 1915), *The Letters of T. S. Eliot* (London: Faber and Faber, 1988), vol. I, p. 97.
3 T. S. Eliot, Letter to Ezra Pound (15 April 1915), *Letters*, vol. I, p. 96.
4 Vivien Eliot, "A Diary of the Rive Gauche," *Criterion* 3.10 (Jan. 1925), 291–92.
5 See Lyndall Gordon, *Eliot's Early Years*, p. 27; T. S. Eliot, Letter to Conrad Aiken (31 Dec. 1914), *Letters*, vol. I, p. 75.
6 Aldous Huxley, Letter to Ottoline Morrell (21 June 1917), in *Ottoline at Garsington*, ed. Robert Gathorne-Hardy (London: Faber and Faber, 1974), p. 207.
7 Bertrand Russell, Letter to Ottoline Morrell (July 1915), in *The Autobiography of Bertrand Russell* (London: Unwin, 1975), p. 278.
8 Gordon, *Eliot's Early Years*, p. 72
9 Stephen Spender, *Eliot* (London: Fontana, 1975), p. 49. On this river interlude, see Eliot's letter to Scofield Thayer (7 May 1916), in *Letters*, vol. I, p. 137.
10 See also *The Waste Land: a Facsimile & Transcript*, ed. Valerie Eliot (London: Faber and Faber, 1971), p. 51, hereafter cited parenthetically as *WLF*.
11 Peter Ackroyd, *T. S. Eliot* (1984; London: Abacus, 1985), p. 62.
12 Gordon, *Eliot's Early Years*, p. 77.
13 Ackroyd, *T. S. Eliot*, p. 62.
14 McKim, *Heredity and Human Progress*, p. 56.
15 Henry H. Goddard, *Feeble-mindedness: its Causes and Consequences* (London: Macmillan, 1914), pp. 4, 547.
16 See McKim, *Heredity and Human Progress*, pp. 56–57; see William J. Robinson, *Eugenics, Marriage, and Birth Control (Practical Eugenics)* (New York: The Critic and Guide, 1917), pp. 100–01.
17 Ackroyd, *T. S. Eliot*, p. 62.
18 Rentoul, *Race Culture*, p. 31.
19 Karl Pearson, *Tuberculosis, Heredity and Environment* (London: Dulau, 1912), p. 21.
20 McKim, *Heredity and Human Progress*, p. 57.
21 On dating "Hysteria," see George Whiteside, "T. S. Eliot: The Psychobiographical Approach," *Southern Review* (Adelaide), 6.1 (March 1973), 11.
22 T. S. Eliot, "Ode," in *Ara Vos Prec* (London, 1919), in James E. Miller, *T. S. Eliot's Personal Waste Land* (University Park, PA and London: Pennsylvania State University Press, 1977), pp. 48–49.
23 Ackroyd, *T. S. Eliot*, p. 62.
24 "Ode," pp. 48–49. Gordon reads the "cheap extinction" as a problem with "premature ejaculation" (*Eliot's Early Years*, p. 75). In *T. S. Eliot's*

Silent Voices (Oxford University Press, 1989), John T. Mayer reads the phrase as an allusion to Eliot's dead friend Jean Verdenal (pp. 196–207).

25 T. S. Eliot, Letter to his father (1 March 1917), *Letters*, vol. 1, p. 160.
26 See Conrad Aiken, Letter to Robert N. Linscott (4 Jan. 1926), in *Selected Letters of Conrad Aiken* , ed. Joseph Killorin (New Haven: Yale University Press, 1978), pp. 109–10.
27 Victor Li, "T. S. Eliot and the Language of Hysteria," *Dalhousie Review*, 77.3 (Autumn 1997), 324–25.
28 Aiken invokes the militant teeth and bruising throat of "Hysteria" (*CPP* p. 32) and the "oval O cropped out with teeth" of "Sweeney Erect" (*CPP* p. 42) when he writes "KOTEX. Used with success by Blue-eyed Claude the Cabin Boy!" and then explains:

> Blue-eyed Claude the cabin boy,
> the clever little nipper
> who filled his ass with broken glass
> and circumcised the skipper.

See Aiken, Letter to Robert N. Linscott.
29 Rentoul, *Race Culture*, p. 31.
30 Sterilization laws differing by state, Harry Laughlin in 1922 proposed a standard state eugenical sterilization law. Because sterilization could be effected by a "score or more of specific operations," and because "[i]n some states existing laws call for operations which will most effectively prevent procreation," practices varied between the least radical and most radical means of achieving sterilization. See Harry Laughlin, "Model Eugenical Sterilization Law," in *Eugenical Sterilization in the United States: a Report of the Psychopathic Laboratory of the Municipal Court of Chicago* (Chicago IL: Municipal Court of Chicago, 1922), rpr. in *Eugenics Then and Now*, ed. Carl Jay Bajema (Stroudsburg, PA: Dowden, Hutchinson & Ross, 1976), p. 147.
31 Kevles, *In the Name of Eugenics*, pp. 47, 94.
32 Jones, *Social Hygiene*, p. 88.
33 McLaren, *Birth Control*, p. 141.
34 R.C. Punnett, "Eliminating Feeblemindedness," *Journal of Heredity*, 8 (1917): 464–65, rpr. in *Eugenics Then and Now*, p. 137.
35 Anthony Julius, *T. S. Eliot, Anti-Semitism, and Literary Form* (Cambridge University Press, 1995), p. 99.
36 Sidney Webb, *The Decline in the Birth Rate*, pp. 16–17.
37 Whetham and Whetham, *The Family and the Nation*, pp. 136–37.
38 Chalmers, "Declining Birth-Rate," 326.
39 B.C. Southam, *A Student's Guide to the Selected Poems of T. S. Eliot*, 6th edn. (London: Faber and Faber, 1994), pp. 82–83.
40 Crawford, *The Savage and the City*, pp. 65–66. See also "Burbank's Improved Fruits," unsigned article, *Nation* (13 July 1911), 39–40. Crawford traces Eliot's engagement with biological and evolutionary study of

plants from his Harvard days to the writing of *The Waste Land* (*The Savage and the City*, pp. 62–72).

41 Luther Burbank, *The Training of the Human Plant* (New York: Century, 1907).

42 Juan Leon, "Meeting Mr. Eugenides," 172.

43 *Ibid.*

44 T. S. Eliot, Letter to Eleanor Hinkley (21 March 1915), *Letters*, vol. 1, p. 92.

45 Matthew Arnold, *Culture and Anarchy*, ed. R.H. Super (1869; rpr. Ann Arbor: University of Michigan Press, 1965), p. 214.

46 Southam, *Student's Guide*, p. 115.

47 Mary Dendy, Letter to Francis Galton (16 Feb. 1909), in Kevles, *In the Name of Eugenics*, p. 107.

48 Pearson, *Tuberculosis, Heredity and Environment*, p. 46.

49 Leonard Darwin, "The Disabled Sailor and Soldier and the Future of Our Race," *The Eugenics Review*, 9.1 (April 1917), 7.

50 Vivien Eliot, Letter to Charlotte C. Eliot (8 April 1917), *Letters*, vol. 1, p. 173; T. S. Eliot, Letter to his mother (11 April 1917), *Letters*, vol. 1, p. 174.

51 T. S. Eliot, Letter to John Quinn (8 Sept. 1918), *Letters*, vol. 1, p. 244.

52 T. S. Eliot, Letter to his father (13 June 1917), *Letters*, vol. 1, p. 183.

53 T. S. Eliot, Letter to his mother (28 May 1917), *Letters*, vol. 1, p. 182.

54 Ackroyd, *T. S. Eliot*, p. 87.

55 T. S. Eliot, Letter to Henry Eliot (23 Aug. 1918), *Letters*, vol. 1, p. 241.

56 See Edward M. Coffman, *The War to End All Wars: the American Military Experience in World War I* (New York: Oxford University Press, 1968), chapter six.

57 T. S. Eliot, Letter to his mother (28 July 1918), *Letters*, vol. 1, p. 238.

58 T. S. Eliot, Letter to Henry Eliot (25 Aug. 1918), *Letters*, vol. 1, p. 241.

59 T. S. Eliot, Letter to Henry Eliot (25 Aug. 1918), *Letters*, vol. 1, p. 241; T. S. Eliot, Letter to John Quinn (8 Sept. 1918), *Letters*, vol. 1, p. 244; T. S. Eliot, Letter to his father (8 Sept. 1918), *Letters*, vol. 1, p. 243.

60 T. S. Eliot, Letter to John Quinn (13 Nov. 1918), *Letters*, vol. 1, p. 254; T. S. Eliot, Letter to Mrs. Jack Gardner (7 Nov. 1918), *Letters*, vol. 1, p. 251.

61 T. S. Eliot, Letter to his mother (13 Nov. 1918), *Letters*, vol. 1, p. 256.

62 Darwin, "The Disabled Sailor," 2, 2, 2, 3–4.

63 T. S. Eliot, Letter to his mother (28 May 1917), *Letters*, vol. 1, p. 182.

64 T. S. Eliot, Letter to John Quinn (13 Nov. 1918), *Letters*, vol. 1, p. 255; T. S. Eliot, Letter to his mother (13 Nov. 1918), *Letters*, vol. 1, p. 256.

65 T. S. Eliot, Letter to his mother (22 Dec. 1917), *Letters*, vol. 1, p. 213.

66 Darwin, "The Disabled Sailor," 8–9.

67 See Dante Alighieri, *The Inferno of Dante Alighieri* (London: Dent, 1908), canto xx, pp. 40–41.

68 T. S. Eliot, Letter to Conrad Aiken (21 August 1916), *Letters*, vol. 1, p. 143.

69 Valerie Eliot, in *The Waste Land: a Facsimile & Transcript*, p. 126.

70 Ezra Pound found this section of the poem "photography"; see *The Waste Land: A Facsimile & Transcript*, p. 11. Mary Hutchinson told Virginia Woolf that the poem was "Tom's biography"; see Woolf, *Diary*, vol. II, p. 178. Eliot revealed to Bertrand Russell that Vivien expected him to see the story of the Eliots in *The Waste Land*: "I must tell you that 18 months ago, before it [*The Waste Land*] was published, Vivien wanted me to send you the MS. to read, because she was sure that you were one of the very few persons who might possibly see anything in it" (T. S. Eliot, Letter to Bertrand Russell [15 Oct. 1923], in *The Autobiography of Bertrand Russell*, p. 409).

71 See Lyndall Gordon's reading of *Burnt Norton* as about the meeting between Eliot and Emily Hale in the garden of Burnt Norton (*Eliot's New Life* [Oxford University Press, 1988], pp. 45–50).

72 Mayer, *T. S. Eliot's Silent Voices*, p. 202.

73 *Ibid.* Mayer discusses Eliot's allusions here to Walt Whitman and Catullus (pp. 202–03), as does Miller, in *T. S. Eliot's Personal Waste Land*, pp. 48–58.

74 Leon, "Meeting Mr. Eugenides," 173.

75 *Ibid.*

76 Vivien Eliot, "Day Book, 1935–1936" (13 Apr. 1936), cited in Gordon, *Eliot's New Life*, p. 54.

6 FATAL FERTILITY IN *THE WASTE LAND*

1 Edmund Wilson, "The Poetry of Drouth," *Dial*, 73 (Dec. 1922), 611.

2 F. R. Leavis, *New Bearings in English Poetry* (London: Chatto & Windus, 1932), pp. 90–93.

3 Cleanth Brooks, "*The Waste Land*: Critique of the Myth," in *The Waste Land: A Collection of Critical Essays*, ed. Jay Martin (Englewood Cliffs, NJ: Prentice-Hall, 1968), p. 86.

4 Northrop Frye, *T. S. Eliot* (Edinburgh: Oliver and Boyd, 1963), pp. 64–65.

5 Spender, *Eliot*, p. 56.

6 Miller, *T. S. Eliot's Personal Waste Land*, p. 73.

7 Sandra M. Gilbert and Susan Gubar, *No Man's Land: the Place of the Woman Writer in the Twentieth Century, volume II: Sexchanges* (New Haven, CT: Yale University Press, 1988), p. 260.

8 Harriet Davidson, *T. S. Eliot and Hermeneutics* (Baton Rouge, LA: Louisiana State University Press, 1985), p. 99.

9 Crawford, *The Savage and the City*, pp. 69–70.

10 Leon, "Meeting Mr. Eugenides," 173.

11 Eliot, Letter to Conrad Aiken (31 Dec. 1914), *Letters*, vol. I, p. 75.

12 Charles B. Davenport, "The Feebly Inhibited: 1. Violent Temper and its Inheritance," *Journal of Nervous and Mental Diseases*, 42 (Sept. 1915), 608; see also Kevles, *In the Name of Eugenics*, p. 53.

13 George Bernard Shaw, Preface to *Three Plays by Brieux* (1909), in *The Complete Prefaces of Bernard Shaw* (London: Paul Hamlyn, 1965), p. 217.

14 Dr. Lindsay, cited in *Problems in Eugenics*, vol. ii, p. 60.

15 McLaren, *Birth Control*, p. 199.

16 Dr. D'Ewart, cited in *Problems in Eugenics*, vol. ii, p. 61.

17 McLaren, *Birth Control*, p. 199.

18 D'Ewart, cited in *Problems in Eugenics*, vol. ii, p. 60.

19 Eliot, "Recent British Periodical Literature in Ethics," 275.

20 "Causes and Effects of the Declining Birth Rate,"147.

21 "The Campaign for Compulsory Notification of Venereal Disease," *Shield*, 3rd ser., 1 (Mar. 2217), 230.

22 "Editorial," *Shield*, 3rd ser., 1 (Oct. 1916), 139.

23 Shaw, Preface to *Three Plays by Brieux*, p. 215.

24 M.H. Abrams, *et al.* (eds.), *The Norton Anthology of English Literature*, 6th edn., 2 vols. (New York: Norton, 1993), vol. ii, p. 2153.

25 C. M. Bowra, *The Creative Experiment* (London: Macmillan, 1949), p. 182.

26 On Australian problems with prostitutes in Egypt, see C. E. W. Bean, *The Story of Anzac*, vol. 1 of *Official History of Australia in the War of 1914–1918*, 2nd rev. edn. (1921; rpr. Sydney: Angus & Robertson 1933), p. 128; Bill Gammage, *The Broken Years: Australian Soldiers in the Great War* (Canberra: Australian National University Press, 1974), p. 37.

27 H. Hallopeau, "On the Prophylaxis of Hereditary Syphilis, and its Effect on Eugenics," in *Problems in Eugenics*, vol. i, p. 348.

28 "Moral Problems Concerning Our Troops in the War Zone and Elsewhere," *Shield*, 3rd ser., 1 (Mar. 1917), 225.

29 "Wrong Methods of Prophylaxis in the Army," *Shield*, 3rd ser., 1 (Mar. 1917), 228–29.

30 Richard Arthur, M.A., M.D. (Sydney), "Some Aspects of the Venereal Problem," *Shield*, 3rd ser., 1 (June 1917), 306.

31 Hallopeau, "Prophylaxis," vol. i, p. 347.

32 Leon, "Meeting Mr. Eugenides," 173.

33 William Blake, "London," in *The Complete Poetry and Prose of William Blake*, ed. David V. Erdman, rev. edn. (Berkeley, CA and Los Angeles, CA: University of California Press, 1982), p. 26.

34 T. S. Eliot, Letter to E. Martin Browne (19 March 1938), in E. Martin Browne, *The Making of T. S. Eliot's Plays* (Cambridge University Press, 1969), pp. 107–08.

35 Frances Swiney, *The Bar of Isis; or the Law of the Mother* 3rd edn. (London: C. W. Daniel, 1912), pp. 16, 32, 46.

36 Greenslade, *Degeneration, Culture and the Novel*, p. 166.

37 Elaine Showalter, "Syphilis, Sexuality and the Fiction of the *Fin de Siècle*," in *Sex, Politics, and Science in the Nineteenth Century Novel*, ed. R. B. Yeazell (Baltimore, MD and London: Johns Hopkins University Press, 1986), p. 88.

38 McLaren, *Birth Control*, p. 199.

39 See Christabel Pankhurst, *The Great Scourge and How to End It* (London: E. Pankhurst, 1913).

40 "Editorial," *Shield*, 3rd ser., 1 (Oct. 1916), 133–34.

41 Eliot, "Recent British Periodical Literature in Ethics," 276–77.

42 "Editorial," *Shield*, 3rd ser., 1 (Oct. 1916), 134; Alison Neilans, "The Protection of Soldiers," *Shield*, 3rd ser., 1 (Mar. 1917), 220 .

43 "Is Rescue Work a Failure?" *Shield*, 3rd ser., 1 (Oct. 1916), 167; Neilans, "The Protection of Soldiers," 221.

44 Eliot, "Recent British Periodical Literature in Ethics," 276.

45 Helen Wilson, Address at the Annual Council of the National Council of Women (Dec. 1916), cited in "The Campaign for Compulsory Notification of Venereal Disease," *Shield*, 3rd series, 1 (Mar. 1917), 235.

46 See R.B. Kerr, Letter to the Editor, *Egoist*, 1.6 (15 June 1914), who quotes Christabel Pankhurst in *The Suffragette* (1 May 1914).

47 Eliot, "Recent British Periodical Literature in Ethics," 276.

48 Isabel Leatham, Letters to the Editor, *Freewoman* (7 Dec. 1911), 52; (4 Jan. 1912), 151.

49 Shaw, Preface, *Three Plays by Brieux*, p. 213.

50 McLaren, *Birth Control*, p. 202.

51 "Wrong Methods of Prophylaxis in the Army," 228.

52 "Editorial," *Shield*, 3rd series, 1 (Oct. 1916), 139.

53 Neilans, "The Protection of Soldiers," 223.

54 Eliot, "Recent British Periodical Literature in Ethics," 276–77.

55 T. S. Eliot, "M. Bourget's Last Novel," *The New Statesman*, 9. 229 (25 Aug. 1917), 500. Eliot's thoughts here may be the result of having considered separation from Vivien, presumably on the advice of Bertrand Russell. See allusions to this matter in letters to Russell in April and May of 1925, cited in *The Autobiography of Bertrand Russell*, p. 410.

56 Eliot, "Recent British Periodical Literature in Ethics," 276. The Bhikku are described as "celibate" in an editorial note to Bhikku Silacara, "Sex-Morality in Burma," *Shield*, 3rd series, 1 (Mar. 1917), 254.

57 Dora Marsden, "Views and Comments," *Egoist*, 1.2 (2 Feb. 1914), 46.

58 H.S.C., Letter to the editor, *Egoist*, 1.2 (16 Feb. 1914), 78.

59 Marsden, "Views and Comments," 46.

60 H.S.C., Letter to the editor, 78.

61 Beebon and Noel Teulon Porter, Letter to the editor, *Egoist*, 1.3 (2 March 1914), 98.

62 Caldwell Harpur, Letter to the editor, *Egoist*, 1.5 (1 May 1914), 179.

63 E.S.P. Haynes, Letter to the editor, *Egoist*, 1.4 (1 Apr. 1914), 139.

64 R.B. Kerr, Letter to the editor, *Egoist*, 1.3 (16 March 1914), 119.

65 E.M. Watson, Letter to the editor, *Egoist*, 1.3 (2 Mar. 1914), 99.

66 Beebon and Noel Teulon Porter, "Chastity," *Egoist*, 1.2 (16 Feb. 1914), 78.

67 Ethel Knott, Letter to the editor, *Egoist*, 1.3 (2 Mar. 1914), 99.

68 Jane Harrison, *Epilegomena to the Study of Greek Religion and Themis: a Study*

of the Social Origins of Greek Religion (New York: University Books, 1962), pp. xlix–liii, liii, liv, lv.

69 McLaren, *Birth Control*, p. 204.

70 Ellis Ethelmer, *Woman Free* (Congleton: Women's Emancipation Union, 1893), pp. 12, 92, 100. Ellis Ethelmer was the pseudonym of Ben Elmy and Mrs. Wolstoneholme Elmy.

71 On strategic frigidity, see McLaren, *Birth Control*, p. 198.

72 "The Declining Birth-Rate: Its Causes and Effects," *Shield*, 3rd series, 1 (Oct. 1916), 142, 144.

73 "Notes and Cuttings," *Shield*, 3rd series, 1 (Oct. 1916), 186–87.

74 "Causes and Effects of the Declining Birth Rate," 142.

75 Chalmers, "Declining Birth-Rate," 322.

76 T. S. Eliot, "London Letter," *Dial*, 73.6 (Dec. 1922), 662.

77 Eliot, "London Letter," *Dial*, 73.6 (Dec. 1922), 662–63. In *Sweeney Agonistes*, the attraction of "a cannibal isle" is "There's no telephones / There's no gramophones / There's no motor cars." Ironically, Doris, a typical inhabitant of a thoroughly modern and civilized London, rejects Sweeney's plan to avoid boredom by observing, "I'd be bored." On Eliot's use of the name Doris to represent aspects of Vivien, on the one hand, and multiple personality disorder, on the other, see Grover Smith, "T. S. Eliot and the Fragmented Selves: From 'Suppressed Complex' to *Sweeney Agonistes*," *Philological Quarterly*, 77.4 (Fall 1998): 417–37.

78 Eliot, "London Letter," *Dial*, 73.6 (Dec. 1922), 659.

79 Bertrand Russell, "Marriage and the Population Question," *International Journal of Ethics*, 26.4 (Jul. 1916), 443–61. See also W.R. Inge, "Marriage," *Eugenics Review*, 8.4 (Jan. 1917), 358–59.

80 See the note to lines 215–56 of *La Terre vaine* in T. S. Eliot, *Poésie*, trad. de Pierre Leyris, édition bilingue (Paris: Editions du Seuil, 1969), p. 97. On this translation and its new notes, see Joan Fillmore Hooker, *T. S. Eliot's Poems in French Translation: Pierre Leyris and Others* (Ann Arbor, MI: University of Michigan Research Press, 1983), p. 6.

81 Russell, "Marriage and the Population Question," 448, 461, 453, 453, 451.

82 Eliot, "London Letter," *Dial*, 73.6 (Dec. 1922), 662.

83 *Ibid.*, 660. On Eliot and the music hall, see Southam, *Student's Guide*, p. 171, and Eliot's "London Letter" in *Dial*, 70.4 (Apr. 1921), 453, and *Dial*, 70.6 (June 1921), 688–89.

84 Eliot, "London Letter," *Dial*, 73.6 (Dec. 1922), 662.

85 Southam, *Student's Guide*, p. 171.

86 Eliot, *Poésie*, pp. 96–97.

87 John Cowen, "The Prostitution Market," *Shield*, 3rd series, 1 (Oct. 1916), 164, 158.

88 Southam, *Student's Guide*, p. 170.

89 Eliot, "London Letter," *Dial*, 73.6 (Dec. 1922), 663.

90 T. S. Eliot, "Commentary," *Criterion*, 3.9. (Oct. 1924), 2–3.

91 MacBride, "The Study of Heredity: Part I," 24–26. Reading MacBride just months after completing his dissertation (in April 1916), Eliot must have noted the coincidence of their shared focus on sea life as the example *par excellence* of primitive life. Arguing that thinking not only reflects the world but helps to make it, Eliot suggests that even "[t]he sea-anemone which accepts or rejects a proffered morsel is thereby relating an idea to the sea-anemone's world . . . a world which is built up from the subject's point of view." Yet "[a]t the same time we must remember that in saying anything about types of consciousness different from our own, we are making statements about worlds which are different from ours, though continuous. Truth on our level is a different thing from truth for the jellyfish, and there must certainly be analogies for truth and error in jellyfish life." (See T. S. Eliot, *Knowledge and Experience in the Philosophy of F. H. Bradley* [London: Faber and Faber, 1964], pp. 44, 165–66.) By his emphasis on the phenomenon of "recapitulation," McBride reinforces biologically Eliot's sense that sea-anemone and jellyfish "worlds" are "continuous" with our own. By his association of "recapitulation" with "the laws of heredity," he reinforces Eliot's sense that the primitive continues to reside as a potential within the modern human being. Thus the Chorus in *Murder in the Cathedral* argues that its intuition of imminent corruption and death is authoritative by claiming precisely the recapitulative, hereditary, continuous experience of which Eliot and McBride speak. On the one hand, we hear: "I have tasted / The living lobster, the crab, the oyster, the whelk and the prawn; / and they live and spawn in my bowels"; on the other hand, we hear: "I have lain on the floor of the sea and breathed with the breathing / of the sea-anemone, swallowed with ingurgitation of the / sponge" (*CPP* p. 270).

92 MacBride, "The Study of Heredity: Part I," 26.

93 T. S. Eliot, "The New Elizabethans and the Old," *Athenaeum*, 4640 (4 Apr. 1919), 135.

94 T. S. Eliot, "The Silurist," *Dial*, 73.3 (Sep. 1927), 263.

95 T. S. Eliot, "London Letter," *Dial*, 71.4 (Oct. 1921), 455.

96 T. S. Eliot, "Baudelaire," in *Selected Essays*, 3rd enlarged edn. (London: Faber & Faber, 1951), pp. 428–29.

97 T. S. Eliot, "Mr. Chesterton (and Stevenson)," *Nation and Athenaeum*, 42.3 (31 Dec. 1927), 516.

98 MacBride, "The Study of Heredity: Part IV," 351.

99 MacBride, "The Study of Heredity: Part III," 240.

100 Regarding the conversation about glands between Eliot and Pound in Italy in May of 1922, see Vivien Eliot, Letter to Ezra Pound (27 June 1922) in *The Letters of T. S. Eliot*, vol. I, p. 532. For the reference to Louis Berman's book *The Glands Regulating Personality: a Study of the Glands of Internal Secretion in Relation to the Types of Human Nature* (New York:

Macmillan, 1921), see T. S. Eliot, Letter to Ezra Pound (19 July 1922), *Letters*, vol. I, p. 549.

101 T. S. Eliot, Letters to Ezra Pound (9 and 19 July 1922), *Letters*, vol. I, pp. 538, 549. Hogben's book was published as *The Comparative Physiology of Internal Secretion* (Cambridge University Press, 1927). Eliot later included "Dr. Berman's hormones" in his list of Pound's "muddle" of beliefs; see T. S. Eliot, "Isolated Superiority," *Dial*, 84.1 (Jan. 1928), 7.

102 Vivien Eliot, Letter to Ezra Pound (27 June 1922), *Letters*, vol. I, p. 532.

103 Ovid, *Metamorphoses*, trans. by Mary Innes (Harmondsworth, England: Penguin, 1955), p. 104.

104 Eliot, "Isolated Superiority," 4–5.

105 T. S. Eliot, "Thoughts after Lambeth," in *Selected Essays*, p. 387.

7 THE LATE EUGENICS OF W. B. YEATS

1 Elizabeth Butler Cullingford, *Gender and History in Yeats's Love Poetry* (Cambridge University Press, 1993); Cullingford, *Yeats, Ireland and Fascism*; Paul Scott Stanfield, *Yeats and Politics in the 1930s*; David Bradshaw, "The Eugenics Movement in the 1930s and the Emergence of *On the Boiler*," in *Yeats Annual No. 9* (London: Macmillan, 1992), pp. 189–215.

2 W. B. Yeats, *On the Boiler*, in *Explorations* (London: Macmillan, 1962), pp. 410, 411, hereafter cited parenthetically in the text as *Ex*.

3 W. B. Yeats, *Purgatory*, in *The Variorum Edition of the Plays of W. B. Yeats*, ed. Russell K. Alspach (London: Macmillan, 1966), pp. 1043–45. *The Variorum Edition of the Plays of W. B. Yeats* is hereafter cited parenthetically in the text as *Plays*.

4 Cullingford, *Yeats, Ireland and Fascism*, pp. 228, 230, 230, 230, 228, 229, 229.

5 Cullingford, *Gender and History*, pp. 284, 284–85; W. B. Yeats, "A Bronze Head," in *The Variorum Edition of the Poems of W. B. Yeats*, ed. Peter Allt and Russell K. Alspach (New York: Macmillan, 1957), 619. *The Variorum Edition of the Poems of W. B. Yeats* is hereafter cited parenthetically in the text as *Poems*.

6 Raymond B. Cattell, *The Fight for our National Intelligence* (London: P.S. King, 1937); see Yeats, *On the Boiler*, p. 423.

7 Stanfield, *Yeats and Politics*, p. 176.

8 Cullingford, *Gender and History*, p. 280.

9 Stanfield, *Yeats and Politics*, p. 176.

10 See *ibid.*, pp. 180–81.

11 *Ibid.*, pp. 162, 166.

12 Bradshaw, "The Eugenics Movement," 190.

13 *Ibid.*, 203.

14 *Ibid.*, 201; W. B. Yeats, "Estrangement: Extracts from a Diary Kept in 1909," in *Autobiographies* (London: Macmillan, 1955), p. 463.

15 Bradshaw, "The Eugenics Movement," 200, 203.
16 Stanfield, *Yeats and Politics*, p. 149.
17 *Ibid.*, p. 151.
18 W. B. Yeats, "If I Were Four-and-Twenty," in *Explorations*, p. 274.
19 Stanfield, *Yeats and Politics*, pp. 169, 152, 169.
20 Bradshaw, "The Eugenics Movement," 199.
21 Edward O'Shea, "The 1920s Catalogue of W. B. Yeats's Library," in *Yeats Annual No. 4* (London: Macmillan, 1986), pp. 279–90.
22 Bradshaw, "The Eugenics Movement," 192.
23 Phyllis Grosskurth, *Havelock Ellis: a Biography* (New York: Knopf, 1980), p. 377.
24 *Encyclopedia of Sexual Knowledge*, general ed. Norman Haire (London: Francis Aldor, 1934); Norman Haire, *How I Run My Birth Control Clinic* (London: Cromer Welfare Clinic, 1929); Norman Haire, *The Comparative Value of Current Contraceptive Methods* (London: Cromer Welfare Centre, 1928); Norman Haire, *Hymen; or the Future of Marriage* (London: Kegan Paul, 1927); Norman Haire, *Rejuvenation: The Work of Steinach, Voronoff, and Others* (London: Allen & Unwin, 1924); Norman Haire, *Recent Developments of Steinach's Work: Part 2 of Rejuvenation: Steinach's Researches on the Sex-glands* (London: British Society for the Study of Sex Psychology, 1923).
25 Grosskurth, *Havelock Ellis*, pp. 377–78.
26 *Ibid.*, pp. 412–13.
27 Bradshaw, "The Eugenics Movement," 192.
28 Paul Kammerer, *The Inheritance of Acquired Characteristics*, trans. A. Paul Maerker-Branden (1924; rpr. New York and London: Garland, 1984), pp. 321–23.
29 J. Sanders, "Measures to Encourage the Fertility of the Gifted," in *A Decade of Progress: Scientific Papers of the Third International Congress of Eugenics* (1934; rpr. New York and London: Garland, 1984), p. 358; Joseph Hone, *W. B. Yeats* (London: Macmillan, 1942), p. 437.
30 Hone, *W. B. Yeats*, p. 437.
31 Eugen Steinach, *Verjungung durch experimentelle Neubelebung der alternden Pubertatsdruse* (Berlin: J. Springer, 1920), p. 20, cited in Virginia D. Pruitt and Raymond D. Pruitt, "Yeats and the Steinach Operation: a Further Analysis," in *Yeats: an Annual of Critical and Textual Studies*, vol. 1, ed. Richard J. Finneran (Ithaca, NY and London: Cornell University Press, 1983), p. 114; Peter Schmidt, *The Conquest of Old Age: Methods to Effect Rejuvenation and to Increase Functional Activity*, trans. Eden and Cedar Paul (London: Routledge, 1931), cited in Pruitt and Pruitt, "Yeats and the Steinach Operation," p. 113; Peter Schmidt, cited in Paul Kammerer, *Rejuvenation and the Prolongation of Human Efficiency: Experiences with the Steinach-operation on Man and Animals* (New York: Boni and Liveright, 1923), p. 156, cited in Pruitt and Pruitt, "Yeats and the Steinach Operation," p. 114.

32 George F. Corners, *Rejuvenation: How Steinach Makes People Young* (New York: Seltzer, 1923), p. 103, cited in Pruitt and Pruitt, "Yeats and the Steinach Operation," p. 115.

33 Harry Benjamin, "Introduction," in Paul Kammerer, *Rejuvenation and the Prolongation of Human Efficiency*, p. 19, cited in Pruitt and Pruitt, "Yeats and the Steinach Operation," p. 114.

34 Haire, *Rejuvenation: The Work of Steinach, Voronoff, and Others*, p. 134, cited in Pruitt and Pruitt, "Yeats and the Steinach Operation," pp. 113–14.

35 Arnold Lorand, *Life Shortening Habits and Rejuvenation* (Philadelphia, PA: F. A. Davis, 1923), pp. 201, 203, 202–03, 209–10.

36 Hone, *W. B. Yeats*, p. 436; Cullingford, *Gender and History*, p. 246.

37 Sanders, "Fertility of the Gifted," p. 358.

38 Joyce, *Portrait of the Artist*, p. 248.

39 Kammerer, *Inheritance of Acquired Characteristics*, pp. 319–20.

40 *Ibid.*, pp. 322, 321, 326.

41 George Briggs Starkweather, *Biogenetic Marvels: the Romance of Biology, Disclosing Man's Infinite Potentialities.* 2 vols. (Washington, DC: Biogenetic Press, 1925), vol. II, pp. 661–62.

42 MacBride, "The Study of Heredity: Part IV," 347, 350.

43 Hone, *W. B. Yeats*, p. 437.

44 *Ibid.*, p. 437.

45 W. B. Yeats, *Ah, Sweet Dancer: W. B. Yeats: Margot Ruddock: a Correspondence*, ed. Roger McHugh (New York: Macmillan, 1970), p. 32; Cullingford, *Gender and History*, p. 245.

46 Yeats, *Ah, Sweet Dancer*, pp. 31–32.

47 See Richard Ellmann, *W. B. Yeats's Second Puberty* (Washington, DC: Library of Congress, 1986), p. 28.

48 Cullingford, *Gender and History*, p. 262.

49 A. Norman Jeffares, *W. B. Yeats: Man and Poet* (New Haven, CT: Yale University Press, 1948), p. 282.

50 Virginia D. Pruitt, "Yeats and the Steinach Operation," *American Imago*, 34 (Fall 1977), 294.

51 Cullingford, *Gender and History*, p. 262.

52 *Ibid.*, p. 263.

53 See C. J. Bond, "Causes of Racial Decay," *Eugenics Review*, 20 (April 1928), 5–19.

54 Cullingford, *Gender and History*, p. 263.

55 Bradshaw, "The Eugenics Movement," 200.

56 William McDougall, *National Welfare and National Decay* (London: Macmillan, 1921), pp. vii, vi, hereafter cited parenthetically within the text.

57 Bradshaw, "The Eugenics Movement," 203.

58 S.H. Halford, "Dysgenic Tendencies," in *Population and Birth-Control* (New York, 1917), p. 232, cited in McDougall, *National Welfare*, p. 154.

59 W. B. Yeats, Letter to Dorothy Wellesley (1938), in *Letters on Poetry to*

Dorothy Wellesley, ed. Dorothy Wellesley (London: Oxford University Press, 1964), p. 178.

60 W. B. Yeats, *The Senate Speeches of W. B. Yeats*, ed. Donald R. Pearce (Bloomington IN: Indiana University Press, 1960), p. 105.

61 *Ibid.*, p. 99.

62 Seamus Deane, *Celtic Revivals: Essays on Modern Irish Literature 1880–1980* (London: Faber and Faber, 1985), p. 29.

63 W. B. Yeats, "Bishop Berkeley" (1931), in *Essays and Introductions* (London: Macmillan, 1969), pp. 401–02.

64 *Ibid.*, p. 403.

65 Deane, *Celtic Revivals*, p. 48.

66 *Ibid.*, p. 48.

67 Florence Farr, *Modern Woman: Her Intentions* (London: Frank Palmer, 1910), p. 65.

68 Bradshaw, "The Eugenics Movement," 200; on Yeats's relationship with Farr, see R.F. Foster, *W. B. Yeats: A Life: vol. 1: The Apprentice Mage 1865–1914* (Oxford University Press, 1997), pp. 290–91.

69 W. B. Yeats, Letter to Augusta Gregory (Oct. 1910), cited in Foster, *Apprentice Mage*, pp. 433, 609.

70 Yeats, "If I Were Four-and-Twenty," p. 274.

71 Cullingford, *Gender and History*, p. 281.

8 YEATS AND STIRPICULTURE

1 Allan Estlake, *The Oneida Community* (London: George Redway, 1900), hereafter cited parenthetically within the text.

2 Edward O'Shea, "The 1920s Catalogue," pp. 279–90.

3 John McKelvie Whitworth, *God's Blueprint: A Sociological Study of Three Utopian Sects* (London and Boston, MA: Routledge & Kegan Paul, 1975), p. 92.

4 John Humphrey Noyes, Letter to David Harrison (15 January 1837), cited in *The Battle-Axe* (1 September 1837), cited in Whitworth, *God's Blueprint*, pp. 95–96.

5 John Humphrey Noyes, *Bible Communism* (Brooklyn, NY: Oneida Community, 1853), cited in *Eugenics Then and Now*, p. 49.

6 John Humphrey Noyes, "Scientific Propagation," in *Eugenics Then and Now*, p. 65.

7 A. N. McGee, "An Experiment in Human Stirpiculture," *The American Anthropologist*, 4.4 (1891), 319–25.

8 Whitworth, *God's Blueprint*, pp. 166, 141, 125.

9 W. B. Yeats, *The Speckled Bird*, ed. William H. O'Donnell (Toronto: McClelland and Stewart, 1976), hereafter cited parenthetically within the text.

10 Oscar Wilde, "The Decay of Lying: An Observation," in *The Complete*

Works of Oscar Wilde, ed. Vyvyan Holland (London and Glasgow: Collins, 1966), pp. 982–83.

11 Walter Pater, *The Renaissance* (New York: Modern Library, 1924), pp. 172–73.

12 See James George Frazer, *The Golden Bough: a Study in Magic and Religion*, one-volume abridged edition (New York: Macmillan, 1951). Yeats returns to this pun about generation as both a measure of time and an act of procreation in the same context of degeneration in his reference to "dying generations" in "Sailing to Byzantium" (*Poems* p. 407).

13 The biological importance for Yeats of imagination and will is evident in *A Vision*, where he uses the example of Lamarck and Darwin (among others) to explain the crucial shift between phases 21 and 22 in the twenty-eight incarnations of the phases of the moon. Lamarck is distinct from Darwin precisely because both he and his system retain a vestige of subjective imagination and will in a world otherwise given over to the objective: "A man of Phase 22 will commonly not only systematize, to the exhaustion of his will, but discover this exhaustion of will in all that he studies. If Lamarck, as is probable, was of Phase 21, Darwin was probably a man of Phase 22, for his theory of development by the survival of fortunate accidental varieties seems to express this exhaustion." See W. B. Yeats, *A Vision*, rev. edn. (New York: Collier Books, 1937), p. 159.

14 John Humphrey Noyes, "John H. Noyes's Religious Experience," cited in Estlake, *Oneida Community*, p. 65.

15 Stanfield, *Yeats and Politics*, p. 146; Katharine Worth, "Introduction," *Where There Is Nothing*, by W. B. Yeats, and *The Unicorn from the Stars*, by W. B. Yeats and Lady Gregory, ed. Katharine Worth (Gerrards Cross: Colin Smythe, 1987), p. 21.

16 Arthur Bingham Walkley, review of *Where There Is Nothing* by W. B. Yeats, *Times Literary Supplement* (26 June 1903), 201–02.

17 W. B. Yeats, Letter to A.B. Walkley (28 June 1903), in *The Collected Letters of W. B. Yeats*, 3 vols., eds. John Kelly and Ronald Schuchard (Oxford: Clarendon Press, 1986–94), vol. III, p. 391.

18 Yeats, *On the Boiler*, p. 437.

19 Yeats, Letter to A. B. Walkley (28 June 1903), *Collected Letters*, vol. III, p. 391.

20 *Ibid.*

21 Stanfield, *Yeats and Politics*, p. 149.

22 *Ibid.*, p. 211.

23 Edward O'Shea, *A Descriptive Catalog of W. B. Yeats's Library* (New York and London: Garland, 1985), p. 323.

24 W. B. Yeats, "Discoveries" (1906), in *Essays and Introductions*, p. 270.

25 W. B. Yeats, *Memoirs: Autobiography – First Draft, Journal*, ed. Denis Donoghue (London: Macmillan, 1972), p. 145.

26 Shaw, *Man and Superman*, p. 149.

27 W. B. Yeats, "The Trembling of the Veil," in *Autobiographies*, pp. 364–65.
28 *Ibid.*, p. 364.
29 *Ibid.*, p. 365.
30 W. B. Yeats, Preface (1903), *Gods and Fighting Men*, by Lady Gregory (London: John Murra, 1904), pp. ix–xxiv, in *The Collected Works of W. B. Yeats*, general eds. Richard J. Finneran and George Mills Harper, 14 volumes, vol. IV, *Prefaces and Introductions*, ed. William H. O'Donnell (New York: Macmillan, 1989), p. 132, hereafter cited parenthetically in the text.
31 Yeats, "The Trembling of the Veil," p. 364.
32 *Ibid.*
33 W. B. Yeats, "Irish Coinage: What We Did or Tried to Do," in *Senate Speeches*, p. 166.

9 YEATS AND *THE SEXUAL QUESTION*

1 See "Forcible Sterilizing Continues, Swiss Told," Reuters News Agency, in *The Globe and Mail*, 29 August 1997.
2 August Forel, *The Sexual Question: a Scientific, Psychological, Hygienic and Sociological Study*, trans. C.F. Marshall (1908; rpr. New York: Physicians and Surgeons Book Company, 1924), hereafter cited parenthetically within the text. Havelock Ellis, *Studies in the Psychology of Sex*, 7 vols. (Philadelphia, PA: F. A. Davis, 1897–1928). Richard Krafft-Ebing, *Psycopathia Sexualis* (1902; rpr. New York: Bell, 1965).
3 Foucault, *The History of Sexuality*, p. 64.
4 *The Encyclopedia of Sexual Behavior*, eds. Albert Ellis and Albert Abarbanel (New York: Jason Aronson, 1973), p. 377.
5 This 1910 paper was published as *Malthusianismus oder Eugenik?* (Munich: E. Reinhardt, 1911).
6 Forel is clearly familiar with Galton's work. See, for example, *The Sexual Question*, pp. 514–15.
7 Foster, *Apprentice Mage*, p. 331.
8 *Ibid.*, p. 330.
9 William Fay, quoted by Foster, *Apprentice Mage*, p. 333.
10 The German first edition was *Die sexuelle Frage* (Munich: E. Reinhardt, 1905). All translations were based on the second edition of 1906.
11 O'Shea, "The 1920s Catalogue of W. B. Yeats's Library."
12 W. B. Yeats, Letter to Lady Gregory (8 March 1909), in *The Letters of W. B. Yeats*, ed. Allan Wade (New York: Macmillan, 1955), p. 525.
13 Allan Wade, *The Letters of W. B. Yeats*, p. 507n3; W. B. Yeats, Letter to Florence Farr (April 1908), in *The Letters of W. B. Yeats*, p. 507.
14 Shaw, *Man and Superman*, pp. 10–12, 13, 14.
15 W. B. Yeats, "J. M. Synge and the Ireland of His Time" (14 September 1910), in *Essays and Introductions*, pp. 314, 314, 341.
16 Yeats, *Memoirs*, p. 223.

17 Yeats, "J. M. Synge and the Ireland of His Time," pp. 311–12.
18 *Ibid.*, p. 313.
19 *Ibid.*, pp. 313, 314.
20 *Ibid.*, pp. 323, 314.
21 W. B. Yeats, "Estrangement: Extracts from a Diary Kept in 1909," in *Autobiographies*, p. 489.
22 See Forel, *The Sexual Question*, pp. 116, 120, 131, 134, 212, 220, 225, 233, 251, 289, 316, 386, 474.
23 Shaw, *Man and Superman*, pp. 209, 47.
24 Yeats, *Memoirs*, p. 176.
25 Vulgar humor in certain jokes and comic scenes on stage and in film still depends on the popular assumption (or suspension of disbelief) that damage to the adult male's sexual organs will immediately create a falsetto voice.
26 Yeats, "J. M. Synge and the Ireland of His Time," p. 314.
27 Yeats, "Estrangement," p. 486.
28 *Ibid.*, p. 487.
29 *Ibid.*, pp. 466–68.
30 *Ibid.*, p. 489.
31 Yeats, *Memoirs*, p. 265.
32 W. B. Yeats, "P.I.A.L. diary" (21 June 1909), cited in Foster, *Apprentice Mage*, p. 407.
33 See Foster, *Apprentice Mage*, pp. 386–96.
34 See *ibid.*, pp. 330–34, 363.
35 Yeats, *Memoirs*, p. 125.
36 *Ibid.*, p. 125–26.
37 *Ibid.*, pp. 125, 127.
38 W. B. Yeats, *Yeats's* Vision *Papers*, 3 vols., vol. II, *The Automatic Scripts: 25 June 1918–29 March 1920*, eds. Steve L. Adams, Barbara J. Frieling, and Sandra L. Sprayberry (Iowa City, Iowa: University of Iowa Press, 1992), p. 349.
39 Yeats, *Memoirs*, pp. 139, 140, 142, 156.
40 *Ibid.*, pp. 140–42.
41 *Ibid.*, p. 155.
42 This is the 1912 version of the poem. See also Yeats, *Memoirs*, p. 245.
43 Yeats, *Memoirs*, pp. 188–89.
44 *Ibid.*, pp. 248, 142, 248–49, 179, 142.
45 *Ibid.*, pp. 140, 156.
46 *Ibid.*, p. 249.
47 *Ibid.*, p. 182.
48 *Ibid.*, pp. 172, 172, 174–75 (emphasis added).
49 *Ibid.*, p. 190.
50 *Ibid.*, p. 174.
51 Yeats, "J. M. Synge and the Ireland of His Time," pp. 331, 331, 331, 331–32.

52 Yeats, *Memoirs*, pp. 156–57, 182, 182.
53 Yeats, "J. M. Synge and the Ireland of His Time," p. 314.
54 See George Moore, "Yeats, Lady Gregory, and Synge," *The English Review*, 16 (January and February 1914): 167–80, 350–64. See also Foster, *Apprentice Mage*, pp. 327–28, 507–09.
55 Foster, *Apprentice Mage*, p. 509.
56 Yeats, *Memoirs*, pp. 270–71.
57 Yeats, "Dramatis Personae," in *Autobiographies*, p. 388.
58 See Foster, *Apprentice Mage*, p. 165.
59 Yeats, *Memoirs*, p. 271.
60 See *ibid.*, p. 271, n. 1.
61 Yeats, *Memoirs*, p. 271.
62 *Ibid.*, p. 142.
63 O'Shea, *A Descriptive Catalog of W. B. Yeats's Library*, p. 205.

Index